Kenneth Slessor

Collected Poems

You know the terror that for poets lurks
Beyond the ferry when to Minos brought.
Poets must utter their Collected Works,
Including Juvenilia. So I thought
That you might warn him. Yes, I think you ought.

— W.H. Auden, 'Letter to Lord Byron'

Kenneth Slessor

Collected Poems

EDITED BY

DENNIS HASKELL AND GEOFFREY DUTTON

Angus&Robertson
An imprint of HarperCollins*Publishers*

An Angus & Robertson Publication

Angus&Robertson, an imprint of
HarperCollinsPublishers
25 Ryde Road, Pymble, Sydney NSW 2073, Australia
31 View Road, Glenfield, Auckland 10, New Zealand
77–85 Fulham Palace Road, London W6 8JB, United Kingdom
10 East 53rd Street, New York NY 10022, USA

First published in Australia in 1994

National Library of Australia
Cataloguing-in-Publication data

Slessor, Kenneth, 1901–1971.
Collected poems.

Bibliography.
Includes index.
ISBN 0 207 17257 9.

I. Haskell, Dennis, 1948– . II. Dutton, Geoffrey, 1922– .
III. Title.

A821.3

Cover image of Ortelius world map of 1570 reproduced with permission from the Rex Nan Kivell Collection, National Library of Australia.
Cover design by Penny Maxwell
Printed by Griffin Paperbacks, Adelaide

9 8 7 6 5 4 3 2 1
97 96 95 94

Contents

Acknowledgements

Acknowledgement is due to Paul Slessor for permission to publish his father's poems, as well as prose works by Kenneth Slessor quoted in the Explanatory Notes. Kenneth Slessor's papers are held in the National Library of Australia and the State Library of New South Wales. Thanks are due to these distinguished libraries for permission to cite material held in their possession, and thanks are owed to their staff for assistance shown on many occasions.

The editors wish to thank the many friends who provided information for the Explanatory Notes in different ways and on various occasions. Further thanks are due to staff of the Australian War Memorial Library and of the Alexander Library and the Reid Library, Western Australia. This work was greatly assisted by grants from the National Library of Australia (under their Harold White Fellowship Scheme) and the Division of Arts and Architecture, the University of Western Australia.

The editors wish to give particular thanks to the secretarial staff of the Department of English at the University of Western Australia; to Alan Dodds for his computer assistance; to Barry Humphries for the loan of Slessor's personal copy of *One Hundred Poems*; and to previous Slessor scholars on whose work we have drawn.

Preface

Kenneth Slessor has long been recognised as one of Australia's major poets; indeed, some would see him as the most important poet Australia has ever produced. Yet his reputation has rested on a surprisingly small output: basically the 103 poems which Slessor in 1957 chose to represent his life's work, under the bland title, Poems. By 1957 Slessor had long ceased to publish any new poetry; Poems added only three new works to One Hundred Poems, which had been published in 1944, and the previous poems were published unchanged. Slessor's silence when at the height of his powers has been one of the great mysteries and disappointments of Australian literature.

That Slessor did not entirely give up writing when he gave up publishing is evidenced by this book, but his output during the last quarter century of his life was slight and sparse. This *Collected Poems* provides a picture of Slessor's whole poetic output, of his development as a poet, and of his decline into silence. It aims to provide accurate texts of all Slessor's poems of any consequence. The poems are presented in the final versions authorised by Slessor, as determined from the poems' last dated publication during his lifetime and his personal papers. Determining final authorisations is not as difficult a process with Slessor as with many other writers. Although a tireless reviser of poems when in manuscript draft, Slessor rarely made changes to poems after their first publication, except for modernising some aspects of his early work. For this reason, textual notes and explanatory notes have been included together.

This book has a number of motivations: a respect for Slessor's poetry as a whole; an interest in the development of that poetry and the relationships between poems written at different times in his writing career; and an awareness of a significant lack of such editions in Australian literature. Although even minor British and American poets have been published in scholarly editions, this is only the second annotated, documented edition of collected poems for any Australian poet (the first being Colin Roderick's 1967–69 edition of Henry

Lawson's verse). Thus, the book provides a record of Slessor's work, and to some extent provides a symbolic assertion about the quality of Australian poetry as a whole.

It must be said that the term 'Collected Poems' is always a more problematic one than it first appears. This volume includes all the completed poems which could with a reasonable degree of certainty be identified as Slessor's except for juvenilia and casual verse. By the term 'juvenilia' the editors mean the verses Slessor wrote as a child, including lines for his family or for his school. The term 'casual verse' covers a mixture of material. Slessor spent his working life as a journalist, during a period in which poetry of a casual sort had a ready place in newspapers. Thus, Slessor would compose a few lines about a well-known person to accompany a sketch or a photograph in a newspaper or would write squibs about contemporary politicians. Similarly, he composed verses such as that for the Artists' Ball of 1950, which begins:

After the Ball is over, after we've made Stan Cross,
When Dorothy Wilson's finished, counting the profit and loss,
After they've woken Geoff. Turton, after the firemen call,
You'll be a cot-case, that's certain,
After the Ball.

Such material we have regarded as 'casual verse', lacking a general interest outside its immediate context or particular audience. Any verse which seems to contain substantial social or satirical comment has been included in the book.

A similar process of editorial judgement is necessary with annotations, since the commentary required by one reader will not be required by another, and Slessor's readership is now extremely diverse: it includes practising poets and critics, international readers, school and university students, lecturers and teachers, and a general Australian readership. Taking this into account, the editors have tended to err on the side of inclusiveness. The annotations follow the order of the poems; the poems are presented in their order of publication in each volume, except that — with the exception of one poem, 'Wild Grapes' — poems included in more than one volume are only printed once. The volumes are presented according to date of publication but with a separation of 'serious' and 'light' verse, and previously uncollected poems are presented in order of composition, with poems that cannot be dated being printed last. The order of the poems in Slessor's selection, *Poems*, and in the anthologies he edited, *Poetry in Australia, 1923* and *The Penguin Book of Modern Australian Verse*, are included in an appendix.

Preparing a book such as this induces a great respect for the compilers of dictionaries, atlases, encyclopaedias and numerous other reference works, as well as for the memories of certain friends. All deficiencies, of course, remain the responsibility of the editors.

Chronology

1901 Kenneth Adolphe Schloesser born 27 March 1901 in Orange, New South Wales, first child of Robert Schloesser and Margaret McInnes

1903 Moves to Sydney with parents

1908 Visits England with parents

1910 Attends Mowbray House School, Chatswood

1914 Robert Schloesser changes family name to 'Slessor'

1915 Attends Sydney Church of England Grammar School ('Shore')

1917 First poem published, 'Goin'' in the *Bulletin*

1918 Wins Victoria League (London) Poetry Prize with 'Jerusalem Set Free'

1919 Attends Sydney Metropolitan Business College

1920 Works as journalist on Sydney *Sun*

1922 Marries Noela Senior
Meets Hugh McCrae, Jack Lindsay and Norman Lindsay

1923–4 Edits *Vision: A Literary Quarterly*, with Jack Lindsay and Frank C. Johnson, and a poetry anthology, *Poetry in Australia, 1923*, with Jack Lindsay

1924 *Thief of the Moon*
Works as journalist on Melbourne *Herald* and sub-editor on Melbourne *Punch*

1926 *Earth-Visitors*
Works as journalist on Sydney *Sun*

1927 Works as journalist (and from 1936 as an editor) on *Smith's Weekly*

1931 *Trio: A Book of Poems* (with Harley Matthews and Colin Simpson)

1932 *Cuckooz Contrey*
Darlinghurst Nights

1933 *Funny Farmyard*

1939 *Five Bells: XX Poems*

1940 Serves as official Australian War Correspondent

1944	Resigns as War Correspondent and rejoins *Sun*
	One Hundred Poems
1945	Noela Slessor dies
	Edits *Australian Poetry 1945*
1946	Affair with Kathleen McShine
1950	*Portrait of Sydney* (prose), ed. Gwen Morton Spencer and Sam Ure Smith
1951	Marries Pauline Wallace
1952	Son, Paul Slessor, born
1956–61	Edits *Southerly*
1957	Works as journalist on *Daily Telegraph*
	Poems
1958	Edits *The Penguin Book of Australian Verse*, with John Thompson and R.G. Howarth
1960	*Australian Profile* (prose)
1961	Divorces Pauline Slessor
	The Penguin Book of Australian Verse revised as *The Penguin Book of Modern Australian Verse*
1965	*Life at the Cross*
1966	*Sydney Harbour*
	Canberra
1970	*Bread and Wine: Selected Prose*
1971	Dies, on 30 June
1983	*Backless Betty from Bondi*, ed. Julian Croft
1985	*The War Diaries of Kenneth Slessor*, ed. Clement Semmler
1987	*The War Despatches of Kenneth Slessor*
1990	*The Sea Poems of Kenneth Slessor*
1992	*Kenneth Slessor*, ed. Dennis Haskell

Slessor also published, probably in the 1960s, two small undated books, *The Grapes are Growing: The Story of Australian Wine* and *Surf: All About It*.

Thief of the Moon

(1924)

She laughed and shook her petticoats . . . 'O, vanity!' she said,
'Now catch me with your kissing if you can!' And off she fled,
Over the walks and arbours as light as a petal shaken . . .
O proud one, who would not be caught . . . O captor I have taken,
Know that I have entrapped your lips, and closer than you think
You're prisoned in a paper cage by bars of printer's ink!

Incongruity

Running with red wet hands from bough to bough,
The sun has drenched ten thousand trees.
    Now night,
Like smoke agrope below them from immense
Black-bubbling bowls of giants' broth, takes flight
Up creeks to steaming mountain-towers. And now
Cold stars, like glaives of silver, palely smite,
    Frigid with hate and old malevolence.

Now in this hour of sinister dismay,
When Lupus beads with evil, I would wait
Robed in the stoles of alchemy, to cry
Defiance to the star-ways, hate for hate,
And counter-charm for planetary sway —
But (fool!) instead I stand and contemplate,
    In pantaloons and coat, the taunting sky —

Whilst even the curlew, puling his old tune,
Has found an echo to the night, and weeps
With ancient grief for some forgotten wrong
That stole from mind an age ago, but keeps
Perpetual trysting with the sombre moon —
And even the nightjar in the valley-deeps
    Accords with evening in his cruel song.

Nuremberg

So quiet it was in that high, sun-steeped room,
So warm and still, that sometimes with the light
Through the great windows, bright with bottle-panes,

There'd float a chime from clock-jacks out of sight,
   Clapping iron mallets on green copper gongs.

But only in blown music from the town's
Quaint horologe could Time intrude . . . you'd say
Clocks had been bolted out, the flux of years
Defied, and that high chamber sealed away
   From earthly change by some old alchemist.

And, oh, those thousand towers of Nuremberg
Flowering like leaden trees outside the panes:
Those gabled roofs with smoking cowls, and those
Encrusted spires of stone, those golden vanes
   On shining housetops paved with scarlet tiles!

And all day nine wrought-pewter manticores
Blinked from their spouting faucets, not five steps
Across the cobbled street, or, peering through
The rounds of glass, espied that sun-flushed room
   With Dürer graving at intaglios.

O happy nine, spouting your dew all day
In green-scaled rows of metal, whilst the town
Moves peacefully below in quiet joy . . .
O happy gargoyles to be gazing down
   On Albrecht Dürer and his plates of iron!

The Ghost

'Bees of old Spanish wine
Pipe at this Inn to-night,
Music and candleshine
   Fill the dim chambers . . .

'Fans toss and ladies pace,
Flutes of cold metal blow,
Maidens like winds of lace
    Tease the dark passages . . .

'Run, you fat kitchen-boys,
Pasties in pyramids
Rise while your masters poise
    Flagons with silver lids . . .

'Ha! Let the platters fume,
Jars wink and bottles drip,
Staining with smoke and spume
    Lips, tables, tapestries . . .

'Wenches with tousled silk,
Mouths warm and bubble eyes,
Tumble those beds of milk
    Under carved canopies . . .

'Now let your lovers dive
Deep to that hurricane . . .
O, to be there alive,
    Breathing again!'

So the ghost cried, and pressed to the dark pane,
Like a white leaf, his face . . . in vain . . . in vain . . .

A Surrender

When to those Venusbergs, thy breasts,
By wars of love and moonlight batteries,
My lips have stormed — O pout thy mouth above,
Lean down those culverins twain, and bid me spike

Their bells with kissing, and their powder steal,
And by night-marches take their garrisons —
No blood shall stain those battlefields of lace
But all their snows run dappled with deep roses,
And thou, I trow, sweet enemy of love,
  Shalt find a conquest in capitulation!

Mangroves

These black bush-waters, heavy with crusted boughs
  Like plumes above dead captains, wake the mind . . .
Uncounted kissing, unremembered vows,
  Nights long forgotten, moons too dark to find,
Or stars too cold . . . all quick things that have fled
  Whilst these old bubbles uprise in older stone,
Return like pale dead faces of children dead,
  Staring unfelt through doors for ever unknown.

O silent ones that drink these timeless pools,
  Eternal brothers, bending so deeply over,
Your branches tremble above my tears again . . .
  And even my songs are stolen from some old lover
Who cried beneath your leaves like other fools,
  While still they whisper 'in vain . . . in vain . . . in vain . . .'

Thief of the Moon

Thief of the moon, thou robber of old delight,
Thy charms have stolen the star-gold, quenched the moon —
Cold, cold are the birds that, bubbling out of night,
Cried once to my ears their unremembered tune —
Dark are those orchards, their leaves no longer shine,

No orange's gold is globed like moonrise there —
O thief of the earth's old loveliness, once mine,
Why dost thou waste all beauty to make thee fair?

Break, break thy strings, thou lutanists of earth,
Thy musics touch me not — let midnight cover
With pitchy seas those leaves of orange and lime,
I'll not repent. The world's no longer worth
One smile from thee, dear pirate of place and time,
Thief of old loves that haunted once thy lover!

Undine

In Undine's mirror the cutpurse found
Five candlesticks by magic drowned,
Like boughs of silver . . . and pale as death,
Biting his beard, till the rogue's own breath
Shook all their gourds of fire, he stopped,
Eyed the gilt baskets, gaped half-round . . .
Then down to the floor his pistol dropped . . .

No sound in the dark rooms . . . the clank
Of metal and beam died fast . . . and flank
Pressed in strange fear to Undine's bed,
The robber stared long, and bent his head
To that soft wave . . . then hand on silk,
Plumbed the warm valley where nightly sank
Undine the water-maid, caved in milk.

And over those pools, the rogue could smell
Rich essences globed and stoppered well
On Undine's table . . . and row by row,

Jars of green china foamed stiff with snow,
And crystal trays and bottles of stone
Bowed like black slaves to that ivory shell,
   The body of Undine . . . but Undine was gone.

Only below the candles' gleam,
In one small casket of waxen cream
With sidelong eyes the thief could follow
That rosy trough, the printed hollow
Of Undine's finger . . . then out to the street
He sprawled and fled . . . but still on the beam
   His pistol waited for Undine's feet!

Good-night

'Good-night, good-night' — sweet maidens all
   Bend golden arms above,
And all their plaits in candlelight
Swing pricked to gilt, while faintly fall
   Those little cries of love —
'Good-night, good-night!'

Now from the stairways winding out
   Lanterns in darkness drown —
Wenches like fire-birds blown to flight
Climb the stone galleries, hover and pout
   Warm gales of kissing down —
Good-night, good-night!

But thou, my friend, brood silent there —
   Now smile — and gape — and try,
With one slow finger, smooth and white,

Thy pistol-wheels — then creep to stare
At coaches pitching by —
Good-night, good-night!

Good-night, good-night, brave turnpike-boy,
Rare, starry toil is ours —
I to my lady's dark delight,
And thou to the moonlit road, employ
By Venus and Mars these waking hours —
Good lad, good-night, good-night!

The Mask

To J.L.

The rout stamps by — now beards of copper
Dance in dark breasts — now music smites
With horns and bells to the candelabra,
Shaking their waxen lights.

Plumes rock — the masquers plunge and riot —
Heat in a steam has drowned the floor —
Dumb with old fears I lurch bewildered,
Beating upon the door.

How came we two to this hot chamber?
What painted marionettes dance here?
It is in vain thy dreams to remember,
It is in vain to fear . . .

But suddenly out of the clang and tumult
I saw thy mask descend,
And I knew thy face revealed for a moment,
And knew thy speech, my friend!

And words we cried that were not mortal,
   Whilst burning in eyes that were not eyes,
There shone the star that shines not ever
   In earth's dark skies . . .

O traveller, greeting! O merry meeting!
   O strange disguise!

Rubens' Innocents

If all those tumbling babes of heaven,
   Plump cherubim with blown cheeks,
Could vault in these warm skies, or leaven
   Our starry silent mountain-peaks —
O painter of chub-faced, shining-thighed
   Fat Ganymedes of God — what noise
Would churn between the clouds and stride
   Far downward from those rose-mouthed boys!

Down to our spires their lusty whooping,
   Fanfares of Paradise, would speed,
Far down to dark-faced clergy stooping
   Round altars of their doleful creed;
And God, whose wings of silver sweep
   Like metal afire on heaven's rim,
Would daze them with a twinkling peep
   Of those young moon-stained cherubim —

Then, for a trice, their skies might sparkle,
   And some gold ichor splash amid
Those most respectable, patriarchal
   Purveyors of stale pardons, hid
Behind their old cathedral closes

From this unguessed, unguessable God,
Shining before their learned noses
Down roads that Peter Rubens trod.

Adventure Bay

Sophie's my world . . . my arm must soon or later
Like Francis Drake turn circumnavigator,
Stem the dark tides, take by the throat strange gales
And toss their spume to stars unknown, as kings
Rain diamonds to the mob . . . then arch my sails
By waterspouts of lace and bubbling rings
Gulfed in deep satin, conquer those warmer waves
Where none but mermaids ride, and the still caves
Untrod by sailors . . . aye, and with needle set,
Rounding Cape Turnagain, take up my way,
And so to the Ivory Coast . . . and farther yet,
Port of all drownéd lovers, Adventure Bay!

Thieves' Kitchen

Good roaring pistol-boys, brave lads of gold,
Good roistering easy maids, blown cock-a-hoop
On floods of tavern-steam, I greet you! Drunk
With wild Canary, drowned in wines of old,
I'll swear your round, red faces dive and swim
Like clouds of fire-fish in a waxen tide,
And these are seas of smoke we thieves behold.

Yet I've a mind I know what arms enchain
With flesh my shoulders . . . aye, and what warm legs

Wind quickly into mine . . . 'tis no pale mermaid,
No water-wench that floats in a smoky main
Betwixt the tankard and my knees . . . in faith,
I know thee, Joan, and by the beard of God,
I'll prove to-night thy mortal parts again!

Leap, leap, fair vagabonds, your lives are short . . .
Dance firelit in your cauldron-fumes, O thieves,
Ram full your bellies with spiced food, gulp deep
Those goblets of thick ale — yea, feast and sport,
Ye Cyprian maids — lie with great, drunken rogues,
Jump by the fire — soon, soon your flesh must crawl
And Tyburn flap with birds, long-necked and swart!

'Quite Modern'

Glassed in dark pools of rosewood,
Some pale composer plays,
Plucking those frozen piano-keys
Like milky fronds from lilac-trees,
To weave their leaves in sprays —
Cold ivory boughs of music blown
Like bells in groves of carven stone,
Whose petals chime always.

Pince-nez and watery diamonds
Drip from each gilded chair;
We nod politely; roll dead eyes
In ravished wisdom . . . words uprise
To rub their sides in air . . .
'Stravinsky? Ah, ma foi, quelle force!' . . .
'Adore him . . . thanks . . . quite modern, of course.'
Alone I stare and stare.

It's only that through the windows
  An old, old air blows in
From some boy whistling miles below,
Whose lips died many an age ago . . .
  Some ancient gaslight din . . .
Oh, Merry Peasant, vulgar bawl . . .
Oh, common boy who scraped that squall . . .
  Once . . . on a violin . . .

Secret Pastures

When twilight strikes the road with fire,
And the moon's cold, crusted fluid
  By some old magic of the night
Leaves thick beneath, on ruts and mire,
  Slow silver scales of light . . .

Softly along the road there goes
An old white stallion, tolling
  With hoofs of chalk on ivory ground,
And earth's all quiet, no whisper blows
  But that slow, hollow sound.

With eyes like jars of darkness and dew,
And nostrils cut from stone . . .
  Lazily, drowsily, bathed in grey,
Down the faint road his feet pursue
  Their ancient, soundless way.

Would I rode with him, through the night
Astride those frozen shoulders,
  That milky mane, those tasselled hoofs,

By miles of houses, powdered-white,
   And miles of moonlit roofs,

And miles of smoking garden-tops,
And miles of grey-tiled villas,
   Past hedges pale with drifted dust,
By lost arcades, forgotten shops,
   And wires long eaten to rust . . .

Would I could seek with him those far,
Sweet, secret pasturages . . .
   Down many a silent, silver street . . .
Where fire-eyed mountain brumbies are,
   And phantom horse-bells beat!

January 18, 1922

Let you remember this January day,
O child of moonlight, shouting your breathless rhymes,
All you who shrine in music the Milky Way,
Or the old, sad loveliness of girls in ivory times —
O lovers of earth, and the moon's cold, guttering dew,
Darkness on starless dunes, and mulberry-birds in leaves,
And the young, marching stars — by these I conjure you
   Remember, remember this January day!

For the days descend and vanish, and soon are over,
Steeping with night the earth in forgetfulness,
And twilight findeth no tears of a broken lover
To cover the graves of dusk, or dawn's pale eyes to bless;
But the Lady Helen is wept, and staves are trolled
By timeless poets, of beauty in fields or fair, dead maids —

And still the grave, beautiful daylight flows as it did of old
    Though the days descend and vanish, and soon are over.

But this dear day, this dear, amazing night,
I'll swear to store for ever in men's minds,
Rescued from time to breathe of past delight
And matchless always, till some miser of moonlight finds
More beauty in far midsummers to adore,
More loveliness to quaff, more charms to cry —
Till then, O lovers of earth, remember for evermore,
    Remember, remember this January night!

Two Nocturnes

1

Cloaked in black furs, like some magnifico
    Come mourning to the catafalque of day,
Night swaggers down the sky to Arakoon —
    A shivering wakes the river-weeds, and lo!
Red in the gums, there swings a smoky moon,
    And dark has driven the thunderbirds away.

How comes the swarthy wash of night upon
    Bay-road, set far from this deserted North
In paven ways, where lazily at dark
    Those oriel-eyed suburban villas don
Soft stoles of velvet, and their front-doors spark
    Like rosy lanterns, dripping phosphor forth?

Do clouds at sunset weigh still, underlined
    With flourishes of God's vermilion ink,
In great grey battlements of candle-grease,
    Whilst day floods west like lava, and behind

All stolen from a Doré frontispiece —
   In sphery Morse, the little planets wink?

2

O cruelly comes dusk to Arakoon,
   And here is darkness dour and terrible;
The weeds of night sweat poisonous, and wrapped
   In far, tremendous reverie, the moon
Distils maleficence, and I am trapped
   By sorceries demoniac from hell.

And, if in sunlight I have glorified
   Those lonely mazes of the bush below,
Now I remember, with a curious ache,
   The panes of Sydney gilt at even-tide,
Like paper lit by candle flame to make
   Some pasteboard setting for a puppet-show . . .

The sizzling steam that blows like cotton-wool
   From clockwork ferries at a toy pontoon . . .
The dear electric signs above the Quay . . .
   And all of Sydney that seems wonderful,
Return to haunt me unendurably,
   Whilst night leans blackly over Arakoon.

Threatenings

Dark's in the air, the moon hangs copper-paned,
   Firing the treetops with her milky mist;
Night's wet panaches droop jetty black, and stained
   Like bloodwood-gum across the sky there twist
The smoking flails of sunset. Small and cold,

Dim planets beat behind, and fragrance blows
Over the globey orange-trees, along
Old riverways and fields of powdered gold,
Whilst washing down the world, the daystream flows
In lilac flumes beyond the Kurrajong.

Why in this tender chemistry of night
And subtle transmutation, should there climb
Cold tides of dread? The trees are blossom-white
Like milky peacock-tails, for eventime
Bends moonlit cheeks above the sleeping earth,
And umber-topped the orangeries loom
Around me. But the stars, the stars, I know
Dance terribly in far, malevolent mirth;
And fears run slyly in the grass below
Like vapours rising from a mummy's tomb.

If cobalt quietness fills the river-pools,
And calm is in the honey-dusted sky . . . .
Oh, hid behind those fragile opuscules
And faint experiments of dusk, there lie
Defiant monsters, far tremendous threats
From powers which made the wattle, and the soft
Flame-painted blossoms of the orange-trees . . .
And past the twilight's opal sarcenets,
Beyond the singing grass, and all of these,
I see red drought, with sulphur suns aloft . . .

Red, scalded steppes of mountain-country, drier
Than brasier-dregs, and desolated strips
Cracked scrofulous by slag-red suns, or fire
In stark, metallic trees, like scarlet whips;
And rotten-steaming skeletons of stock

On silent plains, for green-shot flies to eat;
Or flood-tides from the Murrumbidgee, spouting
Like water-bursts upon the gilded wheat
Round lonely homesteads. And these giants mock
The cobweb Kurrajong with ghastly shouting!

Pan at Lane Cove

Scaly with poison, bright with flame,
Great fungi steam beside the gate,
Run tentacles through flagstone cracks,
Or claw beyond, where meditate
Wet poplars on a pitchy lawn.
Some seignior of colonial fame
Has planted here a stone-cut faun
Whose flute juts like a frozen flame.

O lonely faun, what songs are these
For skies where no Immortals hide?
Why finger in this dour abode
Those Pan-pipes girdled at your side?
Your Gods, and Hellas too, have passed,
Forsaken are the Cyclades,
And surely, faun, you are the last
To pipe such ancient songs as these.

Yet, blow your stone-lipped flute, and blow
Those red-and-silver pipes of Pan.
Cold stars are bubbling round the moon,
Which, like some golden Indiaman
Disgorged by waterspouts and blown
Through heaven's archipelago,

Drives orange bows by clouds of stone . . .
   Blow, blow your flute, you stone boy, blow!

And, Chiron, pipe your centaurs out,
The night has looped a smoky scarf
Round campanili in the town,
And thrown a cloak about Clontarf.
Now earth is ripe for Pan again,
Barbaric ways and Paynim rout,
And revels of old Samian men.
   O Chiron, pipe your centaurs out.

This garden by the dark Lane Cove
Shall spark before thy music dies
With silver sandals; all thy gods
Be conjured from Ionian skies.
Those poplars in a fluting-trice
They'll charm into an olive-grove
And dance a while in Paradise
   Like men of fire above Lane Cove.

Clocks

Who trows he hath Time in his calendars,
   Like moonlight in old almanacs, constrained
By graven sun-dials and the march of stars
To frontiers caged by clocks? Thy brazen wheels,
   O mad arithmetician, roll disdained.

Stare as thou wilt from doméd citadels,

Those bubbles of glass reflect the skies in vain.
Thou canst not chain with astronomic spells
One crack of Time, nor by the stars pin down
This moment to thy pendulum's domain.

Time is a pulse of mutable extent,
Time is a tide that runneth like to blood
Piping in human hearts. 'Tis resident
In mortals only — not an hour-glass drips
Beyond the starstreams in that silent flood.

Only in human veins may Time be found,
Measured by human grief and happiness,
For moons may never sway, nor scape-wheels bound,
Thy heart's horology. O clockwork fools,
'Minute' and 'year' — how futile to assess!

New Magic

At last I know — it's on old ivory jars,
Glassed with old miniatures and garnered once with musk.
I've seen those eyes like smouldering April stars
As carp might see them behind their bubbled skies
In pale green fishponds — they're as green your eyes,
As lakes themselves, changed to green stone at dusk.

At last I know — it's paned in a crystal hoop
On powder-boxes from some dead Italian girl,
I've seen such eyes grow suddenly dark, and droop
Their small, pure lids, as if I'd pried too far
In finding you snared there on that ivory jar
By crusted motes of rose and smoky-pearl.

Oh, well I know what delicate, dark-haired brush,
Cargoed with dragon's-blood and drops of Antwerp blue,
Hath kissed old ivory, and taken that tiptoe flush
Below your lashes, to bind it down with paint
On perfume-jars, or miniatures worked in faint
  Half-lights of chrome and lilac, and all of you.

All this I know which yet my mind recalls
From times when beauty was walled within enamelled skies,
But know not what new magic it is enthralls
My heart to-day, nor whence, beloved, there came
Those gardens of drowsy verdigris and flame
  That shake to forests when I touch your eyes!

For Noela

Like tides of some old sea brimmed years ago
But climbing always, bells are blown to-day
  From over the hills and far, oh far away,
  And nothing but Noel's in the tune they blow —
Now long ago, I gave you Noel gifts —
  Grave seigniors bowed in jewelled lace with spoils
  From Spanish towns to please you, golden coils
Of rope-stuck stones, and silk in ivory drifts . . .

Ah, Noela, no potency's in rhyme
  To conjure those old fairings from the dead,
For poets are tombed below the dust of time
  Despite their music. This I bring instead,
The sweet half-gravity of your laughing eyes
Distilled in timeless words whilst beauty dies.

DECEMBER 25, 1921

Amazement

Time, and the customs of my kind, have staled
That large amazement of my franker years,
When wonder burnt within the hemispheres,
And quaint surprise at life and limbs prevailed
With cosmic humour; nor, as yet, had failed
That dear absurdity of eyes and ears,
Of spiny nose, of laughing, and of tears,
Divined ere life had dulled, or humour paled.

Dear child, remembrance lingers: I can probe
Those lakes of puzzlement behind your eyes,
That stirring mirth, the miracle of flesh . . .
So, too, I solved an undiscovered globe,
Swam in uncharted oceans, mapped the skies,
And strode the Nine Lands of the world afresh.

The Hidden Lands

To-morrow, when our windy pathways pipe
Strident with tumult from a thousand 'planes,
And, strung in wedges like the southing snipe,
Black squadrons beat across the hurricanes:
Then may those nomads of the middle air
Whose cylinders drum faintly from the deeps
High over Dandaloo, lean out and stare
Incredulous . . . whilst in their shadow sleeps
The mystic bush, as it has hotly slept
In prehistoric stillness all those moons,
Ere ever that drowned old Spanish galleon swept
Through coral oceans with her picaroons . . .

And then they'll spy the hidden lands, among
Things quite forgotten when the world was young.

Before the Rain

This is the furtive peace before the rain,
That floods a breathless world with augury;
When the clouds string smudged across the hurricane,
And the pulse of things wanes in expectancy;
When the world is haloed with a nameless glow,
Star-shine in daylight, moonlight *sans* the moon,
And lazily in the street the waggons go,
Crumbling the silence with a creaking tune.

Now should some epic warrior thunder out
To split the stillness with a mighty shout,
Blasting the riotous earth by fire and sword —
Now, now, should some world-hero lead the storm
Tornado-wise amidst a hairy horde,
And maze the planets with his bucklered swarm —
Now should some toppling argosy be hurled
Over the rim of the embattled world —

But still it's hushed — and, rustling down the lane,
Nought but the friendly quietness of the rain . . .

Marco Polo

Reading how Marco Polo came
By bridle-path to Kanbalu,
Forgotten fibres wake to flame,
And smoke old memories anew . . .
For in a bygone life of mine
I watched the carven rampart shine,
Where Kublai's five-clawed dragons glowed
   Like painted wyverns, line on line.

And past those plaster dragon-heads,
Those frescoes cut with curious flowers,
In verdigris and lilac-reds
Old tiles gleamed on the crusted towers,
While bridges cleft of serpent-stone
Bowed by their side, like branches blown
From some high granite Tree of Life
   Whose roots were coiled round Kublai's throne.

O myrtles on the Jasper Mount,
O forest-towered elephants,
And fire-fish in the topaz fount
With red fins blown like water-plants,
And green cornelian tortoise-rows
Below the aqueduct, and those
Gold-feathered cranes, I saw them all,
   How many ages gone, who knows?

I saw tall gilded Tartars pass
Behind their marble balustrades,
With maces made of beaten brass
And turquoise-hafted sabre-blades.
I heard the little golden bells

Blow faintly down the citadels,
And spied those ivory courts within
  Through windows of transparent shells.

But past the fountain-pools I peered,
Beyond the birds, to that divan,
Where, fingering his tawny beard,
In silence dreamed the splendid Khan.
Green china bowls of wine were there,
And oranges and milk-of-mare,
While, stamping on his jewelled wrist,
  A falcon climbed with eyes aflare.

He's gone; and with him, flowers and birds,
And old Venetians too, have died;
Yet burnt in Marco Polo's words,
Those unforgotten splendours hide . . .
And, tired of life's new-fashioned plan,
I long to be barbarian.
I'm sick of modern men, I wish
  You still were living, Kublai-Khan!

Old Chinese Poem

North of the Wall from the Eastern Gate,
Mysterious and desolate
  The distant Graveyard shines;
White aspens whisper round its walks,
  And cypresses and pines.

Beneath the trees the bodies rot
Of men our grandparents forgot,

And the grandparents whom we forget . . .
A thousand years they have lain thus
And shall lie ten thousand yet.

The world spins endless Day and Night,
And the years drip by with dark and light
Till only the Metals and Stones endure . . .
For Man must flee before his Things,
And Death is always sure.

Thy Mourners are buried in their turn;
And all that Saints or Sages learn
Is only . . . that we eat to die:

And it's better to go with Wine and Show
Than shrivel in the Sty!

Taoist

Those friends of Lao-Tzu, those wise old men
Dozing all day in lemon-silken robes,
With tomes of beaten jade spread knee to knee,
And pipe-stem, shining cold with silver, poised
In steaming play, and still a finger free
To dog the path of some forgotten pen;

Almost their bee-sweet ancient words incline
My mind to those old pagan ways, beloved
By mandarins and mages, now but dust
In drowsy pyramids. What creed is this,
Save that which those philosophers discussed
In gold pavilions, over musky wine?

'Repenting always of forgotten wrongs
Will never bring thy heart to rest, for thought
Repairs no whit of evil; rather cast
Thy meditations in that utter void
To which all human deeds resolve at last . . .'

So runs the burden of their thousand songs.

Here, in this dark Star-Chamber of the soul,
You stand arraigned, O slayer of my heart . . .
But I am tired of hoarding up the grist
Of anger, and remember Lao-Tzu.
Revenge is empty to the Taoist,
    And tears of penitence a futile toll!

An Old Harp

The harp is built of cassia and cord;
    And in its strings lie ancient melodies,
Forgotten tunes of wistful emptiness,
    Thin, quavering sonatas, that afford
Small savour in their piping minor keys
To men of newer ways and stranger dress.

The jade upon the stops is dead, and dust
    Lies mistily upon the sorrel strings;
The soul of it has rotted with the years.
    And yet in spite of verdigris and rust,
About the cords a cold, clear music clings.
    Play it or not; you'd surely stop your ears.
You ask me why its melodies must pass?
    Hark to the clamour of the jarring brass!

Chessmen

Chafing on flags of ebony and pearl,
   My paladins are waiting. Loops of smoke
Stoop slowly from the coffee-cups, and curl
   In thin fantastic patterns down the room
By cabinets of chinaware, to whirl
   With milky-blue tobacco-steam, and fume
Together past our pipes, outside the door.

Soon may we lounge in silence, O my friend,
   Behind those carven men-at-arms of chess
Dyed coral-red with dragon's blood, and spend
   The night with noiseless warfare. Queens and rooks
With chiselled ivory warriors must contend
   And counter-plots from old Arabian books
Be conjured to the march of knights and pawns.

April 25

Morning. But does the daystar weep,
   Do the trees weep for the dead?
O false! The lights of sunrise leap
   Through ivory skies instead.

Night smokes afar, the mist-maids cling,
   The world spins on its way;
Only the birds remember, and sing
   What men can never say.

Is it a bird which fills the air
   Over Australia flying?
Somehow it sounds as if somewhere
   A soul is crying.

Simone

Simone in the doorway, as calm and unstirred
  As the lustre that burns on the silk of her hose,
Close-hatted, snug-coated, all muffled and furred
  To the little pink tip of her velvet nose.

So straight in the doorway she stands, so slim and so clear,
So amazingly young, so incredibly dear!

Why should I wonder at seeing her there?
  Save that I thought, and remember it yet,
That sometime, and somehow, somewhere,
  She had stood so, and looked so, and smiled in a life I forget.

Some New Poets

Of sex they prate, these quaint homunculi,
And mope on coffin-worms, or sweat amain
  Much curious jargon — as a madman's brain
  Festers with images, he knows not why —
On reechy love. They like to horrify
  The carefree folk of earth, and sometimes deign
  To fright small babes with maggots from the drain,
Call God a cretin and the world a sty.

On with the danse macabre! The giant dead
  Shine hugely through these vapourings, and soon
All glamour of corruption shall have fled,
  As men remember mountains, and the moon,
Lovers in gardens, children quiet in bed,
  And stars burnt stainless in a black lagoon.

The Embarkation for Cythera

'O, mount thee, Lady, mount!' In the warm lake
There foam a thousand water-girls, blown deep
With rings of silver and bubbles like racing moons —
'O, mount!' — their mouths they hoop, their limbs they shake,
The powdered Marquis on the poop leans out,
  Misty with lace, and showers dark rubies down.

The sweet postillions paid by Venus are these,
With breasts that shake like drops of ivory,
Close-welling to the flesh — their frolicks beat
The waves to milk, and crust with gold the seas
And dolphins wet their hips, when mad for salt,
  They ride on fish-back to the Spanish Main.

Spars net the moon. The moth-blue, pastel air
Swims with a cluster of young cherubim,
Puffing the topsails — undines laugh below
Like bells in water, whilst up that gilded stair
From garden to prow, an arch of petticoats
  Pouts in the breeze — 'O, mount thee, Lady, mount!'

Now the Infanta's maidens take the night
With cloaks and lanterns — now to a buried flute
Great lemans dance, and that little dark-lashed jade
With Cardinals' kisses on her mouth, takes flight
By lawns and bending orange-boughs, to climb
  Warm-tousled on board — 'O, mount thee, Lady, mount!'

Maleine is running in a hundred skirts,
Tumbled with laughter — Alix and Isabelle
Down lanes of statues dawdle — and all those ladies
In patch and paint, and all those ringlet-flirts,

Invade the bulwarks, crying for Cythera —
O, mount thee, ladies: where lies that port of love?

'Tis by the Cyprian's bed — there lovers twine
Darkly with naked thighs — there plumes and diamonds
Vanish by witchery, jewels and laces drop,
Hoops burst asunder, ribbons their task decline,
Satin comes down in pools, and all are conscript,
Sworn alike to Cythera, peers in love.

'O, mount thee, mount thee!' — Ladies and Gallants haste,
Fans clap and sword-knots dance, the Court sweeps down,
The Countess hurries with grass in her powdered hair,
The Duchess with a King's arm round her waist —
And, ah! thou little serving-wench, embark —
Thy mouth is red — 'tis passage enough to Cythera!

The Man of Sentiment

Part One

(A walled garden of York. It is an August Sunday, and the baying of deep church-bells is blown faintly in a warm wind. Laurence Sterne, prebendary, aged forty-six, and Catherine de Fromantel, a girl who sings at Ranelagh, are dawdling through the arbours, and pause at a path which runs between hedges and cypress-trees round a corner some fifty yards away. Catherine has walked down such a path before, it is to be feared, and halts cautiously upon its fringes.)

Laurence:

Nay, 'tis no Devil's walk,
It leads to what? Some leaden Child with lips

Blown open, spouting fountain-dew on birds
That drowsily dive the pool . . . some secret Lawn
Tight locked away in mazes, and trod by none
Save one old crazy Gardener . . . aye, 'tis prick'd
In curious inks on charts of old, I'll vow,
Drown'd in some careless Viscount's library
Five hundred years, and like to rot five more.
Now we, my child, wait idly, toe to brink,
Whilst I must pray thee to walk hand-in-hand
Not fifty steps along a sanded alley . . .

Catherine:

Such paths have led to dangerous lands before,
And many a maid's marched less than fifty steps
To-day no maiden . . . 'tis a well-known Grove,
Thy maze of lime and bergamot, good priest . . .
Plump Notaries would buzz with ivory tablets,
Plaguing the round-tubb'd orange-trees to blab
Could they but speak . . . Oh, trust me, sir, I know
Those leafy Rogues too well!

Laurence:

Nay, Kit, these trees
Are stout duennas, this garden a Dutch garden,
And sure the grass would rust to yellow stalks
If lovers betray'd its beaded innocence.
Come . . . seven steps . . . I'll swear to coax no more . . .
As far as the Cypress . . . not a bee's foot further . . .
As far as the Cypress . . .

Catherine:

No, I tell you, no!
(She allows herself to be led a few steps.)

Laurence:

But here the spices of some little trees,
And certain hot, heavy orchard-essences
From fruits that have molten in their leaves, do tell
Stupendous tales of Paddocks round the turn —
Flat, knee-thick fields of laziness, piping all day
With flies and ants, and most bewhisker'd Bees —
Great solemn Bees, too plump to take a flower
Because their weight might shake the petals down —

Catherine:

Lord, where's the maze, and little carven Lad
He — nay, I will not — nay, sir — fie, a priest,
A prebendary wrestling with a wench
Who's like as not to quaver in dark Taverns —
Oh, sir, have done!

Laurence:

Now here's a mystery —
She'll dawdle from *St. Michael's* with you, walk
With prinking flutters past the choristers,
And take the turnpike, handed by a priest,
But let that saintly gentleman divert
Her footsteps from the vulgar throng, to grant her
Five hundred feet of private ambulation —
Oh, no — those lanes of lime-trees tempt her not —
She'll turn for home!

Catherine:

You know it's not the lanes,
Nor lime-trees either that I like not — priests
Are sable Eunuchs in the public streets,
But passionate rascals in an orangery!

Laurence:

Passion? You tease me, Kit — I keep no passion
In these quiet deeps of Yorkshire — no, and passion
Runs not in veins that time and the church have froze
To pipes of ancient lead — ha, passion, ha, ha!
This torn Divine accus'd of gallantry!
No doubt, a charge of attempted defloration
Of nuns past counting in the convent close
Would next have been preferr'd if my religion
Had but agreed with that of the old ladies!
'Alas, poor Yorick — here lies a three-nun man,'
I thank you for the compliment, dear Slut,
But Love's a dissipation I'm denied —
My reasons are innumerable, chief amongst them
The fact that it disorders my digestion,
And also — most important — I'm a disciple
Of that delicious old philosophy
Which flings us womankind to prime and dandle
And dog forever in the name of *Plato* —
Yes, I — I'm a Platonic — and our friendship
Mere rubbing of dim, spiritual flanks
As legally prescribed in the Symposium . . .
'Tis writ, I warrant you, in authentic Greek,
And must disarm all scruples.

Catherine:

I'm no scholar,
And Greek's but Greek. The body's been my school,
Gilding it, dusting its rounds with Orris-root,
Waxing its lips and silencing its cries —
In Greek I'm lacking, but it seems to me
That when a lad stands tugging a maiden's waist
Near snapping a Lace that oughtn't to be snapp'd —
He may quote *Plato*, but his bent's the same.

Laurence:

'Tis monstrous wrong! I'll swear no bones of mine
Have taboured it to Love — or if they have
They've groaned like skeletons in *Holbein's* Dance —
Aye, creaked and jarred with miserable joy
To cheerless ends. I'm no Voluptuary
New-greased with Love's pomatum — look at me,
My name's the Reverend *Tristram* . . . *Laurie Sterne* . . .
Or *Yorick*, as you like . . . aged in the suburbs
Of thirty-five or thereabouts . . . gaunt, long-legged,
Peruked grotesquely on the north-west border
With powdered wool, a trifle disarranged.
Poor *Tristram* . . . all he quests are cast-off things,
A smile tossed like a cherry to the birds,
The casual brush of eyes across a Counter,
Some careless touch of skin like flutter'd silk,
Or sweet munificence of Beauty thrown
Like pennies to the Post-boy . . . secret breasts
Like ivory fruits, unbared a bending-trice
Whilst *Janatone* leans over apricocks
To bite their stalks off . . . aye, and silken knees

Reveal'd in twinkling foams of Dimity
When Libertine winds run under maidens' Frocks —
And when those Frocks are tugg'd, small naked shoulders
That suddenly rise from ruffs of Mechlin lace,
Veined with sly, riotous roses, then subside
In quicksands of wild Satin and bubbling Silk . . .
Poor *Tristram* . . . all he seeks are these, but Life
Bequeaths him only Sorrows . . .
Do you call it weak to have one's eyes brimmed up
With tears of pity . . . an ye do, I'm weak . . .

Catherine:

Tears, Master *Laurence*?

Laurence:

I weep internally.
Taunt me not, Kit, my heart is old and broken.

Catherine:

But wherefore tears?

Laurence:

They rise like stones of crystal,
And whence they come, who knows? Perchance my Wife!

Catherine:

Poor man — she's fast in France —

Laurence:

Her deeds remain.
Oh, pity me, sweet child, I need thy tears.

Catherine:

Come, let me take thee to this bench of stone,
I would thy heart were happier —

Laurence:

Nay, not here —
'Tis cold — and there's a mound of twisted flowers
Beyond the turn, five paces past the Fish-pond,
Would net no less than two, no more than one,
In most prodigious comfort —

Catherine:

Poor, poor *Yorick*,
I'll dab thy tears upon my petticoat . . .

Laurence:

Delightful Girl!

Catherine:

Nay, wait sir, — wait, sir — O!
(They are heard talking for a while behind the corner hedge.)

The Man of Sentiment

PART TWO

(Meard's Court, Soho. An August nightfall, 1760. Catherine is seated at a small pianoforte, Catherine's mother is examining the contents of a chest. 'Tristram Shandy' has plunged Sterne into the drawing-rooms of London, and Catherine has followed.)

Mother:

Ten bottles of Calcavillo . . . one pot of Honey . . .
A jar of Comfits — (*sniffs*) — some Eau de Chypre . . .
The phial's of Crystal — (*sniffs*) — some few dead Posies . . .
Fourteen Epistles, dabbed with gilded sand
And sealed with crusts of lilac wax beneath . . .
Three sheets of music . . . boughpots filled with flowers . . .
Cards for the *Fête Aqueuse* . . . O, monstrous fine!
A mirror of Bronze (I doubt it's but some favour
From a Cotillon) . . . Fans, they're from the Ball . . .
A print by *Mr Campbell*, with Lions' Heads,
And '*STERNE*' surmounted by a loop of Roses,
Most witching smart . . . a frame of Chinese lacker
To hold th' engraving fast . . . romantic truly!
Your priest's a garter'd nobleman, and leaks
Prodigious generosity . . . in faith,
He's monstrous kind . . . aye, look you, in a fortnight
Full fifty-seven gifts he hath despatch'd
In various paquets . . . aye, and written to boot
One hundred pages Quarto . . . there's a man
I call of true nobility . . . though, in faith,
He's come no closer than scroll'd Signatures
For thirteen weeks . . . no doubt he's held in leash
By Satin thongs to some Duchess . . . 'tis hard,
I do protest, to interrupt a Rout
With kissing girls in Soho . . .

Catherine:

Light the candles,
And leave me, an you love me.

Mother:

Aye, 'tis true.
I love you, Kit. Priests do no more than that,
And *Laurie Sterne* no —

Catherine:

Peace! Have done. I'm tired.

Mother:

Ah, *Catherine*, you've played the trick too well
For scolding — see to it, child, I pray
That York's not drown'd in town, nor *Yorick* either.
Those red-heel'd Ladies cage him in their Hoops
Whilst he indites Epistles to *'Dear Kitty'* —
He's but a tearful babe, and may be drawn
By aught of the turns you know — a Stocking's top
Rimm'd with quick flesh — some string across the shoulder
Slipp'd from the bodice — aye, or peeps of Lace
Would snare that heart which flaps inconstantly
Like lanthorns in great Winds —

Catherine:

Leave me, I'm tired.
(*Exit Mother. Catherine plays slowly, and meanwhile Sterne enters and listens in the darkness of the door.*)

Laurence:

Oh, Kit!

Catherine:

Who's that?

Laurence:

A wretched Gentleman,
Once known in York, now lost in London's ways.

Catherine:

'Tis — oh, you fright me —

Laurence:

'Tis but wretched *Yorick*,
Sad *Tristram* —

Catherine:

Bring you news of that poor Priest?
'Tis many a week since last I heard of him,
And being a trifle concern'd in his success,
Pray speak of him — he's near forgotten here,
And might be dead —

Laurence:

She jests — but Kit, I love you!

Catherine:

'Dear Kit — I love you — Laurence.' So 'tis said
In fifty-seven manners, wrote with flourishes
In that poor Priest's extensive correspondence.

Laurence:

Nay, Kit — I love you — not a moment longer
Could aught of Business, Authorship or Rank
Imprison me in cold Pall Mall — I love you!

Catherine:

'Tis a moment then too late. I love not you!

Laurence:

Nay, I protest you tease me. O, *Catherine*
Have you no heart for pity —

Catherine:

What, more pity?
Yea, miserable wretch, I grieve for you —
By *Plato*, I commiserate your woes —
Poor *Tristram*, doom'd to everlasting Routs,
Meshed in Ridottos, pent in *Fêtes Champêtres* —
O, yes, by heaven, I sympathise indeed!

Laurence:

You mock me. 'Tis unworthy, Kit. I'll vow
No lover has danced in town more wretchedly

Than I at Carlton House — my jaws were wet —
I'll swear were wet with weeping . . . night by night
I'd steal by candlelight from Dukes and Barons,
Climb to my Room, and consecrate sad hours
To dreams of thee . . .

Catherine:

O, *Laurence*, come away . . .
Back, back to Yorkshire. 'Tis a year this morning
Since that hot day in August — do you remember?

Laurence:

Yes, I remember. 'Twas a day like this,
I rowed thee down by Ouse . . . O, happy Boat!

Catherine:

Nay, 'tis in vain. You know not what I mean.
No lovers pace those hedges now, the Garden
Sleeps once again . . .

Laurence:

Ah, heavens, the Garden, Kit!
Nay, I protest I do remember . . .

Catherine:

You!
Nay, you remember *Plato* and your tears,
Plato and your digestion . . .

Laurence:

Heavens, yes, *Plato*,
My sweet Platonic . . .

Catherine:

Sure the philosophy
Affords more true delight to its professor
Than to the obedient novice. Nay, 'tis vain.
I love you not . . . no, not if you coached home
And fee'd the Gods to pipe in Yorkshire gardens.

Laurence:

Catherine!

Catherine:

Nay.

Laurence:

O *Catherine*, I'll repent —
By heaven, I'll swear to post away instanter.
Run back with me to that one leaden Child
Whose cheeks were blown in smiles above our bed,
Sweet Kit of the Garden — aye, the pool drips now,
The fountain spouts again, the birds dive under,
That August morn returns — return thou with it!

Catherine:

Oh, leave — oh, leave —

Laurence:

Ah, *Catherine*, I love you.
Doubt me not, sweet, 'tis true. I've proved that vow
Too often since last August — aye and more,
I've naught but misery in London — fame
Hath little delight for lovers — Balls and Routs
Without your voice resolve to mere mechanics.
Believe me, Kit, I stop but long enough
To foster my luck — and with thine aid, sweet Child,
Poor *Laurence Sterne*, the rustic priest, shall swim,
Thee on his shoulders, down the gutter of Time.

Catherine:

I would your — oh, 'tis vain — leave me, I beg.

Laurence:

No, no. I love you!

Catherine:

Nay, you love me not.
You love your Wife.

Laurence:

That fume of a woman! No!

Catherine:

You love no woman, *Tristram* — nay, no woman.
You love but Eyes whose lakes of darkness mirror

Poor *Laurence Sterne* — you love but Ears whose mazes
Resound with *Yorick's* words, and blow them back
To *Yorick* himself — you love but Lips that know
Sweet means of kissing *Yorick*, and since all lips
Accomplish kissing, in faith, you love all lips,
And most your own. Aye, Sir, you're true enough
In your own manner to all you love on earth —
What's that? The oil'd machinery of Love,
The cogs that twist in Venus — and after that,
Yes, after that, you feast on *'sentiment'* —
'Tis your own word — weep tender nights away
With sad, delicious memories of a kiss
When if you chose you might reap more than kissing —
You love — of course, you love (O sentimental!)
You tickle your heart with sweetness of emotion,
Glut on romantic thrills, enjoy rich passions,
Most luscious martyrdoms — plump, tasty sorrows —
By God, I've done with playing that touching role,
'The Girl I Left Behind Me' — here am I,
'The Girl Who Wouldn't be Left Behind', and trust me,
I'll smash those chaste affections of your soul,
You pudding of stale sentiment!

Laurence:

O, *Catherine*!

Catherine:

No more. I've done. Find other fools to dream of,
And I'll find other lads with lips more hot
Who'll clip me for a Month, perhaps, or less,
And leave me — and forget . . .

Laurence:

O, *Catherine!*

Catherine:

Weep, little man!

Laurence:

O Kit of the Garden! Kit . . .

(Exit Sterne. Catherine remains staring over the keyboard. After a pause, enter her mother.)

Mother:

He's gone — you've vexed him — O, to think he's gone
In tears and temper — you're a fool, you Slut . . .
You've botched it all . . . you should have heeded me.
Eh, lass, a Bodice carelessly open'd up
Can tempt a backward Gallant . . . what's the use!
He's gone, you fool . . . and here's that handsome Mirror
Fallen and broken . . .

Earth-Visitors

(1926)

Winter Dawn

At five I wake, rise, rub on the smoking pane
A port to see — water breathing in the air,
Boughs broken. The sun comes up in a golden stain,
Floats like a glassy sea-fruit. There is mist everywhere,
White and humid, and the Harbour is like plated stone,
Dull flakes of ice. One light drips out alone,
One bead of winter-red, smouldering in the steam,
Quietly over the roof-tops — another window
Touched with a crystal fire in the sun's gullies,
One lonely star of the morning, where no stars gleam.

Far away on the rim of this great misty cup,
The sun gilds the dead suburbs as he rises up,
Diamonds the wind-cocks, makes glitter the crusted spikes
On moss-drowned gables. Now the tiles drip scarlet-wet,
Swim like birds' paving-stones, and sunlight strikes
Their watery mirrors with a moister rivulet,
Acid and cold. Here lie those mummied Kings,
Men sleeping in houses, embalmed in stony coffins,
Till the Last Trumpet calls their galleries up,
And the suburbs rise with distant murmurings.

O buried dolls, O men sleeping invisible there,
I stare above your mounds of stone, lean down,
Marooned and lonely in this bitter air,
And in one moment deny your frozen town,
Renounce your bodies — earth falls in clouds away,
Stones lose their meaning, substance is lost in clay,
Roofs fade, and that small smoking forgotten heap,
The city, dissolves to a shell of bricks and paper,
Empty, without purpose, a thing not comprehended,
A broken tomb, where ghosts unknown sleep.

And the least crystal weed, shaken with frost,
The furred herbs of silver, the daisies round-eyed and tart,
Painted in antic china, the smallest night-flower tossed
Like a bright penny on the lawn, stirs more my heart,
Strikes deeper this morning air, than mortal towers
Dried to a common blindness, fainter than flowers,
Fordone, extinguished, as the vapours break,
And dead in the dawn. O Sun that kills with life,
And brings to breath all silent things — O Dawn,
Waken me with old earth, keep me awake!

Music

I

Music, on the air's edge, rides alone,
  Plumed like empastured Caesars of the sky
  With a god's helmet; now, in the gold dye
Of sunlight, the iron cloak, the Tuscan stone,
Melt to enchanted flesh — a voice is blown
  Down from the windy pit, like a star falling.
  Men think it is a lost eagle calling,
But the fool and the lover know it for Music's cry.

He is running with the Valkyrs on a road of manes,
  Darkness draws back its fur, the stars course by,
Fighting the windy beaks of hurricanes
  To keep their stations in the sky —
Away, away! The little earth-light wanes,
  The moon has drowned herself, cold music rings,
The battering of a thousand Vulcanals

Hammers the blood; a thousand horsemen fly
Belly to air, away! Now Music sings
Harshly, like horns of Tartars blown on high.

II

A ship in hell marooned;
He lies under the mast,
Caked with the sticky unguents of the sun.
Sluggishly at his wound,
The rat Pain, biting with bloody teeth
And broken nails, is fed at last,
The tale is done.
Let the shell of bleeding flesh remain,
This crusted finery is nothing worth.
He flings his body carelessly to Pain,
Meat for the earth.
Trumpets of godhood! The voice of Music sings,
Lost in the dark forest, riding out,
Louder and nearer, with triumphant wings,
Music and his eternal cavaliers —
Now *Tristan* rises with a mighty shout.
Nobody hears.

III

O, silent night, dark beach,
Drowning like lovers, each in each,
Uncharge thy musky boughs, unbend
Thy mouths of air, and give them speech —

Then, like a nest of thieves,
The golden, tattling leaves
Will sell their mask for bravoes' love,
Or cry their fruit to stranger Eves,

And voices ride
By foam and field
Of drowsy lovers, lips unsealed,
Blown to the lazy tide —

'With love we put the planets out,
With kissing drowned the bells,
And struck the clambering moon to ice;
Now we shall sleep and hide . . .'
I sang with Nonie, side by side,
Sunk in a drift of tumbled laces,
Till Music breathed his enormous flute
Over our small, upturned faces.

IV

In the pans of straw-coned country
This river is the solitary traveller;
Nothing else moves, the sky lies empty,
Birds there are none, and cattle not many.
Now it is sunlight, what is the difference?
Nothing. The sun is as white as moonlight.
Wind has buffeted flat the grasses,
Long, long ago; but now there is nothing,
Wind gone and men gone, only the water
Stumbling over the stones in silence —
Nothing but fields with roots gone rotten,
Paddocks unploughed and clotted marshes.
Even the wind that stirred them has vanished,
Only the river remains with its water,
Shambling over the straw-coned country.
Nothing else moves, the sky lies empty,
Only the river remains with its water,
And droughts will come . . .

V

In and out the countryfolk, the carriages and carnival,
Pastry-cooks in all directions push to barter their confections,
Trays of little gilded cakes, caramels in painted flakes,
Marzipan of various makes and macaroons of all complexions,
Riding on a tide of country faces.
Up and down the smoke and crying,
Girls with apple-eyes are flying,
Country boys in costly braces
Run with red, pneumatic faces;
Trumpets gleam, whistles scream,
Organs cough their coloured steam out,
Dogs are worming, sniffing, squirming;
Air-balloons and paper moons,
Roundabouts with curdled tunes,
Drowned bassoons and waggon-jacks;
Tents like flowers of candle-wax;
'Buy, buy, buy, buy!
Cotton ties, cakes and pies, what a size, test your eyes, hair-dyes, candy-shies, all a prize, penny tries, no lies, watch it rise, buy, buy, buy, buy!'
So everybody buys.

Gently the doctor of magic mutters,
Opens his puppet-stall,
Pulls back the painted shutters,
Ruffles the golden lace.
Ha! The crowd flutters . . .
Reddened and sharp and small,
O, *Petroushka's* face!

VI

Torches and running fire; the flagstones drip
Like a black mirror, wet from killing. Smoke goes up,
Clouding the gilded rafter-birds, and the flying cup
That floats with magic wine to Konchak's lip.

Then the Khan claps his beard, and harps are brushed
Clear in the darkness; dancers' bells far off
Blab at their ankles. Now, from the gold trough,
We have dipped bowls of mare's milk; all is hushed.

Suddenly, dull bubbling drums uprise, grow thicker,
Split with a scream of metal — glazed in the flare,
Tartar girls rapidly whirl in storms of animal hair,
Spinning in islands of movement, quicker and quicker.

In the middle of the dance, smiling at his whim,
Khan Konchak rose, and left the golden hall.
Soon there was silent darkness over all.
One of the dancers was sent after him.

VII

In the apple-country, in the apple-trees,
The boughs are bubbling with pink snow
To frost the fields. A thousand birds fall crying,
Sharp and sweet, like morning-stars, in seas
Deeper than air. A thousand blossoms blow,
Drops of gold blood, like flowers gone flying,
Drowning with foam the drowsy girls below.

These country-girls, in hats of straw,
Take kissing as a natural law,
Put up their cheeks, like rosy saucers,
Gravely on tiptoe waiting.

They plainly do not know the dangers
This practice breeds from courteous strangers,
Who find, on airing their politeness,
Such local customs captivating.

As for my part, under the trees,
I found a girl with tawny knees,
Pretty enough, at a hurried view.
We lay on blossoms, glassed with dew.
I didn't notice her till we kissed.
How pleasant, a sentimentalist!

VIII

Open! It is the moon knocking with fists of air
To break thy doors down, it is the lusty moon
More clamorous than hunting-cries, come tramping
With lanterns to uprouse thee, drown the fields
In drifts of crystal, waken the farms with light,
And lovers call to buffet the rough smoke
From valleys rising up — then, like the juice
Of Juno's apples, the rich, Indian glow
Shall cast them out of Time, and all be running,
Dancing and kissing, in this headlong, breathless moon,
This moon pulling at old hinges, bawling through keyholes,
Crying out *'Siegmund! Siegmund! Siegmund!'*
The door flies open.

In this house, there is anger, in the forest, night,
But love is under my laughter, and under my cloak, flight.
O, hast thou not yet woken?
In night, there is bitterness, in sorrow, tears to weep,
But love is under my music, and under my cloak, sleep.
O, Lady, hast thou spoken?

In tears, there is remembering, in memory, no release,
But love is under my kissing, and under my cloak, peace.
O, hide beneath my cloak!

So shall we steal into the deeps of Spring,
Clasped each to each, and swim the merry tide,
Rounding the world, on the green floods astride,
Till, drowned in a bubble of flowers, too dazed to cling,
We're thrown up, pink and naked castaways,
On some old beach, where Time is put to rout,
And the world a buried star, not talked about —
So shall we daunt the gods, conceal their gaze.

IX

Once, at your words, I would have struck to flame
The ground I strode on, all the hives of blood
Gone bursting mad — but now, congealed and thick,
Anger, the wine, chokes me, hoods me with stone,
Clogs and corrodes me with its marish flood.
Suddenly, as though to metal grown,
I stand immovable, feel strangely sick,
And hear your voice far off, crying my name.

The clouds dissolve. Now I can see your face,
Immense and sweating; the room has fallen in,
Tiny beside it — your face, immense and sweating,
Blurred into mockery at the words that fill you.
Come, then. You wish to crush me. Let us begin;
Since it is obvious I shall have to kill you,
Have done with useless voices and regretting.
I want to get it over, and leave this place.

Then, like some god on a stone pedestal
Who stirs by night with unfamiliar limbs,

I turn to an automaton, upraise
Half-wondering an arm I find in the air,
Clammy with grappled iron. Everything swims,
Fogged in the coughing gas-light. Blindly I stare,
And stab once or twice . . . stabbing in a daze . . .
No need for more. He is dead, this animal.

Dead, dead. There was no need to strike
So many times, there is no need to hide —
It's nothing to be ashamed of nowadays.
He was my enemy. Now he has perished,
Charred in the smoking ovens of my pride.
Why should the splendid fury that I cherished
Seem now to be a cold and fruitless blaze?
Good God! Can't I kill my enemy if I like!

X

Nothing grows on the stone trees
But lanterns, frosty gourds of colour,
Melting their bloody drops in water
Over the dark seas.

These peaks of stucco, smoking light,
These Venice-roads, the pools and channels,
Tunnel the night with a thousand planets,
Daubing their glaze of white,

Where belfries glitter, spire on spire,
Shining on men with paper faces,
And boats, in the glass billow fading,
Beetles of cloudy fire.

Faintly the dripping, crystal strings
Unlock their Spanish airs, their festival

Which, far away, resolves to emptiness,
Echoes of bitter things,

Far away music, cold and small,
Which, like a child's delight remembered,
Falls to mocked effigy for ever,
Melancholy to recall.

XI

Come in your painted coaches, friends of mine,
We'll keep the stars night-company with wine,
Morning shall find us bending to the flute,
And daybreak mock us at our candleshine.

Pile all thy jewelled berries in a heap,
Almonds and musk and sweetmeats, all for thee —
We'll rest on silk a thousand cushions deep,
Wake up and shake the cassia-tree,
And eat a sticky cake, and sleep,
And slee — . . .

XII

Look up! Thou hast a shining Guest
   Whose body in the dews hath lain,
His face like a strange wafer pressed
   Secret and starry, at thy pane;
And he shall sing with human tongue
Old music men have never sung
Since Orpheus on earth was young,
   And shall not sing again.

But life and all its lies of stone
   Shall crack to fumes and disappear,
Thy little golden shells be blown

Like stars in water, far and near,
And thou shalt wake behind the Glass,
In stone dissolved, and phantom brass —
O, deaf! The bells of Music pass,
Not can, but darest, thou hear!

Realities

To the etchings of Norman Lindsay

Now the statues lean over each to each, and sing,
Gravely in warm plaster turning; the hedges are dark.
The trees come suddenly to flower with moonlight,
The water-gardens to glassy fire, and the night, the night,
Breaks in a rain of stars. O, now the statues wake,
Poise on their leaden stems, and dive into the lake —
And the old Gardener, who has grown old with raking,
Bends by his flickering candle, and hears the noise,
And is nodding his head at a music of copper shaking,
And Mercury whispering to some little graven Boys.

And Venus with Venus is walking in a misty grove,
Their mouths breathless with great lies of Jove,
And the green-silver moon flows quivering down their sides,
Till each is lined in light.
'And this Brass Tower?' she said —
But a stone Faun, clawed to the branches overhead,
Could hold his breath no longer, downward slides,
And crashes in a storm of leaves. — O, look, the lake!
O, the great dolphins from the fountain-rim,
And the rusty Tritons — and O, the branches break —
A flute of ivory shines — it is Apollo come to swim!

Then the skies open with a light from no moon or star,
The dark terraces tremble, melt in a shower of petals;
Flowers turn to faces; faces, like small gold panes,
Are bodied with a mist of limbs — no dark remains,
Nor silence, but there is laughter like bells in air,
A rushing wind of music, torches, dancers everywhere,
And lovers no farther. It is not night nor day,
The world's tissue has utterly crumbled away,
Time is a crusty pond, and that old Mirror, Life,
Has broken, and the ghosts of flesh are stirred
With a new blood, the fluid of eternity,
And mouths that have never spoken, ears that have never heard,
Eyes that have never seen, speak now, and hear, and see.

And I, who have climbed in these unrooted boughs
Behind the world, find substance there and flesh,
Thoughts more infrangible than windy vows,
Love that's more bodily, and kisses longer,
And Cythera lovelier, and the girls of moonlight stronger
Than all earth's ladies, webbed in their bony mesh.
The statues dance, and the old Gardener is asleep,
And golden bodies tread the paths — O, happy shapes,
O, shining ones! Could I for ever keep
Within your radiance, made absolute at last,
No more amongst earth's phantoms to be cast,
No more in the shadowy race of the world exist,
But, born into reality, remember Life
As men see ghosts at midnight — so with me
Might all those aery textures, the world's mist,
Melt into Beauty's actuality!

Earth-Visitors

To N.L.

There were strange riders once, came gusting down
Cloaked in dark furs, with faces grave and sweet,
And white as air. None knew them, they were strangers —
Princes gone feasting, barons with gipsy eyes
And names that rang like viols — perchance, who knows,
Kings of old Tartary, forgotten, swept from Asia,
Blown on raven chargers across the world,
For ever smiling sadly in their beards
    And stamping abruptly into courtyards at midnight.

Post-boys would run, lanterns hang frostily, horses fume,
The strangers wake the Inn. Men, staring outside
Past watery glass, thick panes, could watch them eat,
Dyed with gold vapours in the candleflame,
Clapping their gloves, and stuck with crusted stones,
Their garments foreign, their talk a strange tongue,
    But sweet as pineapple — it was Archdukes, they must be.

In daylight, nothing; only their prints remained
Bitten in snow. They'd gone, no one knew where,
Or when, or by what road — no one could guess —
None but some sleepy girls, half tangled in dreams,
Mixing up miracle and desire; laughing, at first,
Then staring with bright eyes at their beds, opening their lips,
Plucking a crushed gold feather in their fingers,
And laughing again, eyes closed. But one remembered,
Between strange kisses and cambric, in the dark,
That unearthly beard had lifted . . . 'Your name, child?'
'Sophia, sir — and what to call your Grace?'
    Like a bubble of gilt, he had laughed 'Mercury!'

It is long now since great daemons walked on earth,
Staining with wild radiance a country bed,
And leaving only a confusion of sharp dreams
To vex a farm-girl — that, and perhaps a feather,
Some thread of the Cloth of Gold, a scale of metal,
Caught in her hair. The unpastured Gods have gone,
They are above those fiery-coasted clouds
Floating like fins of stone in the burnt air,
And earth is only a troubled thought to them
That sometimes drifts like wind across the bodies
   Of the sky's women.

There is one yet comes knocking in the night,
The drums of sweet conspiracy on the pane,
When darkness has arched his hands over the bush
And Springwood steams with dew, and the stars look down
On that one lonely chamber . . .
She is there suddenly, lit by no torch or moon,
But by the shining of her naked body.
Her breasts are berries broken in snow; her hair
Blows in a gold rain over and over them.
She flings her kisses like warm guineas of love,
   And when she walks, the stars walk with her above.

She knocks. The door swings open, shuts again.
'Your name, child?'
   A thousand birds cry 'Venus!'

Next Turn

No pause! The buried pipes ring out,
   The flour-faced Antic runs from sight;

Now Colombine, with scarlet pout,
Floats in the smoking moon of light.

Now programmes wave, heads bend between —
The roaring Years go past in file.
Soon there's the Transformation Scene —
And then the Footmen down the aisle.

For you must wait, before you leave
This Theatre of Varieties,
Their frozen fingers on your sleeve,
Their most respectful 'Now, sir, please!'

Out in the night, the Carriage stands,
Plumed with black trees. The Post-boys grin.
The Coachman beats upon his hands.
Turn after Turn goes on within.

A Sunset

The old Quarry, Sun, with bleeding scales,
Flaps up the gullies, wets their crystal pebbles,
Floating with waters of gold; darkness exhales
Brutishly in the valley; smoke rises in bubbles;
Suddenly we stop at the meeting of two trails.
'Do you remember?'
'But now everything is changed —
Trees ringed with death, the creek with its bells clanking
Dried like white bone.' Even our voices are estranged.
Darkness chokes the river; so nearly what I am thinking
It echoes, the whole thing might have been arranged!

Heine in Paris

Late: a cold smear of sunlight bathes the room;
The gilt lime of winter, a sun grown melancholy old,
Streams in the glass. Outside, ten thousand chimneys fume,
Looping the weather-birds with rings of gold;
The spires of Paris, pricked in an iron spume,
Uprise like stars of water, and mail the sky.
Night comes: the wind is cold.

La Mouche has lit the candles, cleared up the mess.
She is talking, this merry little girl, of the new clown,
Mercutio in red spots, and Miss Nellie, the Equine Princess,
Who can ride three terrible horses upside-down . . .
'Mon dieu, quelle cirque!' . . . and Madame Stephanie's dress . . .
'As true as I live' . . . the clear little voice trickles on,
All over the Circus, on and on, and all over the town.

Now she has creaked downstairs. Heine is left alone,
Knees hugged in bed, the drug purring in his brain,
And the windows turning blue. He can see some clouds being blown,
Scraping their big, soft bellies on the pane:
'Take me, O Clouds!' — but in a puff they've flown.
So once they fled in *Eighteen Twenty-Nine*
From — Hamburg, was it? — in a damp disdain . . .

Hamburg — those roofs of tulip-red, those floating trees,
Those black masts clotting the air, and swart cigars,
And puffed old bankers panting along the quays,
And Uncle Solomon shouting amongst the spars,
And Uncle Solomon's cargoes, coffee and cheese,
And Uncle Solomon's face, like a copper moon,
And Uncle Solomon's daughter, and the stars, the stars.

O, Hamburg and Amalie — the stars and dung —
He remembered suddenly that night he stood below,
Dark in the street, with stinging heart and helpless tongue,
And her face passed in the pane, like paper to and fro.
But in a thousand songs that song was never sung.
Amalie, Amalie, who was only a foaming of thought,
A thing thought of, and forgotten, long ago.

And Louise, Diana, and Jenny, and all those bright,
Mad girls who had scrawled their names inside his mind —
All vanished, all gone; and all of them forged in a night,
Conspired of dreams, and leaving no dream behind,
Ungrateful for their dreaming — flight after flight
Of musings wrapped in satin, fancies in silk,
And a thousand thoughts of naked roses and milk,
By love and the moon designed.

But now it seemed that these were only one thought,
One stone of Venus, cut with a hundred sides,
One girl revealed ten thousand times, and caught
Ten thousand times from out those amorous tides.
Now she was gone. They were all gone, those girls that he had sought,
All gone, or paunched in marriage, or crushed in graves,
Or promised for other men's brides.

And it was only a ghost's hair that had spilt,
Fur of the night, in kissing dark and strange,
To choke his lips. And all of those worlds he'd built,
The girls he'd conjured before his dreams took mange,
The rogues he'd stamped on, harlot, trollop, and jilt,
The fools he'd blistered — all of them passed and forgotten;
But that — *that* did not change.

Men crumbled, man lived on. In that animal's face,
'Twas but a squirt aimed at the moon, to fling contempt.
Meyerbeer, Borne, and Klopstock vanished, but in their place
New Klopstocks, Meyerbeers blown again, and Bornes undreamt,
Sprang up like fungi, and there remained no trace
Of lashings past. Men, men he could flog for ever,
But man was still exempt.

That did not change — always the world remained,
Breathing and sleeping; loving and taking in love;
Fighting and coupling; life by the belly constrained,
Stupid in roads of flesh; eating, but never enough;
Ravening, never to cease; warring, but nothing gained;
Babbling to silent Christs; climbing to heavens of the brain,
Unknown, unanswering, above.

All these remained, words passed. The paper he'd filled,
Deep to the lips in bitter salt, with fury and tears,
No man remembered; anger and fools were stilled
In dust alike — and out of those roaring years,
What now was left of all the passion he'd spilled,
The fire he'd struck? A cadence or two of love,
A song that had stroked men's ears.

All wrong, all wasted. Now, in this winter snow,
In the black winds from Russia, and the printed mane of night,
Heine looked out, and gazed at the world below,
Thick with old chemicals, breaking far out of sight
With ageless tides of man — ah, granite flow,
Eternal, changeless flux of humanity,
Undying darkness and light!

Not treading those floods could save him — not striking stone,
Not damming the world could serve — only to fly,
Careless of men and their shouting — untouched — alone —
Snatched by his own gods from a falling sky,
And singing his own way — clutching his own, his own,
Blind to the world — yes, that was the road of Heine —
Up to the sun, solitary, a speck in the ether —

'Ha, now, Christ Jesus and Jehovah, I choose to die!'

Stars

'These are the floating berries of the night,
They drop their harvest in dark alleys down,
Softly far down on groves of Venus, or on a little town
Forgotten at the world's edge — and O, their light
Unlocks all closed things, eyes and mouths, and drifts
Quietly over kisses in a golden rain,
Drowning their flight, till suddenly the Cyprian lifts
Her small, white face to the moon, then hides again.

'They are the warm candles of beauty, hung in blessing on high,
Poised like bright comrades on boughs of night above:
They are the link-boys of Queen Venus, running out of the sky,
Spilling their friendly radiance on all her ways of love.

'Should the girl's eyes be lit with swimming fire,
O do not kiss it away, it is a star, a star!'
So cried the passionate poet to his great, romantic guitar.

But I was beating off the stars, gazing, not rhyming.
I saw the bottomless, black cups of space
Between their clusters, and the planets climbing
Dizzily in sick airs, and desired to hide my face.
But I could not escape those tunnels of nothingness,
The cracks in the spinning Cross, nor hold my brain
From rushing for ever down that terrible lane,
Infinity's trap-door, eternal and merciless.

The Night-Ride

Gas flaring on the yellow platform; voices running up and down;
Milk-tins in cold dented silver; half-awake I stare,
Pull up the blind, blink out — all sounds are drugged;
The slow blowing of passengers asleep;
Engines yawning; water in heavy drips;
Black, sinister travellers, lumbering up the station,
One moment in the window, hooked over bags;
Hurrying, unknown faces — boxes with strange labels —
All groping clumsily to mysterious ends,
Out of the gaslight, dragged by private Fates.
Their echoes die. The dark train shakes and plunges;
Bells cry out; the night-ride starts again.
Soon I shall look out into nothing but blackness,
Pale, windy fields. The old roar and knock of the rails
Melts in dull fury. Pull down the blind. Sleep. Sleep.
Nothing but grey, rushing rivers of bush outside.
Gaslight and milk-cans. Of Rapptown I recall nothing else.

Melbourne

Melbourne, this mastodon of bleeding stone
  Sprawled on earth's dugs, repeats its type again,
Boasting, as archaeologists have shown,
  A giant's body and a louse's brain.

City Nightfall

Smoke upon smoke; over the stone lips
Of chimneys bleeding, a darker fume descends.
Night, the old nun, in voiceless pity bends
  To kiss corruption, so fabulous her pity.

All drowns in night. Even the lazar drowns
In earth at last, and rises up afresh,
Married to dust with an Infanta's flesh —
  So night, like earth, receives this poisoned city,

Charging its air with beauty, coasting its lanterns
With mains of darkness, till the leprous clay
Dissolves, and pavements drift away,
  And there is only the quiet noise of planets feeding.

And those who chafe here, limed on the iron twigs,
No greater seem than sparrows, all their cries,
Their clockwork and their merchandise,
  Frolic of painted dolls. I pass unheeding.

Cuckooz Contrey

(1932)

The Atlas

1 The King of Cuckooz

'The Platt of Argier and the Pts. adioning within the view thereof made by Robert Norton the Muster Mr. of his Ma't's Fleet ther Ao Di 1620 & by his owne carfull & dilligent observations then not without danger.'

The King of Cuckooz Contrey
Hangs peaked above Argier
With Janzaries and Marabutts
To bid a sailor fear —

With lantern-eyed astrologers
Who walk upon the walls
And ram with stars their basilisks
Instead of cannon-balls.

And in that floating castle
(I tell you it is so)
Five thousand naked Concubines
With dulcimers do go.

Each rosy nose anoints a tile,
Bang, bang! the fort salutes,
When He, the King of Cuckooz Land,
Comes forth in satin boots,

Each rosy darling flies before
When he desires his tent,
Or, like a tempest driving flowers,
Inspects a battlement.

And this I spied by moonlight
Behind a royal bamboo —

That Monarch in a curricle
Which ninety virgins drew;

That Monarch drinking nectar
(Lord God, my tale attest!)
Milked from a snow-white elephant
As white as *your* white breast!

And this is no vain fable
As other knaves may lie —
Have I not got that Fowl aboard
Which no man may deny?

The King's own hunting-falcon
I limed across the side
When by the Bayes of Africa
King James's Fleet did ride.

What crest is there emblazoned,
Whose mark is this, I beg,
Stamped on the silver manacle
Around that dainty leg?

Let this be news to you, my dear,
How Man should be revered;
Though I'm no King of Cuckooz Land,
Behold as fierce a beard!

I have as huge an appetite,
As deep a kiss, my girl,
And *somewhere*, for the hand that seeks,
Perhaps a Sultan's pearl!

2 Post-roads

'The Traveller's Guide, or a Most Exact Description of the Roads of England; being Mr. Ogilby's Actual Survey and Mensuration by the Wheel, &c.'

Post-roads that clapped with tympan heels
Of tilburies and whiskys rapidly spanking,
Where's now the tireless ghost of *Ogilby*?
Post-roads
That buoyed the rich and plunging springs
Of coaches vaster than Escurials,
Where now does *Ogilby* propel that Wheel,
What milestones does he pause to reprimand,
In what unmapped savanna of dumb shades?

Ye know not — ye are silent — brutish ducts
Numbed by the bastinadoes of iron boots,
Three hundred years asnore. Do you forget
The phaetons and fiacres, flys and breaks,
The world of dead men staring out of glass
That drummed upon your bones? Do you forget
Those nostrils oozing smoke, those floating tails,
Those criniers whipped with air?

And kidnapped lights,
Floats of rubbed yellow towed from window-panes,
Rushing their lozenges through headlong stones;
And smells of hackneys, mohair sour with damp,
Leather and slopped madeira, partridge-pies
Long-buried under floors; and yawning Fares
With bumping flap-dark spatulas of cards —
'Knave takes the ten . . . oh, God, I wish that it,
I wish that it was Guildford' . . .

Ogilby
Did not forget, could not escape such ecstasies,
Even in the monasteries of mensuration,
Could not forget the roads that he had gone
In fog and shining air. Each line was joy,
Each computation a beatitude,
A diagram of Ogilby's eye and ear
With soundings for the nose. Wherefore I think,

Wherefore I think some English gentleman,
Some learned doctor of the steak-houses,
Ending late dinner, having strolled outside
To quell the frivolous hawthorn, may behold
There in the moonshine, rolling up an hill,
Steered by no fleshly hand, with spokes of light,
The *Wheel* — *John Ogilby's Wheel* — the *WHEEL* hiss by,
Measuring mileposts of eternity.

3 Dutch Seacoast

'Toonneel der Steden van vereenighde Nederlanden met hare Beschrijvingen uytgegeven by Joan. Blaeu.'

No wind of Life may strike within
This little country's crystal bin,
Nor calendar compute the days
Tubed in their capsule of soft glaze.

Naked and rinsed, the bubble-clear
Canals of Amsterdam appear,
The blue-tiled turrets, china clocks
And glittering beaks of weathercocks.

A gulf of sweet and winking hoops
Whereon there ride 500 poops

With flying mouths and fleeting hair
Of saints hung up like candles there —

Fox-coloured mansions, lean and tall,
That burst in air but never fall,
Whose bolted shadows, row by row,
Float changeless on the stones below —

Sky full of ships, bay full of town,
A port of waters jellied brown:
Such is the world no tide may stir,
Sealed by the great cartographer.

O, could he but clap up like this
My decomposed metropolis,
Those other countries of the mind,
So tousled, dark and undefined!

4 MERMAIDS

'A new and Accurat Map of the World, in two Hemispheres, Western and Eastern, with the Heavens and Elements, a Figure of the Spheare, the Eclipse of the Sunne, the Eclipse of the Moon.' — J. Speed, 1675

Once Mermaids mocked your ships
With wet and scarlet lips
And fish-dark difficult hips, Conquistador;
Then Ondines danced with Sirens on the shore,
Then from his cloudy stall, you heard the Kraken call,
And, mad with twisting flame, the Firedrake roar.

Such old-established Ladies
No mariner eyed askance,
But, coming on deck, would swivel his neck
To watch the darlings dance,

Or in the gulping dark of nights
Would cast his tranquil eyes
On singular kinds of Hermaphrodites
Without the least surprise.

Then portulano maps were scrolled
With compass-roses, green and gold,
That fired the stiff old Needle with their dyes
And wagged their petals over parchment skies.

Then seas were full of Dolphins' fins,
Full of swept bones and flying Jinns,
Beaches were filled with Anthropophagi
And Antient Africa with Palanquins.

Then sailors, with a flaked and rice-pale flesh
Staring from maps in sweet and poisoned places,
Diced the old Skeleton afresh
In brigs no bigger than their moon-bunched faces.

Those well-known and respected Harpies
Dance no more on the shore to and fro;
All that has ended long ago;
Nor do they sing outside the captain's porthole,
A proceeding fiercely reprehended
By the governors of the P. & O.

Nor do they tumble in the sponges of the moon
For the benefit of tourists in the First Saloon,
Nor fork their foaming lily-fins below the side
On the ranges of the ale-clear tide.

And scientists now, with binocular-eyes,
Remark in a tone of complacent surprise:
'Those pisciform mammals — pure Spectres, I fear —
Must be Doctor Gerbrandus's *Mermaids*, my dear!'

But before they can cause the philosopher trouble,
They are *GONE* like the cracking of a bubble.

5 The Seafight

'Archipelague du Mexique ou sont les Isles de Cuba, Espagnole Jamaique, &c.' — Sanson, 1692

Here in a gulf of golden leaf
You'll find a seafight ringed with flame;
Cannons that cry Tirduf, Tirduf,
Daggers that collop, guns that maim;
Jaws beaked with blood, men flung to hell,
Men blasting trumpets, men that flee,
Men crimped by death, and under all
Old patient, baleful, spying Sea —

Old Sea, that in a dicebox rolls
Their trundling skulls, their jacks of bone,
That sucks them out of broken hulls
When other mumbling mouths have gone —
Old hungry Sea, that holds our flesh
In the huge forceps of the storm,
And they are given to the fish
And we plucked forth, and we made warm.

But ye that kill, why heed the face
Of Ocean? Not alone you slay,
Since deeper seas are dammed in space
And fiercer storms can scream in clay;
Existence has as bitter teeth,
But we can always find a minute
For the festivities of death
Who sail upon this dangerous planet.

Captain Dobbin

Captain Dobbin, having retired from the South Seas
In the dumb tides of 1900, with a handful of shells,
A few poisoned arrows, a cask of pearls,
And five thousand pounds in the colonial funds,
Now sails the street in a brick villa, 'Laburnum Villa',
In whose blank windows the harbour hangs
Like a fog against the glass,
Golden and smoky, or stoned with a white glitter,
And boats go by, suspended in the pane,
Blue Funnel, Red Funnel, Messageries Maritimes,
Lugged down the port like sea-beasts taken alive
That scrape their bellies on sharp sands,
Of which particulars Captain Dobbin keeps
A ledger sticky with ink,
Entries of time and weather, state of the moon,
Nature of cargo and captain's name,
For some mysterious and awful purpose
Never divulged.
For at night, when the stars mock themselves with lanterns,
So late the chimes blow loud and faint
Like a hand shutting and unshutting over the bells,
Captain Dobbin, having observed from bed
The lights, like a great fiery snake, of the *Comorin*
Going to sea, will note the hour
For subsequent recording in his gazette.

But the sea is really closer to him than this,
Closer to him than a dead, lovely woman,
For he keeps bits of it, like old letters,
Salt tied up in bundles
Or pressed flat,
What you might call a lock of the sea's hair,

So Captain Dobbin keeps his dwarfed memento,
His urn-burial, a chest of mummied waves,
Gales fixed in print, and the sweet dangerous countries
Of shark and casuarina-tree,
Stolen and put in coloured maps,
Like a flask of seawater, or a bottled ship,
A schooner caught in a glass bottle;
But Captain Dobbin keeps them in books,
Crags of varnished leather
Pimply with gilt, by learned mariners
And masters of hydrostatics, or the childish tales
Of simple heroes, taken by Turks or dropsy.
So nightly he sails from shelf to shelf
Or to the quadrants, dangling with rusty screws,
Or the hanging-gardens of old charts,
So old they bear the authentic protractor-lines,
Traced in faint ink, as fine as Chinese hairs.

Over the flat and painted atlas-leaves
His reading-glass would tremble,
Over the fathoms, pricked in tiny rows,
Water shelving to the coast.
Quietly the bone-rimmed lens would float
Till, through the glass, he felt the barbéd rush
Of bubbles foaming, spied the albicores,
The blue-finned admirals, heard the wind-swallowed cries
Of planters running on the beach
Who filched their swags of yams and ambergris,
Birds' nests and sandalwood, from pastures numbed
By the sun's yellow, too meek for honest theft;
But he, less delicate robber, climbed the walls,
Broke into dozing houses
Crammed with black bottles, marish wine

Crusty and salt-corroded, fading prints,
Sparkle-daubed almanacs and playing cards,
With rusty cannon, left by the French outside,
Half-buried in sand,
Even to the castle of Queen Pomaree
In the Yankee's footsteps, and found her throne-room piled
With golden candelabras, mildewed swords,
Guitars and fowling-pieces, tossed in heaps
With greasy cakes and flung-down calabashes.

Then Captain Dobbin's eye,
That eye of wild and wispy scudding blue,
Voluptuously prying, would light up
Like mica scratched by gully-suns,
And he would be fearful to look upon
And shattering in his conversation;
Nor would he tolerate the harmless chanty,
No *'Shenandoah'*, or the dainty mew
That landsmen offer in a silver dish
To Neptune, sung to pianos in candlelight.
Of these he spoke in scorn,
For there was but one way of singing *'Stormalong'*,
He said, and that was not really singing,
But howling, rather — shrieked in the wind's jaws
By furious men; not tinkled in drawing-rooms
By lap-dogs in clean shirts.
And, at these words,
The galleries of photographs, men with rich beards,
Pea-jackets and brass buttons, with folded arms,
Would scowl approval, for they were shipmates, too,
Companions of no cruise by reading-glass,
But fellows of storm and honey from the past —
'The Charlotte, Java, '93,'
'Knuckle and Fred at Port au Prince,'

'William in his New Rig,'
Even that notorious scoundrel, Captain Baggs,
Who, as all knew, owed Dobbin Twenty Pounds
Lost at fair cribbage, but he never paid,
Or paid 'with the slack of the tops'l sheets'
As Captain Dobbin frequently expressed it.

There were their faces, grilled a trifle now,
Cigar-hued in various spots
By the brown breath of sodium-eating years,
On quarter-decks long burnt to the water's edge,
A resurrection of the dead by chemicals.
And the voyages they had made,
Their labours in a country of water,
Were they not marked by inadequate lines
On charts tied up like skins in a rack?
Or his own Odysseys, his lonely travels,
His trading days, an autobiography
Of angles and triangles and lozenges
Ruled tack by tack across the sheet,
That with a single scratch expressed the stars,
Merak and Alamak and Alpherat,
The wind, the moon, the sun, the clambering sea,
Sails bleached with light, salt in the eyes,
Bamboos and Tahiti oranges,
From some forgotten countless day,
One foundered day from a forgotten month,
A year sucked quietly from the blood,
Dead with the rest, remembered by no more
Than a scratch on a dry chart —
Or when the return grew too choking bitter-sweet
And laburnum-berries manifestly tossed
Beyond the window, not the fabulous leaves

Of Hotoo or canoe-tree or palmetto,
There were the wanderings of other keels,
Magellan, Bougainville and Cook,
Who found no greater a memorial
Than footprints over a lithograph.

For Cook he worshipped, that captain with the sad
And fine white face, who never lost a man
Or flinched a peril; and of Bougainville
He spoke with graceful courtesy, as a rival
To whom the honours of the hunting-field
Must be accorded. Not so with the Spaniard,
Sebastian Juan del Cano, at whom he sneered
Openly, calling him a fool of fortune
Blown to a sailors' abbey by chance winds
And blindfold currents, who slept in a fine cabin,
Blundered through five degrees of latitude,
Was bullied by mutineers a hundred more,
And woke and found himself across the world.

Coldly in the window,
Like a fog rubbed up and down the glass
The harbour, bony with mist
And ropes of water, glittered; and the blind tide
That crawls it knows not where, nor for what gain,
Pushed its drowned shoulders against the wheel,
Against the wheel of the mill.
Flowers rocked far down
And white, dead bodies that were anchored there
In marshes of spent light.
Blue Funnel, Red Funnel,
The ships went over them, and bells in engine-rooms
Cried to their bowels of flaring oil,

And stokers groaned and sweated with burnt skins,
Clawed to their shovels.
But quietly in his room,
In his little cemetery of sweet essences
With fond memorial-stones and lines of grace,
Captain Dobbin went on reading about the sea.

Talbingo

'Talbingo River' — as one says of bones:
'Captain' or 'Commodore' that smelt gunpowder
In old engagements no one quite believes
Or understands. Talbingo had its blood
As they did, ran with waters huge and clear
Lopping down mountains,
Turning crags to banks.

Now it's a sort of aching valley,
Basalt shaggy with scales,
A funnel of tobacco-coloured clay,
Smoulders of puffed earth
And pebbles and shell-bodied flies
And water thickening to stone in pocks.

That's what we're like out here,
Beds of dried-up passions.

Gulliver

I'll kick your walls to bits, I'll die scratching a tunnel,
If you'll give me a wall, if you'll give me a simple stone,
If you'll do me the honour of a dungeon —
Anything but this tyranny of sinews.
Lashed with a hundred ropes of nerve and bone
I lie, poor helpless Gulliver,
In a twopenny dock for the want of a penny,
Tied up with stuff too cheap, and strings too many.
One chain is usually sufficient for a cur.

Hair over hair, I pick my cables loose,
But still the ridiculous manacles confine me.
I snap them, swollen with sobbing. What's the use?
One hair I break, ten thousand hairs entwine me.
Love, hunger, drunkenness, neuralgia, debt,
Cold weather, hot weather, sleep and age —
If I could only unloose their spongy fingers,
I'd have a chance yet, slip through the cage.
But who ever heard of a cage of hairs?
You can't scrape tunnels in a net.

If you'd give me a chain, if you'd give me honest iron,
If you'd graciously give me a turnkey,
I could break my teeth on a chain, I could bite through metal,
But what can you do with hairs?
For God's sake, call the hangman.

Crow Country

Gutted of station, noise alone,
The crow's voice trembles down the sky

As if this nitrous flange of stone
Wept suddenly with such a cry;
As if the rock found lips to sigh,
The riven earth a mouth to moan;
But we that hear them, stumbling by,
Confuse their torments with our own.

Over the huge abraded rind,
Crow-countries graped with dung, we go,
Past gullies that no longer flow
And wells that nobody can find,
Lashed by the screaming of the crow,
Stabbed by the needles of the mind.

Glubbdubdrib

'. . . and we all three entered the gate of the palace between two rows of guards, armed and dressed after a very antique manner, and something in their countenances that made my flesh creep with a horror I cannot express.' — A Voyage to Laputa.

In the castle of Glubbdubdrib
How splendidly we dine
On flesh from magic potagers
And cups of dead men's wine,

Dead men who run with bottles,
Lackeys of silent air,
A ghost in gilded livery
Fawning behind each chair.

Beckon, and flunkey Caesars
Bring us their phantom bread.

Once they were gods and emperors;
Now, of course, they are dead.

The governor of Glubbdubdrib
(Two ghosts cringe on each side)
Bows to congratulations,
Filled with a careless pride.

'Really, the servant problem . . .
You mean that Roman youth?
Catullus. Oh, yes, brisk enough,
But — you know — so uncouth.

'There's Plato in the passage,
They tell me he's quite droll.
He says some devilish clever things;
A heathen, though, poor soul . . .'

The governor of Glubbdubdrib
Resumes his drinking-cup.
As for the guests and visitors,
They hadn't even looked up.

The Nabob

To the memory of William Hickey, Esq.

Coming out of India with ten thousand a year
Exchanged for flesh and temper, a dry Faust
Whose devil barters with digestion, has he paid dear
For dipping his fingers in the Roc's valley?

Who knows? It's certain that he owns a rage,
A face like shark-skin, full of Yellow Jack,

And that unreckoning tyranny of age
That calls for turtles' eggs in Twickenham.

Sometimes, by moonlight, in a barge he'll float
Whilst hirelings blow their skulking flageolets,
Served by a Rajah in a golden coat
With pigeon-pie . . . Madeira . . . and Madeira . . .

Or in his Bon de Paris with silver frogs
He rolls puff-bellied in an equipage,
Elegant chariot, through a gulf of fogs
To dine on dolphin-steak with Post-Captains.

Who knows? There are worse things than steak, perhaps,
Worse things than oyster-sauces and tureens
And worlds of provender like painted maps
Pricked out with ports of claret and pitchcocked eels,

And hubbubs of billiard-matches, burnt champagne,
Beautiful ladies 'of the establishment'
Always in tempers, or melting out again,
Bailiffs and Burgundy and writs of judgment —

Thus to inhabit huge, lugubrious halls
Damp with the steam of entrees, glazed with smoke,
Raw drinking, greasy eating, bussing and brawls,
Drinking and eating and bursting into bed-chambers.

But, in the end, one says farewell to them;
And if he'd curse to-day — God damn your blood! —
Even his curses I'd not altogether condemn,
Not altogether scorn; and if phantoms ate —

Hickey, I'd say, sit down, pull up, set to:
Here's knife and fork, there's wine, and there's a barmaid.

Let us submerge ourselves in onion-soup,
Anything but this 'damned profession of writing'.

Five Visions of Captain Cook

I

Cook was a captain of the Admiralty
When sea-captains had the evil eye,
Or should have, what with beating krakens off
And casting nativities of ships;
Cook was a captain of the powder-days
When captains, you might have said, if you had been
Fixed by their glittering stare, half-down the side,
Or gaping at them up companionways,
Were more like warlocks than a humble man —
And men were humble then who gazed at them,
Poor horn-eyed sailors, bullied by devils' fists
Of wind or water, or the want of both,
Childlike and trusting, filled with eager trust —
Cook was a captain of the sailing days
When sea-captains were kings like this,
Not cold executives of company-rules
Cracking their boilers for a dividend
Or bidding their engineers go wink
At bells and telegraphs, so plates would hold
Another pound. Those captains drove their ships
By their own blood, no laws of schoolbook steam,
Till yards were sprung, and masts went overboard —
Daemons in periwigs, doling magic out,
Who read fair alphabets in stars
Where humbler men found but a mess of sparks,
Who steered their crews by mysteries

And strange, half-dreadful sortilege with books,
Used medicines that only gods could know
The sense of, but sailors drank
In simple faith. That was the captain
Cook was when he came to the Coral Sea
And chose a passage into the dark.

How many mariners had made that choice
Paused on the brink of mystery! 'Choose now!'
The winds roared, blowing home, blowing home,
Over the Coral Sea. 'Choose now!' the trades
Cried once to Tasman, throwing him for choice
Their teeth or shoulders, and the Dutchman chose
The wind's way, turning north. 'Choose, Bougainville!'
The wind cried once, and Bougainville had heard
The voice of God, calling him prudently
Out of the dead lee shore, and chose the north,
The wind's way. So, too, Cook made choice,
Over the brink, into the devil's mouth,
With four months' food, and sailors wild with dreams
Of English beer, the smoking barns of home.
So Cook made choice, so Cook sailed westabout,
So men write poems in Australia.

II

Flowers turned to stone! Not all the botany
Of Joseph Banks, hung pensive in a porthole,
Could find the Latin for this loveliness,
Could put the Barrier Reef in a glass box
Tagged by the horrid Gorgon squint
Of horticulture. Stone turned to flowers
It seemed — you'd snap a crystal twig,
One petal even of the water-garden,
And have it dying like a cherry-bough.

They'd sailed all day outside a coral hedge,
And half the night. Cook sailed at night,
Let there be reefs a fathom from the keel
And empty charts. The sailors didn't ask,
Nor Joseph Banks. Who cared? It was the spell
Of Cook that lulled them, bade them turn below,
Kick off their sea-boots, puff themselves to sleep,
Though there were more shoals outside
Than teeth in a shark's head. Cook snored loudest himself.

One day, a morning of light airs and calms,
They slid towards a reef that would have knifed
Their boards to mash, and murdered every man.
So close it sucked them, one wave shook their keel,
The next blew past the coral. Three officers,
In gilt and buttons, languidly on deck
Pointed their sextants at the sun. One yawned,
One held a pencil, one put eye to lens:
Three very peaceful English mariners
Taking their sights for longitude.
I've never heard
Of sailors aching for the longitude
Of shipwrecks before or since. It was the spell
Of Cook did this, the phylacteries of Cook.
Men who ride broomsticks with a mesmerist
Mock the typhoon. So, too, it was with Cook.

III

Two chronometers the captain had,
One by Arnold that ran like mad,
One by Kendal in a walnut case,
Poor devoted creature with a hangdog face.

Arnold always hurried with a crazed click-click
Dancing over Greenwich like a lunatic,
Kendal panted faithfully his watch-dog beat,
Climbing out of Yesterday with sticky little feet.

Arnold choked with appetite to wolf up time,
Madly round the numerals his hands would climb,
His cogs rushed over and his wheels ran miles,
Dragging Captain Cook to the Sandwich Isles.

But Kendal dawdled in the tombstoned past,
With a sentimental prejudice to going fast,
And he thought very often of a haberdasher's door
And a yellow-haired boy who would knock no more.

All through the night-time, clock talked to clock,
In the captain's cabin, tock-tock-tock,
One ticked fast and one ticked slow,
And Time went over them a hundred years ago.

IV

Sometimes the god would fold his wings
And, stone of Caesars turned to flesh,
Talk of the most important things
That serious-minded midshipmen could wish,

Of plantains, and the lack of rum
Or spearing sea-cows — things like this
That hungry schoolboys, five days dumb,
In jolly-boats are wonted to discuss.

What midshipman would pause to mourn
The sun that beat about his ears,
Or curse the tide, if he could horn
His fists by tugging on those lumbering oars?

Let rum-tanned mariners prefer
To hug the weather-side of yards;
'Cats to catch mice' before they purr,
Those were the captain's enigmatic words.

Here, in this jolly-boat they graced,
Were food and freedom, wind and storm,
While, fowling-piece across his waist,
Cook mapped the coast, with one eye cocked for game.

V

After the candles had gone out, and those
Who listened had gone out, and a last wave
Of chimney-haloes caked their smoky rings
Like fish-scales on the ceiling, a Yellow Sea
Of swimming circles, the old man,
Old Captain-in-the-Corner, drank his rum
With friendly gestures to four chairs. They stood
Empty, still warm from haunches, with rubbed nails
And leather glazed, like agéd serving-men
Feeding a king's delight, the sticky, drugged
Sweet agony of habitual anecdotes.
But these, his chairs, could bear an old man's tongue,
Sleep when he slept, be flattering when he woke,
And wink to hear the same eternal name
From lips new-dipped in rum.

'Then Captain Cook,
I heard him, told them they could go
If so they chose, but he would get them back,
Dead or alive, he'd have them,'
The old man screeched, half-thinking to hear 'Cook!
Cook again! Cook! It's other cooks he'll need,
Cooks who can bake a dinner out of pence,

That's what he lives on, talks on, half-a-crown
A day, and sits there full of Cook.
Who'd do your cooking now, I'd like to ask,
If someone didn't grind her bones away?
But that's the truth, six children and half-a-crown
A day, and a man gone daft with Cook.'

That was his wife,
Elizabeth, a noble wife but brisk,
Who lived in a present full of kitchen-fumes
And had no past. He had not seen her
For seven years, being blind, and that of course
Was why he'd had to strike a deal with chairs,
Not knowing when those who chafed them had gone to sleep
Or stolen away. Darkness and empty chairs,
This was the port that Alexander Home
Had come to with his useless cutlass-wounds
And tales of Cook, and half-a-crown a day —
This was the creek he'd run his timbers to,
Where grateful countrymen repaid his wounds
At half-a-crown a day. Too good, too good,
This eloquent offering of birdcages
To gulls, and Greenwich Hospital to Cook,
Britannia's mission to the sea-fowl.

It was not blindness picked his flesh away,
Nor want of sight made penny-blank the eyes
Of Captain Home, but that he lived like this
In one place, and gazed elsewhere. His body moved
In Scotland, but his eyes were dazzle-full
Of skies and water farther round the world —
Air soaked with blue, so thick it dripped like snow
On spice-tree boughs, and water diamond-green,

Beaches wind-glittering with crumbs of gilt,
And birds more scarlet than a duchy's seal
That had come whistling long ago, and far
Away. His body had gone back,
Here it sat drinking rum in Berwickshire,
But not his eyes — they were left floating there
Half-round the earth, blinking at beaches milked
By suck-mouth tides, foaming with ropes of bubbles
And huge half-moons of surf. Thus it had been
When Cook was carried on a sailor's back,
Vengeance in a cocked hat, to claim his price,
A prince in barter for a longboat.
And then the trumpery springs of fate — a stone,
A musket-shot, a round of gunpowder,
And puzzled animals, killing they knew not what
Or why, but killing . . . the surge of goatish flanks
Armoured in feathers, like cruel birds:
Wild, childish faces, killing; a moment seen,
Marines with crimson coats and puffs of smoke
Toppling face-down; and a knife of English iron,
Forged aboard ship, that had been changed for pigs,
Given back to Cook between the shoulder-blades.
There he had dropped, and the old floundering sea,
The old, fumbling, witless lover-enemy,
Had taken his breath, last office of salt water.

Cook died. The body of Alexander Home
Flowed round the world and back again, with eyes
Marooned already, and came to English coasts,
The vague ancestral darknesses of home,
Seeing them faintly through a glass of gold,
Dim fog-shapes, ghosted like the ribs of trees
Against his blazing waters and blue air.

But soon they faded, and there was nothing left,
Only the sugar-cane and the wild granaries
Of sand, and palm-trees and the flying blood
Of cardinal-birds; and putting out one hand
Tremulously in the direction of the beach,
He felt a chair in Scotland. And sat down.

A Bushranger

Jackey Jackey gallops on a horse like a swallow
Where the carbines bark and the blackboys hollo.
When the traps give chase (may the Devil take his power!)
He can ride ten miles in a quarter of an hour.

Take a horse and follow, and you'll hurt no feelings;
He can fly down waterfalls and jump through ceilings,
He can shoot off hats, for to have a bit of fun,
With a bulldog bigger than a buffalo-gun.

Honeyed and profound is his conversation
When he bails up Mails on Long Tom Station,
In a flyaway coat with a black cravat,
A snow-white collar and a cabbage-tree hat.

Flowers in his button-hole and pearls in his pocket,
He comes like a ghost and he goes like a rocket
With a lightfoot heel on a blood-mare's flank
And a bagful of notes from the Joint Stock Bank.

Many pretty ladies he could witch out of marriage,
Though he prig but a kiss in a bigwig's carriage;

For the cock of an eye or the lift of his reins,
They would run barefoot through Patrick's Plains.

The Country Ride

'. . . Of all the Journeys that ever I made, this was the merriest, and I was in a strange mood for mirth.' — Samuel Pepys, 11 April, 1661

Earth which has known so many passages
Of April air, so many marriages
Of strange and lovely atoms breeding light,
Never may find again that lost delight.

In the sharp sky, the frosty deepnesses,
There are still birds to barb the silences,
There are still fields to meet the morning on,
But those who made them beautiful have gone.

Diamonds are flung by other smoking springs,
But where is he that cropped their offerings —
The pick-purse of enchantments, riding by,
Whistling his *'Go and Be Hanged, That's Twice Good-bye'*?

Who such a frolic pomp of blessing made
To kiss a little pretty dairymaid . . .
And country wives with bare and earth-burnt knees,
And boys with beer, and smiles from balconies . . .

The greensleeve girl, apprentice-equerry,
Tending great men with slant-eye mockery:
'Then Mr Sam says, "Riding's hot," he says,
Tasting their ale and waving twopences . . .'

Into one gaze they swam, a moment swirled,
One fiery paintbox of the body's world —
Into Sam's eye, that flying bushranger —
Swinging their torches for earth's voyager.

And how the blood sang, and the senses leapt,
And cells that under tents of horn had slept
Rose dancing, at the black and faceless bale
Of gallows-flesh that had not girl nor ale!

Elegy in a Botanic Gardens

The smell of birds' nests faintly burning
Is autumn. In the autumn I came
Where spring had used me better,
To the clear red pebbles and the men of stone
And foundered beetles, to the broken Meleager
And thousands of white circles drifting past,
Cold suns in water; even to the dead grove
Where we had kissed, to the Tristania tree
Where we had kissed so awkwardly,
Noted by swans with damp, accusing eyes,
All gone to-day; only the leaves remain,
Gaunt paddles ribbed with herringbones
Of watermelon-pink. Never before
Had I assented to the hateful name
Meryta Macrophylla, on a tin tag.
That was no time for botany. But now the schools,
The horticulturists, come forth
Triumphantly with Latin. So be it now,
Meryta Macrophylla, and the old house,

Ringed with black stone, no Georgian Headlong Hall
With glass-eye windows winking candles forth,
Stuffed with French horns, globes, air-pumps, telescopes
And Cupid in a wig, playing the flute,
But truly, and without escape,
THE NATIONAL HERBARIUM,
Repeated dryly in Roman capitals,
THE NATIONAL HERBARIUM.

Toilet of a Dandy

Transports of filed nerves; a wistful cough;
One sensual hairbrush reluctantly concludes
The Great Harry's excruciations and beatitudes,
Delicately and gravely putting things on and off.

Shouting through shirts, dipping out liquid flowers,
All the accoutrements and mysteries,
The awful engines of the toilet — presses, trees,
And huge voluptuous bootjacks, for two shuddering hours.

But in the glass navel of his dressing-room,
Nests of diminishing mirrors, Narcissus peers,
Too nicely shined, parting the cracked, refracted sneers,
And meets the Corpse in Evening Dress; Caruso's tomb.

Serenade

Thou moon, like a white Christus hanging
At the sky's cross-roads, I'll court thee not,
Though travellers bend up, and seek thy grace.
Let them go truckle with their gifts and singing,
I'll ask no favours of thy cocker face.

Moonlight's a viand sucked by the world's lovers,
Captains and peasants, all that are young and have luck.
They take the moon. Nobody asked them to.
Let the musicians lout to thee for favours;
Personally, I have other things to do.

To Myself

After all, you are my rather tedious hero;
It is impossible (damn it!) to avoid
Looking at you through keyholes.
But come! At least you might try to be
Even, let us say, a Graceful Zero
Or an Eminent Molecule, gorgeously employed.

Have you not played Hamlet's father in the wings
Long enough, listening to poets groan,
Seeking a false catharsis
In flesh not yours, through doors ajar
In the houses of dead kings,
In the gods' tombs, in the coffins of cracked stone?

Have you not poured yourself, thin fluid mind,
Down the dried-up canals, the powdering creeks,
Whose waters none remember

Either to praise them or condemn,
Whose fabulous cataracts none can find
Save one who has forgotten what he seeks?

Your uncle, the Great Harry, left after him
The memory of a cravat, a taste in cheese,
And a way of saying 'I am honoured.'
Such things, when men and beasts have gone,
Smell sweetly to the seraphim.
Believe, fool, there are worse gifts than these.

Wild Grapes

The old orchard, full of smoking air,
Full of sour marsh and broken boughs, is there,
But kept no more by vanished Mulligans,
Or Hartigans, long drowned in earth themselves,
Who gave this bitter fruit their care.

Here's where the cherries grew that birds forgot,
And apples bright as dogstars; now there is not
An apple or a cherry; only grapes,
But wild ones, Isabella grapes they're called,
Small, pointed, black, like boughs of musket-shot.

Eating their flesh, half-savage with black fur,
Acid and gipsy-sweet, I thought of her,
Isabella, the dead girl, who has lingered on
Defiantly when all have gone away,
In an old orchard where swallows never stir.

Isabella grapes, outlaws of a strange bough,
That in their harsh sweetness remind me somehow

Of dark hair swinging and silver pins,
A girl half-fierce, half-melting, as these grapes,
Kissed here — or killed here — but who remembers now?

Waters

This Water, like a sky that no one uses,
Air turned to stone, ridden by stars and birds
No longer, but with clouds of crystal swimming,
I'll not forget, nor men can lose, though words
Dissolve with music, gradually dimming.
So let them die; whatever the mind loses,
Water remains, cables and bells remain,
Night comes, the sailors burn their riding-lamps,
And strangers, pitching on our graves their camps,
Will break through branches to the surf again.

Darkness comes down. The Harbour shakes its mane,
Glazed with a leaf of amber; lights appear
Like thieves too early, dropping their swag by night,
Red, gold and green, down trap-doors glassy-clear,
And lanterns over Pinchgut float with light
Where they so long have lain.
All this will last, but I who gaze must go
On water stranger and less clear, and melt
With flesh away; and stars that I have felt,
And loved, shall shine for eyes I do not know.

Burying Friends

'. . . for a little of our vital essence goes into the grave of a friend.' —
'The Succubus', N. Lindsay

Burying friends is not a pomp,
Not, indeed, Roman:
Lacking the monument,
Heroic stone;
Nor is it an obscuring parasol,
The pad of customary gloves and cries
And a black leather mourning-carriage
Hung between death and the beholder's eyes.

This little bin of cancelled flesh
Strode the earth once,
Rubbed against men —
But that's all done.
A gentle elegy, a tear or two,
May charm the grave-diggers, no doubt,
But nothing can count to these incongruous ruins.
Their commercial value is not worth speaking about.

Only it seems not a burial
Of irrelevant sods,
But a lopped member
From this my body;
Almost, in fact, a tiny amputation,
A paring of biography, thrown in there.
And he has thieved his own life away
And something from mine. Farewell, thou pilferer!

Metempsychosis

Suddenly to become John Benbow, walking down William Street
With a tin trunk and a five-pound note, looking for a place to eat,
And a peajacket the colour of a shark's behind
That a Jew might buy in the morning . . .

To fry potatoes (God save us!) if you feel inclined,
Or to kiss the landlady's daughter, and no one mind,
In a peel-papered bedroom with a whistling jet
And a picture of the Holy Virgin . . .

Wake in a shaggy bale of blankets with a fished-up cigarette,
Picking over 'Turfbird's Tattle' for a Saturday morning bet,
With a bottle in the wardrobe easy to reach
And a blast of onions from the landing . . .

Tattooed with foreign ladies' tokens, a heart and dagger each,
In places that make the delicate female inquirer screech,
And over a chest smoky with gunpowder-blue —
Behold! — a mermaid piping through a coach-horn!

Banjo-playing, firing off guns, and other momentous things to do,
Such as blowing through peashooters at hawkers to improve the view —

Suddenly paid-off and forgotten in Woolloomooloo . . .

Suddenly to become John Benbow . . .

Rubens' Hell

Venus with rosy-cloven rump
And rings of straw-bright flying hair
Looks in the glass that slaves are plying
Not for her own face floating there,
But for the sly and curious gaze
Of Rubens, through the keyhole prying.

Warm flesh of gods, by light embayed,
And drifting daemon-bones within
That sweep like music up and down
To pouts and cups of ivory skin,
Firm-valleyed croup, and swagging arm
In whose embankment bracelets drown —

Do you remain, you strokes of paint,
With Venus mocked and Rubens dead
And Beauty sold for an antique
And microscopes raised up instead?
Still are your old adherents true;
Rubens is there, if he could speak.

Rubens is there in your high room,
Rubens it is who blows his breath
To fix you laughing in the glass,
Who keeps a castle here from death
While schools go out and fashions fall
And microscopes and movements pass.

This castle-keep of joys conceived
But never sucked is Rubens' hell,
Is Rubens' limbo, cut and won
From darkness. Here he comes to dwell.

Man's heaven is the place he builds
By thoughts imagined and things done.

Some choose a paradise of gas,
And some, by pious deeds below,
The heavenly butter-hatch for flunkeys;
Who dream of nought to nothing go.
Therefore I'd sooner Rubens' hell
Than go to heaven with the donkeys.

La Dame du Palais de la Reine

Sophie, in shocks of scarlet lace,
Receives her usual embrace
Beneath a hedge, behind a curtain,
Or in the chambers of His Grace.
Whether a kiss be worth the care
Five minions wasted on her hair,
Sophie herself is half uncertain,
Paused in adorable despair.

When past beseeching Man she floats
In golden-coasted petticoats,
A shaft of irritation passes;
Like colic; but with antidotes.
Then serious doubts occur of Love
That spoils the Peacock, sours the Dove,
And mixes up the lower classes
So hopelessly with those above.

Is the bird Passion worth the lime?
Can the small Amor turn to crime

By ruining skirts — and the digestion?
Such problems occupy her time.
But often these objections thaw
To counts with viols — or grooms with straw —
And Sophie, giving up the question,
Bends to some strange but natural law.

With books of music, diamond rings,
Spaniels and roses, fireworks, swings,
Her lovers come. But Sophie sighs,
Whose thoughts are fixed on Higher Things.
Between the sleepy kisses given,
Her mind by grave debate is driven,
Perplexity distracts those eyes
Which, lovers vow, are lost in Heaven!

Country Towns

Country towns, with your willows and squares,
And farmers bouncing on barrel mares
To public-houses of yellow wood
With '1860' over their doors,
And that mysterious race of Hogans
Which always keeps General Stores . . .

At the School of Arts, a broadsheet lies
Sprayed with the sarcasm of flies:
'The Great Golightly Family
Of Entertainers Here To-night' —
Dated a year and a half ago,
But left there, less from carelessness
Than from a wish to seem polite.

Verandas baked with musky sleep,
Mulberry faces dozing deep,
And dogs that lick the sunlight up
Like paste of gold — or, roused in vain
By far, mysterious buggy-wheels,
Lower their ears, and drowse again . . .

Country towns with your schooner bees,
And locusts burnt in the pepper-trees,
Drown me with syrups, arch your boughs,
Find me a bench, and let me snore,
Till, charged with ale and unconcern,
I'll think it's noon at half-past four!

Mephistopheles Perverted

(Or Goethe for the Times)

Once long ago lived a Flea
Who kept such a fine, fat King,
Not that he held with royalty,
But more for the appearance of the thing,

And gave his Majesty to hold
(Such pageantries are far too few)
A sword of ruby-hilted gold
That possibly might hack a cheese in two;

But lest this glory might begin
To prove the regency too far,
His thunderbolt they made of tin,
And changed his godship for another Star.

Thus when the Monarch drove abroad,
With stars like buttons round his chest,
God-fearing Fleas would all applaud,
And alien Lice be grudgingly impressed.

Such relics every Flea must flaunt,
If only as the final trump
That mocks Materialism's taunt,
Proving there's more in life than Suck and Jump.

Once long ago — but not so long —
A King went curing scrofula . . .
The chorus of this charming song,
I'm told reliably, is Ha, Ha, Ha.

Crustacean Rejoinder

Take your great light away, your music end;
I'm off to feed myself as quick as I can.
You're perfectly impossible to comprehend,
I'm such a busy man.

Good God, haven't you got a circumference?
There's not a moment I can call my own —
My clocks, my keys, my wheels and instruments
And that fierce Ethiop, the telephone.

No doubt, it's very charming out in the sun,
But there are other things, you know. In any case,
I've got no time, no time. There's much to be done.
Thank God for this, my faithful carapace!

Trade Circular

To the Poets' Ladies

Shall I give you the Bourbon-sugars
Of sherry and yellow sky
And a girl in a country curricle
Merrily bowling by?

Or darkness flying with crystals,
And the great Miser, Night,
Rubbing a mountain's breast-bone
With an old rind of light?

Wake up the handcuffed angels,
Muster the marble kings,
Till the blood swims in their bodies
And the stone captain sings?

Ask for a cage of comets,
Poets will give you this —
But if you should ask them for nothing,
They'll see how dead girls kiss.

Fixed Ideas

Ranks of electroplated cubes, dwindling to glitters,
Like the other pasture, the trigonometry of marble,
Death's candy-bed. Stone caked on stone,
Dry pyramids and racks of iron balls.
Life is observed, a precipitate of pellets,
Or grammarians freeze it into spar,
Their rhomboids, as for instance, the finest crystal
Fixing a snowfall under glass. Gods are laid out

In alabaster, with horny cartilage
And zinc ribs; or systems of ecstasy
Baked into bricks. There is a gallery of sculpture,
Bleached bones of heroes, Gorgon masks of bushrangers;
But the quarries are of more use than this,
Filled with the rolling of huge granite dice,
Ideas and judgments: vivisection, the Baptist Church,
Good men and bad men, polygamy, birth-control . . .

Frail tinkling rush
Water-hair streaming
Prickles and glitters
Cloudy with bristles
River of thought
Swimming the pebbles —
Undo, loosen your bubbles!

The Old Play

'. . . Madame, connaissez-vous cette vieille pièce? C'est une pièce tout à fait distinguée, seulement un peu trop mélancolique.' — H. Heine, *Tambour Legrand*

I

In an old play-house, in an old play,
In an old piece that has been done to death,
We dance, kind ladies, noble friends.
Observe our modishness, I pray,
What dignity the music lends.
Our sighs, no doubt, are only a doll's breath,
But gravely done — indeed, we're all devotion,
All pride and fury and pitiful elegance.
The importance of these antics, who may doubt?

Do you deny us the honour of emotion
Because another has danced this, our dance?
Let us jump it out.

II

In the old play-house, in the watery flare
Of gilt and candlesticks, in a dim pit
Furred with a powder of corroded plush,
Paint fallen from angels floating in mid-air,
The gods in languor sit.
Their talk they hush,
Their eyes' bright stony suction
Freezes to silence as we come
With our proud masks to act.
Who knows? Our poor induction
May take the ear, may still, perchance, distract.

Unspeakable tedium!
Is there nothing new in this old theatre, nothing new?
Are there no bristles left to prick
With monstrous tunes the music-box of flesh?
Hope dies away; the dance, absurd, antique,
Fatigues their monocles; the gods pursue
Their ageless colloquy afresh.

III

Marduk his jewelled finger flips
To greet a friend. Bald-headed, lean,
He wets his red transparent lips,
Taps his pince-nez, and gapes unseen.

Hequet to Mama Cocha cranes
Her horny beak. 'These fools who drink

Hemlock with love deserve their pains.
They're so conventional, I think.'

Limply she ceases to employ
Her little ivory spying-lens.
'I much prefer the Egyptian boy
Who poisoned Thua in the fens.'

IV

But who are we to sneer,
Who are we to count the rhymes
Or the authorized postures of the heart
Filched from a dynasty of mimes?
Each has a part;

We do not hear
The mockers at our little, minion ardours,
Our darling hatreds and adulteries,
Our griefs and ecstasies,
Our festivals and murders.

And who are we, who are we,
That would despise the lawful ceremonies
Condoned by the coming of five Christs,
By the beating of an infinitude of breasts,
By Adam's tears, by the dead man's pennies,
Who are we?

V

And who are we to argue with our lutes,
How would we change the play?
Are we Lucifers with hell in our boots?
There are no Lucifers to-day.

By no means. It is never like this,
Never like this. One does not fall.
How should we find, like Lucifer, an abyss?
Never like that at all.

And who are we to pester Azrael,
Importunate for funeral plumes
And all the graces Death can sell —
Death in cocked feathers, Death in drawing-rooms,
Death with a sword-cane, stabbing down the stairs?
It is not like this at all,
Never, never like this.
Death is the humblest of affairs,
It is really incredibly small:
The dropping of a degree or less,
The tightening of a vein, such gradual things.
And then
How should we guess
The slow Capuan poison, the soft strings,
Of Death with leather jaws come tasting men?

VI

Camazotz and Anubis
Go no more to the *coulisses*.
Once they'd wait for hours,
Grateful for a few excuses,
Hiding their snouts in flowers,
Merely as a tribute to the Muses.

Those were the days of serenades,
Prima donnas and appointments.
Now they think longer of pomades,
Less of the heart and more of ointments.

Anubis dabbles with the world;
A charming man, perhaps a trifle sinister,
But with his stars on, and his tendrils curled,
Really, you'd take him for the Persian Minister.

But Camazotz has grown jaded
And likes an arm-chair in the stalls,
Being by brute necessity persuaded
That perfect love inevitably palls;

Such the divine adversity
Of passion twisting on its stem,
Seeking a vague and cloudier trophy
Beyond the usual diadem.

'More balconies! More lilac-trees!
Let us go out to the private bar.
I am so tired of young men like these,
Besides, I note he is carrying a guitar.'

VII

'Shang Ya! I want to be your friend' —
That was the fashion in our termitary,
In the gas-lit cellules of virtuous young men —
'Shang Ya! I want to be your friend.'
Often I think, if we had gone then
Waving the torches of demoniac theory,
We should have melted stone, astonished God,
Overturned kings, exalted scullions,
And ridden the hairy beast outside
Into our stables to be shod —
Such was the infection of our pride,
Almost a confederation of Napoleons.

Though in Yuëh it is usual
  To behead a cock and dog,
Such was not considered binding
  In our bloodless decalogue.

But the tail-piece to the chapter
  We so fierily began
Resembled an old song-book
  From the golden days of Han.

Ours was the Life-Parting
Which made the poets so elegantly tragic.
On and on, always on and on,
By fears and families, by a sudden plague of logic,
By an agreeable ossification,
By a thousand tiny particles of space
Widening the fissures of our brotherhood,
We were impelled from place to place,
Dismembered by necessitude.

Who could have called that soft, adhesive nag
We bounced our lives on, a wild horse?
We were given palfreys in the place of stallions;
As for the kings and scullions,
We should, no doubt, have brought them to our flag
Had we not forgotten the prescribed discourse.

On and on, driven by flabby whips,
To the Nine Lands, to the world's end,
We have been scattered by the sea-captains of ships,
Crying no more with bright and childish lips,
Even if we wanted to pretend,
'Shang Ya! Let me be your friend.'

VIII

This is really a Complete Life and Works,
The memorial of a great man
Who was born with Excalibur in his fist
And finished by asking questions.

Woken by a star falling on his tiles,
He rushed out, defying devils —
'Come forth, you monster!' Only neighbours peeped
Fish-eyed at this ferocity.

Repeatedly inviting the rogue to stand,
He hunted with a naked sword,
But though general admiration and sympathy were expressed,
The scoundrel was not detected.

At last, regrettable to state, he stopped.
Why honour a coward with pursuit?
So he began to use Excalibur in the kitchen,
Or on occasion as a hay-rake.

How did he know that Time at length would gnaw
The rascal's face with quicklime?
Gradually the print faded, a fog blew down,
He even forgot the nature of the outrage.

However, he managed to live very tolerably,
And now, in a substantial villa,
Having saved enough to purchase an annuity,
Is piously glad he never found anyone.

But Gutumdug and Vukub-Cakix,
Having already seen many great men,

May surely be pardoned if with foundered chins
They doze a little . . .

Phew . . . heu . . .
Doze a little.

IX

A bird sang in the jaws of night,
Like a star lost in space —
O, dauntless molecule to smite
With joy that giant face!

I heard you mock the lonely air,
The bitter dark, with song,
Waking again the old Despair
That had been dead so long,

That had been covered up with clay
And never talked about,
So none with bony claws could say
They'd dig my coffin out.

But you, with music clear and brave,
Have shamed the buried thing;
It rises dripping from the grave
And tries in vain to sing.

O, could the bleeding mouth reply,
The broken flesh but moan,
The tongues of skeletons would cry,
And Death push back his stone!

X

My strings I break, my breast I beat,
The immemorial tears repeat,
But Beli, yawning in the pit,
Is not at all impressed by it.

Fresh lachrymations to endure!
He champs a gilded comfiture —
'The song was stale five Acts ago;
Besides, it isn't Life, you know.'

XI

But Life we know, but Life we know,
Is full of visions and vertigo,
Full of God's blowpipes belching rubies forth,
And God's ambiguous grape-shot maiming saints,
Full of emancipations and restraints —
Thou poor, bewildered earth!

Thou givest us neither doom nor expiation,
Nor palm-trees bursting into praise;
Blow down thy fruit, we snatch our stomachful,
Thou turnest not thy gaze,
Knowing we do but rob a little time;
A flight of air; thou takest back the spoils.
O, for some thunder on our brother's crime,
Even a little harmless flagellation
Or a few miserable boils!

But thou! Thou dost not turn thy face
Either to buffet or explore.
The devils bask, the martyrs weep.
Art thou too proud in a high place,

Or too befuddled in thy sleep?
Art thou too languorous to roar?

XII

You that we raised
To the high places,
With painted eyes
And cloudy faces,
You that are named,
But no one finds,
Made out of nothing
By men's minds —
Be true to us,
Play us not false;
Be cruel, O Gods,
Not fabulous.

You were our statues
Cut from space,
Gorgon's eyes
And dragon's face;
Fail us not,
You that we made,
When the stars go out
And the suns fade.
You were our hope
Death to bless —
Leave us not crying
In emptiness.

Five Bells

(1939)

To the memory of
an Australian poet
John Alexander Ross McKellar
1904–1932

Five Bells

Time that is moved by little fidget wheels
Is not my Time, the flood that does not flow.
Between the double and the single bell
Of a ship's hour, between a round of bells
From the dark warship riding there below,
I have lived many lives, and this one life
Of Joe, long dead, who lives between five bells.

Deep and dissolving verticals of light
Ferry the falls of moonshine down. Five bells
Coldly rung out in a machine's voice. Night and water
Pour to one rip of darkness, the Harbour floats
In air, the Cross hangs upside-down in water.

Why do I think of you, dead man, why thieve
These profitless lodgings from the flukes of thought
Anchored in Time? You have gone from earth,
Gone even from the meaning of a name;
Yet something's there, yet something forms its lips
And hits and cries against the ports of space,
Beating their sides to make its fury heard.

Are you shouting at me, dead man, squeezing your face
In agonies of speech on speechless panes?
Cry louder, beat the windows, bawl your name!

But I hear nothing, nothing . . . only bells,
Five bells, the bumpkin calculus of Time.
Your echoes die, your voice is dowsed by Life,
There's not a mouth can fly the pygmy strait —
Nothing except the memory of some bones

Long shoved away, and sucked away, in mud;
And unimportant things you might have done,
Or once I thought you did; but you forgot,
And all have now forgotten — looks and words
And slops of beer; your coat with buttons off,
Your gaunt chin and pricked eye, and raging tales
Of Irish kings and English perfidy,
And dirtier perfidy of publicans
Groaning to God from Darlinghurst.

Five bells.

Then I saw the road, I heard the thunder
Tumble, and felt the talons of the rain
The night we came to Moorebank in slab-dark,
So dark you bore no body, had no face,
But a sheer voice that rattled out of air
(As now you'd cry if I could break the glass),
A voice that spoke beside me in the bush,
Loud for a breath or bitten off by wind,
Of Milton, melons, and the Rights of Man,
And blowing flutes, and how Tahitian girls
Are brown and angry-tongued, and Sydney girls
Are white and angry-tongued, or so you'd found.
But all I heard was words that didn't join
So Milton became melons, melons girls,
And fifty mouths, it seemed, were out that night,
And in each tree an Ear was bending down,
Or something had just run, gone behind grass,
When, blank and bone-white, like a maniac's thought,
The naphtha-flash of lightning slit the sky,
Knifing the dark with deathly photographs.
There's not so many with so poor a purse
Or fierce a need, must fare by night like that,

Five miles in darkness on a country track,
But when you do, that's what you think.

Five bells.

In Melbourne, your appetite had gone,
Your angers too; they had been leeched away
By the soft archery of summer rains
And the sponge-paws of wetness, the slow damp
That stuck the leaves of living, snailed the mind,
And showed your bones, that had been sharp with rage,
The sodden ecstasies of rectitude.
I thought of what you'd written in faint ink,
Your journal with the sawn-off lock, that stayed behind
With other things you left, all without use,
All without meaning now, except a sign
That someone had been living who now was dead:
'At Labassa. Room 6 x 8
On top of the tower; because of this, very dark
And cold in winter. Everything has been stowed
Into this room — 500 books all shapes
And colours, dealt across the floor
And over sills and on the laps of chairs;
Guns, photoes of many differant things
And differant curioes that I obtained . . .'

In Sydney, by the spent aquarium-flare
Of penny gaslight on pink wallpaper,
We argued about blowing up the world,
But you were living backward, so each night
You crept a moment closer to the breast,
And they were living, all of them, those frames
And shapes of flesh that had perplexed your youth,
And most your father, the old man gone blind,

With fingers always round a fiddle's neck,
That graveyard mason whose fair monuments
And tablets cut with dreams of piety
Rest on the bosoms of a thousand men
Staked bone by bone, in quiet astonishment
At cargoes they had never thought to bear,
These funeral-cakes of sweet and sculptured stone.

Where have you gone? The tide is over you,
The turn of midnight water's over you,
As Time is over you, and mystery,
And memory, the flood that does not flow.
You have no suburb, like those easier dead
In private berths of dissolution laid —
The tide goes over, the waves ride over you
And let their shadows down like shining hair,
But they are Water; and the sea-pinks bend
Like lilies in your teeth, but they are Weed;
And you are only part of an Idea.
I felt the wet push its black thumb-balls in,
The night you died, I felt your eardrums crack,
And the short agony, the longer dream,
The Nothing that was neither long nor short;
But I was bound, and could not go that way,
But I was blind, and could not feel your hand.
If I could find an answer, could only find
Your meaning, or could say why you were here
Who now are gone, what purpose gave you breath
Or seized it back, might I not hear your voice?

I looked out of my window in the dark
At waves with diamond quills and combs of light
That arched their mackerel-backs and smacked the sand

In the moon's drench, that straight enormous glaze,
And ships far off asleep, and Harbour-buoys
Tossing their fireballs wearily each to each,
And tried to hear your voice, but all I heard
Was a boat's whistle, and the scraping squeal
Of seabirds' voices far away, and bells,
Five bells. Five bells coldly ringing out.

Five bells.

Sleep

Do you give yourself to me utterly,
   Body and no-body, flesh and no-flesh,
Not as a fugitive, blindly or bitterly,
   But as a child might, with no other wish?
Yes, utterly.

Then I shall bear you down my estuary,
Carry you and ferry you to burial mysteriously,
Take you and receive you,
Consume you, engulf you,
In the huge cave, my belly, lave you
With huger waves continually.

And you shall cling and clamber there
And slumber there, in that dumb chamber,
Beat with my blood's beat, hear my heart move
Blindly in bones that ride above you,
Delve in my flesh, dissolved and bedded,
Through viewless valves embodied so —

Till daylight, the expulsion and awakening,
The riving and the driving forth,
Life with remorseless forceps beckoning —
Pangs and betrayal of harsh birth.

To the Poetry of Hugh McCrae*

Uncles who burst on childhood, from the East,
Blown from air, like bearded ghosts arriving,
And are, indeed, a kind of guessed-at ghost
Through mumbled names at dinner-tables moving,

Bearers of parrots, bonfires of blazing stones,
Their pockets fat with riches out of reason,
Meerschaum and sharks'-teeth, ropes of China coins,
And weeds and seeds and berries blowzed with poison —

So, from the baleful Kimberleys of thought,
From the mad continent of dreams, you wander,
Spending your trophies at our bloodless feet,
Mocking our fortunes with more desperate plunder;

So with your boomerangs of rhyme you come,
With blossoms wrenched from sweet and deadly branches,
And we, pale Crusoes in the moment's tomb,
Watch, turn aside, and touch again those riches,

Nor ask what beaches of the mind you trod,
What skies endured, and unimagined rivers,
Or whiteness trenched by what mysterious tide,
And aching silence of the Never-Nevers;

* Poetry: An art practised by the ancients.

Watch, turn aside, and touch with easy faith
Your chest of miracles, but counting nothing,
Or dumbly, that you stole them out of death,
Out of death's pyramids, to prove us breathing.

We breathe, who beat the sides of emptiness,
We live, who die by statute in steel hearses,
We dance, whose only posture gives us grace
To squeeze the greasy udders of our purses —

(Look in this harsher glass, and I will show you
The daylight after the darkness, and the morning
After the midnight, and after the night the day
After the year after, terribly returning).

We live by these, your masks and images,
We breathe in this, your quick and borrowed body;
But you take passage on the ruffian seas,
And you are vanished in the dark already.

Last Trams

I

That street washed with violet
Writes like a tablet
Of living here; that pavement
Is the metal embodiment
Of living here; those terraces
Filled with dumb presences
Lobbed over mattresses,
Lusts and repentances,

Ardours and solaces,
Passions and hatreds
And love in brass bedsteads . . .
Lost now in emptiness
Deep now in darkness
Nothing but nakedness,
Rails like a ribbon
And sickness of carbon
Dying in distances.

II

Then, from the skeletons of trams,
Gazing at lighted rooms, you'll find
The black and Röntgen diagrams
Of window-plants across the blind

That print their knuckleduster sticks,
Their buds of gum, against the light
Like negatives of candlesticks
Whose wicks are lit by fluorite;

And shapes look out, or bodies pass,
Between the darkness and the flare,
Between the curtain and the glass,
Of men and women moving there.

So through the moment's needle-eye,
Like phantoms in the window-chink,
Their faces brush you as they fly,
Fixed in the shutters of a blink;

But whose they are, intent on what,
Who knows? They rattle into void,

Stars of a film without a plot,
Snippings of idiot celluloid.

Lesbia's Daughter

Lesbia's daughter, I shall tell no lie,
Here's no fit amber for such a dainty fly.
Let them embalm your beauty whoso can
In boastful odes, I'm a more honest man.

Lovers' abodes with poets' words are paved,
But prudent girls would get those vows engraved,
For brass than paper being something stronger
May last, it's more than like, a fortnight longer.

Where's the fine music that the fossil men
Of lost Lemuria brandished on a pen?
All tossed in earth — men, music, lovers gone —
And where's the lust a skull has for a bone?

If joy can turn a moment to a year,
Why take to Then and There what's meant for Here,
Or nurture for a cemetery tense
The curious pleasures of impermanence?

Look for no lovers on that later scene,
Let it avail you Are, who shall have Been,
Burnt utterly the stick you had to burn,
Lived once, loved well, gave thanks, and won't return.

Out of Time

I

I saw Time flowing like the hundred yachts
That fly behind the daylight, foxed with air;
Or piercing, like the quince-bright, bitter slats
Of sun gone thrusting under Harbour's hair.

So Time, the wave, enfolds me in its bed,
Or Time, the bony knife, it runs me through.
'Skulker, take heart,' I thought my own heart said,
'The flood, the blade, go by — Time flows, not you!'

Vilely, continuously, stupidly,
Time takes me, drills me, drives through bone and vein,
So water bends the seaweeds in the sea,
The tide goes over, but the weeds remain.

Time, you must cry farewell, take up the track,
And leave this lovely moment at your back!

II

Time leaves the lovely moment at his back,
Eager to quench and ripen, kiss or kill;
To-morrow begs him, breathless for his lack,
Or beauty dead entreats him to be still.

His fate pursues him; he must open doors,
Or close them, for that pale and faceless host
Without a flag, whose agony implores
Birth, to be flesh, or funeral, to be ghost.

Out of all reckoning, out of dark and light,
Over the edges of dead Nows and Heres,
Blindly and softly, as a mistress might,
He keeps appointments with a million years.

I and the moment laugh, and let him go,
Leaning against his golden undertow.

III

Leaning against the golden undertow,
Backward, I saw the birds begin to climb
With bodies hailstone-clear, and shadows flow,
Fixed in a sweet meniscus, out of Time,

Out of the torrent, like the fainter land
Lensed in a bubble's ghostly camera,
The lighted beach, the sharp and china sand,
Glitters and waters and peninsula —

The moment's world, it was; and I was part,
Fleshless and ageless, changeless and made free.
'Fool, would you leave this country?' cried my heart,
But I was taken by the suck of sea.

The gulls go down, the body dies and rots,
And Time flows past them like a hundred yachts.

North Country

North Country, filled with gesturing wood,
With trees that fence, like archers' volleys,
The flanks of hidden valleys
Where nothing's left to hide

But verticals and perpendiculars,
Like rain gone wooden, fixed in falling,
Or fingers blindly feeling
For what nobody cares;

Or trunks of pewter, bangled by greedy death,
Stuck with black staghorns, quietly sucking,
And trees whose boughs go seeking,
And trees like broken teeth

With smoky antlers broken in the sky;
Or trunks that lie grotesquely rigid,
Like bodies blank and wretched
After a fool's battue,

As if they've secret ways of dying here
And secret places for their anguish
When boughs at last relinquish
Their clench of blowing air —

But this gaunt country, filled with mills and saws,
With butter-works and railway-stations
And public institutions,
And scornful rumps of cows,

North Country, filled with gesturing wood —
Timber's the end it gives to branches,
Cut off in cubic inches,
Dripping red with blood.

South Country

After the whey-faced anonymity
Of river-gums and scribbly-gums and bush,
After the rubbing and the hit of brush,
You come to the South Country

As if the argument of trees were done,
The doubts and quarrelling, the plots and pains,
All ended by these clear and gliding planes
Like an abrupt solution.

And over the flat earth of empty farms
The monstrous continent of air floats back
Coloured with rotting sunlight and the black,
Bruised flesh of thunderstorms:

Air arched, enormous, pounding the bony ridge,
Ditches and hutches, with a drench of light,
So huge, from such infinities of height,
You walk on the sky's beach

While even the dwindled hills are small and bare,
As if, rebellious, buried, pitiful,
Something below pushed up a knob of skull,
Feeling its way to air.

William Street

The red globes of light, the liquor-green,
The pulsing arrows and the running fire
Spilt on the stones, go deeper than a stream;
You find this ugly, I find it lovely.

Ghosts' trousers, like the dangle of hung men,
In pawnshop-windows, bumping knee by knee,
But none inside to suffer or condemn;
You find this ugly, I find it lovely.

Smells rich and rasping, smoke and fat and fish
And puffs of paraffin that crimp the nose,
Or grease that blesses onions with a hiss;
You find it ugly, I find it lovely.

The dips and molls, with flip and shiny gaze
(Death at their elbows, hunger at their heels)
Ranging the pavements of their pasturage;
You find it ugly, I find it lovely.

Cock-Crow

The cock's far cry
From lonely yards
Burdens the night
With boastful birds
That mop their wings
To make response —
A mess of songs
And broken sense.

So, when I slept,
I heard your call
(If lips long dead
Could answer still)
And snapped-off thoughts
Broke into clamour,

Like the night's throats
Heard by a dreamer.

The Knife

The plough that marks on Harley's field
   In flying earth its print
Thows up, like death itself concealed,
   A fang of rosy flint,

A flake of stone, by fingers hewed
   Whose buried bones are gone,
All gone, with fingers, hunters, food,
   But still the knife lives on.

And well I know, when bones are nought,
   The blade of stone survives —
I, too, from clods of aching thought,
   Have turned up sharper knives.

To a Friend

Adam, because on the mind's roads
   Your mouth is always in a hurry,
Because you know 500 odes
   And 19 ways to make a curry,

Because you fall in love with words
   And whistle beauty forth to kiss them,
And blow the tails from China birds
   Whilst I continually miss them,

Because you top my angry best
   At billiards, fugues or pulling corks out,
And whisk a fritter from its nest
   Before there's time to hand the forks out,

Because you saw the Romans wink,
   Because your senses dance to metre,
Because, no matter what I drink,
   You'll hold at least another litre,

Because you've got a gipsy's eye
   That melts the rage of catamountains,
And metaphors that pass me by
   Burst from your lips in lovely fountains,

Because you've bitten the harsh foods
   Of Life, grabbed every dish that passes,
And walked amongst the multitudes
   Without the curse of looking-glasses,

Because I burn the selfsame flame
   No falls of dirty earth may smother,
Oh, in your Abbey of Thélème,
   Enlist me as a serving-brother!

Vesper-Song of the Reverend Samuel Marsden

My cure of souls, my cage of brutes,
Go lick and learn at these my boots!
When tainted highways tear a hole,
I bid my cobbler welt the sole.

O, ye that wear the boots of Hell,
Shall I not welt a soul as well?
  O, souls that leak with holes of sin,
  Shall I not let God's leather in,
  Or hit with sacramental knout
  Your twice-convicted vileness out?

Lord, I have sung with ceaseless lips
A tinker's litany of whips,
Have graved another Testament
On backs bowed down and bodies bent.
My stripes of jewelled blood repeat
A scarlet Grace for holy meat.
  Not mine, the Hand that writes the weal
  On this, my vellum of puffed veal,
  Not mine, the glory that endures,
  But Yours, dear God, entirely Yours.

Are there not Saints in holier skies
Who have been scourged to Paradise?
O, Lord, when I have come to that,
Grant there may be a Heavenly Cat
With twice as many tails as here —
  And make me, God, Your Overseer.
  But if the veins of Saints be dead,
  Grant me a whip in Hell instead,
  Where blood is not so hard to fetch.

But I, Lord, am Your humble wretch.

Full Orchestra

My words are the poor footmen of your pride,
Of what you cry, you trumpets, each to each
With mouths of air; my speech is the dog-speech
Of yours, the Roman tongue — but mine is tied
By harsher bridles, dumb with breath and bone.
Vainly it mocks the dingo strings, the stops,
The pear-tree flying in the flute, with drops
Of music, quenched and scattered by your own.

So serving-men, who run all night with wine,
And whet their ears, and crouch upon the floor,
Sigh broken words no man has heard before
Or since, but ravished in the candleshine,
Between the push and shutting of a door,
From the great table where their masters dine.

Advice to Psychologists

You spies that pierce the mind with trenches,
   Feasting your eyes through private panes,
Who, not content with Heavenly stenches,
   Insist on taking up the drains,

For you I've only two suggestions,
   Who prowl with torches in this Bog —
Small good you'll get from asking questions;
   Walk on your nostrils, like a dog.

Sensuality

Feeling hunger and cold, feeling
Food, feeling fire, feeling
Pity and pain, tasting
Time in a kiss, tasting
Anger and tears, touching
Eyelids with lips, touching
Plague, touching flesh, knowing
Blood in the mouth, knowing
Laughter like flame, holding
Pickaxe and pen, holding
Death in the hand, hearing
Boilers and bells, hearing
Birds, hearing hail, smelling
Cedar and sweat, smelling
Petrol and sea, feeling
Hunger and cold, feeling
Food, feeling fire . . .

Feeling.

Cannibal Street

'Buy, who'll buy,' the pedlar sings,
'Bones of beggars, loins of kings,
Ribs of murder, haunch of hate,
And Beauty's head on a butcher's plate!'

Hook by hook, on steaming stalls,
The hero hangs, the harlot sprawls;
For Helen's flesh, in such a street,
Is only a kind of dearer meat.

'Buy, who'll buy,' the pedlar begs,
'Angel-wings and lady-legs,
Tender bits and dainty parts —
Buy, who'll buy my skewered hearts?'

Buy, who'll buy? The cleavers fall,
The dead men creak, the live men call,
And I (God save me) bargained there,
Paid my pennies and ate my share.

from Poems

(1957)

Polarities

Sometimes she is like sherry, like the sun through a vessel
of glass,
Like light through an oriel window in a room of yellow
wood;
Sometimes she is the colour of lions, of sand in the fire of
noon,
Sometimes as bruised with shadows as the afternoon.

Sometimes she moves like rivers, sometimes like trees;
Or tranced and fixed like South Pole silences;
Sometimes she is beauty, sometimes fury, sometimes
neither,
Sometimes nothing, drained of meaning, null as water.

Sometimes, when she makes pea-soup or plays me
Schumann,
I love her one way; sometimes I love her another
More disturbing way when she opens her mouth in
the dark;
Sometimes I like her with camellias, sometimes with a
parsley-stalk,
Sometimes I like her swimming in a mirror on the wall;
Sometimes I don't like her at all.

*An Inscription for Dog River**

Our general was the greatest and bravest of generals.
For his deeds, look around you on this coast —
Here is his name cut next to Ashur-Bani-Pal's,
Nebuchadnezzar's and the Roman host;
And we, though our identities have been lost,

Lacking the validity of stone or metal,
We, too, are part of his memorial,
Having been put in for the cost,

Having bestowed on him all we had to give
In battles few can recollect,
Our strength, obedience and endurance,
Our wits, our bodies, our existence,
Even our descendants' right to live —
Having given him everything, in fact,
Except respect.

*'At this point the hills approach the sea and rise high above the river; together they form a very serious obstacle which had to be negotiated by every army marching along the shore. Here the Egyptian Pharaohs therefore commemorated their successes, and their example was followed by all subsequent conquerors, Assyrian, Babylonian, Roman (and French) down to 1920.' — *Steimatzky's Guide to Syria and the Lebanon*. In 1942, General Sir Thomas Blamey had an inscription cut to celebrate the capture of Damour by Australian troops under his command.

Beach Burial

Softly and humbly to the Gulf of Arabs
The convoys of dead sailors come;
At night they sway and wander in the waters far under,
But morning rolls them in the foam.

Between the sob and clubbing of the gunfire
Someone, it seems, has time for this,
To pluck them from the shallows and bury them in burrows
And tread the sand upon their nakedness;

And each cross, the driven stake of tidewood,
Bears the last signature of men,
Written with such perplexity, with such bewildered pity,
The words choke as they begin —

'Unknown seaman' — the ghostly pencil
Wavers and fades, the purple drips,
The breath of the wet season has washed their inscriptions
As blue as drowned men's lips,

Dead seamen, gone in search of the same landfall,
Whether as enemies they fought,
Or fought with us, or neither; the sand joins them together,
Enlisted on the other front.

EL ALAMEIN

Funny Farmyard

Nursery Rhymes and Painting Book

(1933)

Katie Cat

Oh, what can Katie Cat
    Be at,
And what can she be doing?
She's doing nothing, it would seem,
But looking round for cream,
                                        cream,
                                            cream,
And mewing,
        mewing,
            mewing!

Hatty Hen

Hatty Hen —
She's tired of men,
Tired of talking, tired of squawking,
Laying eggs till who knows when.
Week by week,
She supplies
Eggs of large and noble size;
People sneak
(What's the use?)
All that Hatty can produce;
Days and days,
Hatty lays
Eggs that stupify the gaze —
Robbers take the lot, and then
Hatty lays an egg again.

Bill Bunny

This distinguished-looking figure,
   If politeness is your habit,
With a haughty sort of snigger
   You'll address as '*William Rabbit*'.

But formality offends,
   Where it isn't merely funny,
And he'd *much* prefer his friends
   To address him as 'BILL BUNNY'.

Timothy, the Terrier

Could anyone be merrier
Than Timothy, the Terrier,
Or bear a madder twinkle in the eye, eye, eye?
He'll make a meal, by gosh, from the heel of a golosh
Or the upper of a slipper on the sly, sly, sly!

Peter

If you ask me what breeding is Peter,
He's a kind of an amateur setter —
(At least, I *believe* he's a setter,
Perhaps just a Bitzer* is better) —
No galloping greyhound is fleeter
(At least, as an *eater* than Peter)
So neatly and sweetly
And very completely
Attired in this elegant sweater!

*Bitzer this and Bitzer that.

Rufus Rooster

Rufus the Rooster
Believes in publicity —
Blowing and crowing and likewise whatoh-ing,
In accents so glowing,
Will beat electricity —
'Listen, my lad,'
(He says) 'to your dad,
Here's the original newspaper ad. —
A whirr of his wings,
And Rufus, he sings:–
'EGGS to be had!
Eggs to be HAD!'

Daniel Duck

Daniel Duck
Is hard to know —
He doesn't cluck,
He doesn't crow;
When chickens nod,
He gives a sniff —
He is so very
Proud and stiff.

Should you be fond
Enough to lend
A handy pond,
He'll condescend
To fish for worms —
But, here's the joke,
He wouldn't speak
To common folk!

Gran'pa Goat

Oh, hear the tale of Gran'pa Goat,
On big top-hats he used to dote;
His heart would flutter pit-a-pat
With envy for a big top-hat;
The fairies heard his wistful prayer,
And put this hat on, then and there,
But, fixed so firmly, there and then,
He couldn't get it off again —
Such would be strange for you or me,
But then, he IS a goat, you see.

Little Letty Lamb

Little Letty Lamb
Has had to leave her pram
Behind her in the nursery
and
Take
A
Tram.
Though riding in a pram was once her practice,
(And much as she adores a pram), the fact is
She bade her pram adieu,
And grew
And *grew*,
And GREW,
Till now, if you should mention 'pram'
Within five yards of Letty Lamb,
You plainly show
You do not know
What tact is.

Darlinghurst Nights

(1933)

and Morning Glories
Being 47 strange sights
Observed from eleventh storeys,
In a land of cream puffs and crime,
By a Flat-roof Professor;
And here set forth in sketch and rhyme
by 'Virgil' and Kenneth Slessor

Delicatessen

Little, round cherries in little, round glasses,
Oysters in bottles, and soup a la can,
Over the counter, the grocery passes,
All for the love of a man —
All for the sake of some far-away someone
Chafing with hunger in far-away state,
Snatching from Mammon a mouthful of salmon,
Banging a fork on his plate.

Still is the pistol of Smith and of Wesson,
Stilled is the wish of the gunman to roam,
Delicatessen, delicatessen,
Delicatessen, come home!

Ladies who linger too late with a bargain,
Chauffeurs whose mistresses peer from their cars,
All down the counter, they crowd with their jargon
Buying their dinner in jars;
Food for the flat, and a snack for the wealthy,
Arrogant truffles and vulgar sardines,
Herrings and custard and mushrooms and mustard,
Caviar, chicken, and beans.

Vain is the lore of the cookery-lesson,
Faced by the fangs of a ravenous male —
Delicatessen, delicatessen,
Delicatessen for sale!

Ham, pink as roses, and peaches and pickles,
Onions in crystal, like globules of gold,
Out of the window, the treasury trickles,
Greedily, speedily sold;

Olives and gherkins and sauerkraut and whitebait,
   Pork and asparagus, captive in tin —
Searching for any marked 'Tasty, One Penny',
   Faces gaze wistfully in.

Misting the glass of the windows they press on,
   Snub, little noses pushed flat with a sigh —
Delicatessen, delicatessen,
   Delicatessen, good-bye!

Country Eyes

Diana is down from the station,
   A fortnight from Heaven-Knows-Where —
Her favourite hobby is down in the lobby
   With gratification
   To sit in a chair.

The lords and the ladies, the beautiful ladies,
The lords and the ladies are noble to see,
In sables and satins, they tinkle Manhattans
Or dabble their diamonds in butter and tea.

The music is always by Tosti,
   Delightfully wicked and gay;
Each waiter that passes has 500 glasses,
   All pink, green, and frosty,
   That shine on his tray.

And the lords and the ladies, the sweet, pretty ladies,
The lords and the ladies take supper in sips,
In satins and sables at little round tables,
With little round cocktails and little round lips.

And Spanish ambassadors linger
In elegant gloom with their beer —
Magnificent creatures with classical features —
While twiddling one finger,
There's Cuthbert de Vere!

But the lords and the ladies, the wonderful ladies,
The lords and the ladies look round in surprise —
Mouth open, heart beating, too breathless for eating
Diana sits watching with shining great eyes.

The lords have a habit of lying,
The archdukes are out of a job.
The frolicsome ladies are Cohens and Gradys,
And Cuthbert is dying
To borrow two bob.

All the touts at their tables, the middle-aged Mabels
The second-hand butterflies, mumble and peer;
The Dresden princesses have dirt on their dresses.
Diana is twenty — Romance is so near!

The Green Rolls-Royce

Where the iceman doesn't cater
For the idle millionaire
With his private Kelvinator
And his faithful Frigidaire,
Where the windows gleam with money
And the wine is never sly,
And the world is always sunny
And the rent is always high,

And the landlord says with passion
   The locality is 'choice',
In a condescending fashion
   Goes the green Rolls-Royce.

Where the Black Marias clatter,
   And peculiar ladies nod,
And the flats are rather flatter,
   And the lodgers rather odd,
Where the night is full of dangers
   And the darkness full of fear,
And eleven hundred strangers
   Live on aspirin and beer,
Where the gas-lights flare and flutter
   And the phonographs rejoice,
Like an archduke in the gutter
   Goes the green Rolls-Royce.

If you care to do some prying,
   And you want to get some thrills,
You can hear a lady sighing
   To a pocketful of bills:
'Here's the rent-day getting closer,
   I can't bear things as they are,
You will have to pay the grocer
   Or I'll have to sell the car.'
But no sooner has she said it
   In a melancholy voice,
Than she goes and gets some credit
   With the green Rolls-Royce.

The Tiger in the Rose

Rosie at the Stadium
  Flaunts around her neck
Rubies rare as radium.
  Diamonds by the peck;
Furs of real peschaniki,
  Staggering the Press,
Make the neighbours panicky
  Not in evening dress.
Rosie's not the simple little angel you suppose,
Down behind a dimple there's a Tiger
                                        in
                                            the
                                                Rose!

Eyes like infant violets
  Shine in Rosie's face,
Serenades and triolets
  Hang around the place,
Talk of possibilities,
  Pansies in a rage —
Once they start hostilities,
  Rosie goes Stone Age.
Shouting all the louder, 'Paste him on the nose!'
Underneath the powder, there's a Tiger
                                        in
                                            the
                                                Rose!

Jungle creatures loitering
  Down in Rosie's heart,
Leap out reconnoitring

When the fighters start;
Fairies love ferocity —
Rosie starts to shout,
Filled with animosity,
'Bust him on the snout!'
Never mind the posy, disregard the pose,
Have a look at Rosie! There's a Tiger
in
the
Rose!

Choker's Lane

In Choker's Lane, the doors appear
Like black and shining coffin-lids,
Whose fill of flesh, long buried here,
Familiar visiting forbids.

But sometimes, when their bells are twirled,
They'll show, like Hades, through the chink,
The green and watery gaslight world
Where girls have faces white as zinc.

And sometimes thieves go smoothly past,
Or pad by moonlight home again,
For even thieves come home at last,
Even the thieves of Choker's Lane.

And sometimes you can feel the breath
Of beasts decaying in their den —
The soft, unhurrying teeth of Death
With leather jaws come tasting men.

Then sunlight comes, the tradesmen nod,
   The pavement rings with careless feet,
And Choker's Lane — how very odd! —
   Is just an ordinary street.

The Voice on the Wire

If angels could speak on a city exchange,
   Or fairies blow flutes in the battery,
I wouldn't consider your murmur so strange
   Nor choke the receiver with flattery,
But Postmaster-Generals frown at the flute,
   And angels don't argue with Nemesis,
One memo from Kitto makes nightingales mute
   And fairies are warned off the premises.

Oh, Mr Jones, you do say things!
   It's breaking regulations,
And every time your number rings
   You start these conversations,
The monitor gets so enraged,
   It's very aggravating.
What's that? No, madam. Line's engaged.
   Twopence, please. Waiting. Waiting.

I'd pay ninety guineas, not 2d a call,
   If only I had the felicity
To carry you off, with your headphones and all,
   Away from accursed electricity,
To carry you off like a sylph of the air,
   Away on a magic trajectory,
Where bells never ring, and subscribers don't swear,
   And nobody owns a directory.

Oh, Mr Jones, you've got a nerve,
   I've wasted time already.
It's really more than you deserve.
   The idea! Call you Freddy?
You keep your fancies to the 'phone,
   It's years since I've been carried.
I'm 39, eleven stone,
   And, Mr Jones, I'm married.

Kimono Cora

Kimono Cora, she's like an aurora,
   She blazes with bangles of brass,
She wears a pearl necklace, her rubies are reckless
   (You'd never suspect they were glass).
The tramguards look round as she leaps from the ground,
   The taximen yearn as they pass,
The passengers stiffen, so sheer is her chiffon,
   She brandishes such an extent —
All stockings and singlet, two shoes and a ringlet,
   She's covered with satin and scent.

Kimono Cora, Kimono Cora,
   Kimono Cora's in town.
She knows how to speak like a thousand a week,
   But she frequently hasn't a brown.
Well, diamonds can roll in the gutter,
   And lilies can blossom in grime,
But no one supposes that attar of roses
   Can grow out of potage de slime.

Kimono Cora has such a plethora
   Of dashing society friends,

But, gossip or lover, they never discover
  The stairway that Cora ascends.
She waves them goodbye with a spark of the eye,
  Then — suddenly — everything ends.
No longer the flapper, she flings on a wrapper
  Bedraggled with ages of dirt,
Sour perfume still lingers, there's grime on her fingers,
  And grease on the edge of her skirt . . .

Kimono Cora, Kimono Cora,
  Kimono Cora's come back,
To her dirt and her debts and her stale cigarettes,
  And a pile of foul plates in her track.
Well, stars are reflected in quagmires,
  And wines don't depend on the cup,
And Cora emerges in satins and serges
  From mystery — seven floors up!

Carmen of the Chorus

When Carmen capers floating
  So dangerously nice,
The stalls are full of doting,
  The boxes full of Zeiss.
In thistledown defiance
  Her rosy ankles twist —
O, Limbs that baffle science,
  O, Curves that Euclid missed!
Carmen of the Chorus, scandalously simple,
Her brain is partly porous, but she waves a wicked dimple;
She may be rather silly, as chorus-ladies go,

But she dances like a lily
In the Very
Front
Row!

As eight o'clock is jangling,
Her feet in pirouettes
Are punctually dangling
Their golden pantalettes.

The noblest leg in drama
Kicks wisdom to the heights —
O, Princess of Pyjama,
O, Pretty One in Tights!
Let them sneer and snigger and classify geraniums,
YOU possess a Figure, which is more than clever craniums;
Professors are all crazy, as most professors know,
And could THEY dance like a daisy
In the Very
FARTHEST
Row?

The Girl in the Window

The girl in the window
Looks over the square
At a girl in a window
With pearls in her hair,
With diamonds to dangle
And feathers to preen,
A comb and a bangle,
As proud as a queen,

In a flat so becoming,
   So silken and sleek,
With hot and cold plumbing
   (Ten guineas a week),
Where life is no harder
   For paying a price,
With fowls in the larder
   And Heidsieck on ice.
No need to be thrifty
   Or spend and repent,
With 'Papa' aged fifty
   To fix up the rent.

   The girl in the window
      Looks over the square
   And sees, in a mirror,
      Herself standing there!

The girl in the window
   Looks over the square
At a girl in a window
   With eyes of despair,
In a cheap little attic,
   A cheap little dress,
All cotton and Batik
   (Ten shillings or less),
A trunk with no label,
   A ricketty bed,
A broken-down table,
   A banquet of bread,
The wallpaper peeling,
   A crack in the door,
Dirt on the ceiling,

And dust on the floor;
No hope for to-morrow,
The money all spent,
A fortnight of sorrow
Behind in the rent.

The girl in the window
Looks over the square
At a girl in a window —
Herself! — standing there.

It, If and Also!

When skyscrapers burst into lilac,
And Burgundy foams by the tank,
And nightingales carol their joy by the barrel,
Or nest in the Commonwealth Bank;
When constables faint upon duty,
And 'buses collide with a sigh —
By tokens of similar beauty,
You'll know that it's Clara —
Adorable Clara —
The Girl who has IT passing by.

What makes the tram-guard turn his head,
What makes the traffic stall so?
You can follow in a daze to investigate her ways,
She's the Girl who added IF and ALSO!

Like Venus disguised in a jumper,
She brightens the dingiest home,
With charm and chinchilla converting a villa

To Somebody's Palace at Rome.
Her followers never diminish,
Her manners, you've got to admit,
Improve the original Glynnish
By adding Conjunctions —
Important Conjunctions —
By adding Conjunctions to IT.

What wins the simple millionaire?
What makes the peerage fall so?
It's the wisdom and the wit, and the little bit of IT.
And the IF
and the HOW
and the ALSO!

Gardens in the Sky

There's a golden hocus-pocus
Where the buried people eat,
For the air is full of crocus
Blowing down to William Street —
Oh, behold the Roman candles
Of the window-boxes burst,
As the fairies tap their sandals
On the Alps of Darlinghurst!

Everywhere, everywhere, flowers are fleeting in the air,
Lovers greeting, poets meeting, flowers are fleeting everywhere.

Where the stars are lit by Neon,
Where the fried potato fumes,

And the ghost of Mr Villon
    Still inhabits single rooms,
And the girls lean out from heaven
    Over lightwells, thumping mops,
While the gent in 57
    Cooks his pound of mutton chops —

Even there, even there, flowers are floating in the air;
Eyes are gloating, boarders doting, flowers are floating even
    there.

With a teacup full of water
    And a proud possessive eye,
You can see the landlord's daughter
    Damping gardens in the sky;
While her parent, having planted
    Half-a-yard of daffodils
(Is the butter-box enchanted?)
    Mows the lawn on window-sills.

Up the stair, down the stair, flowers are flying everywhere;
Birds are crying, bailiffs sighing, flowers are flying
here
and
there!

Ticket in Tatts!

Ride a Blue Cab to the top of King's Cross,
Don't mind the money, don't think of the loss,
Three cheers for Flemington,
Bah to the Remington,
Farewell to Pitman, good-bye to the boss,
No more dictation and no more comptometers,
Blow up the office and burn the chronometers,
Buy a few diamonds and price a few hats,
Flaunt a few furs and inspect a few flats,
No more economy,
Here's to gastronomy!
Daisy's won — how much?
FIVE
THOUSAND
IN TATTS!

Farewell finances that wrinkle the brow,
Good-bye to trams, we use Cadillacs now,
Hickory, dickory,
Gas-rings and chicory,
Watch us drink nothing but Moët — and how!
Bring out your truffles, we'll dine upon venison,
Smile at Sir Samuel, hobnob with Denison,
Flirt with George Cohen in ten-guinea hats,
Fox-trot with no one who doesn't wear spats —
In a kind of paralysis,
Picturing palaces,
Daisy dreams on,
WITH A
TICKET IN
TATTS!

Good-bye Iceman!

Ladies always standing on the first-floor landing
Ladies in the el-
                    e-
                      vator,
Ladies, looking, looking, while the sausages are cooking,
Looking at the ice in the refrig-
                                         er-
                                            ator —
Once there was an Iceman, full of burning smirks,
Cupid's Casanova from the freezing works;
Now there's only porcelain, cupboards, and duplicity,
Pipes and wheels and switches, and stupid electricity,
And girls grow sick of the cold click, click
Of the
      New
         Re-
            frig-
               er-
                 ator.

And why do you listen, little pink lady,
What are you waiting for there all day?
Oh, a sigh or a sound from a ghost on his round,
And the tramp of a foot far away!

There's the great invention, full of condescension,
Waiting like a deaf dumb-waiter,
But you don't get passion in any sort of fashion
From an up-to-date respectable
Re-
   frig-
      er-
         ator!

Once there was an Iceman, took us all by storm,
His ice was cold, but his heart was warm,
Now there's only clockwork, motors and thermometers,
Whirligigs in cylinders, and gases in gasometers,
And it isn't half as nice, it's a sneaking sort of ice
From the
New
Re-
frig-
er-
ator!

So listen no longer, little pink lady,
No one is tramping to knock at your door.
There's no more romance in the iceman's glance,
And he doesn't come round any more.

Mannequins

Mannequin, mannequin, floating up in taffeta,
Dressing up for palaces, living in a flat —
'Very, very striking! Cut to Madam's liking!'
Says the Ninety Guinea Model in the
BIG BLACK HAT.

Up and down in Lanvin, up and down in Poiret,
Scornful in the elbow, haughty in the eye,
There she goes in bangles, there she goes in spangles.
There she goes in beauty that a cheque can't buy.

Dowagers in diamonds, double chins and lap-dogs,
Full of adiposity, cabbages and cash —
'Madam would be thinner if she went without her dinner,'
Says the Champs Elysees Costume with the
PINK SILK SASH.

Up and down in Redfern, up and down in Paquin,
Curling up her Kissproof, tossing up her head;
Petal of the peerage, sniffing at the steerage,
Adding up expenses — saveloys and bed.

Mannequin, mannequin, going home in jitneys,
Going home in buses to a Crown Street flat.
Poverty and squalor — 'Lend us half-a-dollar!'
Says the Renovated Model in the
FIVE BOB HAT.

Up and down in Remnants, up and down in Greasespots,
Cutting up potatoes on the fourth floor back —
Pie and pickle Clarice, far away from Paris,
Lady Creme de Woolworth's frightened of the Sack!

Caretaker's Daughters

Caretaker's daughters go taking the air
Where only a fairy could follow;
They're easy to tease with a mezzanine stare,
But harder to catch than a swallow.
They'll drop you a kiss from a door in the sky
Or gaze at your waving in wonder —
For caretakers dwell so infernally high,
You're always a floor or two under.

You chase them up ledges and race them up planks,
By parapet-edges and ladders and tanks,
They laugh on the heights, while sore in the hoof
You toil up nine flights to the Girl on the Roof!

Be off with your impudent waving Down There,
Away with your candy and roses!

You're down in the basement, they're up in the air,
    Or scraping the sky with their noses.
No matter what passion your bosom declares,
    With frenzied affection expanding,
You'll wear out your ankles up 99 stairs,
    Or faint with fatigue on the landing.

For caretaker's quarters are up on the roof;
No wonder their daughters are rather aloof —
On footing more firm, and with notions less high
You wave like a worm at a Girl in the Sky!

Eleven O'Clock

Miss What's-Her-Name has vanished like a fairy,
She's left the carbon-copies in a heap,
    There are yards of potted Pitman
    Like mysterious works by Whitman,
And the Underwood is yawning in its sleep.

Poor Miss What's-Her-Name,
    Dear little thing,
Works every morning
    At a big
        gas
            ring.

There's steam round THEM
    Like smoke from a loco —
At eleven a.m.
    She makes
        us
            cocoa!

Miss What's-Her-Name is home again from dancing.
She flops herself exhausted in a chair,
With a few well-chosen phrases
She has kicked her shoes to blazes,
And her mother (fifty-seven) combs her hair.
Poor Miss What's-Her-Name,
Dear little thing,
Works every night
For a rhine-
stone
ring;

And supper? Ahem!
There's a parent in loco.
At eleven p.m.
MA
makes
cocoa!

The Lady in the Lift

Oh, why this constant to-and-fro,
This frequent bustling to the basement
By men, two Saturdays ago
Notorious for self-effacement?
And why does Jackson scowl at Jones,
And Brogan blush at Thompson's notice?
The answer comes in ringing tones —
We've got a Lady in our Otis!
If you're waiting up on Seven, press the button, ring the bell,

She can take you up to Heaven, she can drop you down to Hell;
Let the Second Storey sneer at you for boasting your affection,
She may pause a while and peer at you —
STOPPED
FOR
INSPECTION.

Such quantities of things to shift,
Such passengers in mad collision,
Before she came to drive our lift
Were never seen by human vision.
In vain, to pester her with pearls —
You mustn't only BE, but STAY good —
Such things may do for other girls
Who drive, perhaps, a Standard Waygood.

She will drop you seven storeys, with your stomach in the air,
While you contemplate the glories of her shoulders and her hair;
You can ask her out to sup, but it won't affect her frown —
UP,
UP,
She will run you up, or she'll take you down,
DOWN,
DOWN.

Pay-Day

Away with your bills and your budgets,
   Pooh, pooh, to your paltry accounts!
A fig for tinned salmon, we're dining with Mammon,
   Inflated with mighty amounts.
We're Astors and Fords and Infantas,
   We sniff at the mob in disgust;
We're elegant houris with diamonds for dowries,
   And twenty-five shillings to bust.

   O, honied existence!
      We're bolder than bisons,
   Our banknotes outdistance
      The late Jimmy Tyson's;
   They talk more together
      Than talkies by Warner,
   With dear Mr Heather-
      shaw's name in the corner.

Let's blow all our bullion at Woolworth's,
   Or laze in the lounge like an earl —
Get thoroughly reckless and purchase a necklace
   With pearls that might really be pearl.
We're off in a cab to Romano's
   With rajahs too haughty to speak —
And nobody guesses that Payday Princesses
   Eat kippers the rest of the week.

   Conceal your derision,
      Cashiers in your cages,
   Nor mock at the vision
      When counting our wages.
   It's Heathershaw's heyday,

So fold 'em up tidy —
There's only one payday
And that day is Friday!

Residential

Phyllis from the country
With lips as fresh as berries,
Eyes that stare without a care,
And cheeks like cherries.

Up and down the terrace
Innocently flitting,
Trying scores of funny doors
To find a 'bed and sitting'.

Such a nice old lady
Beckons from the landing —
Rather quaint, and caked with paint,
But full of understanding.

'Down from Molong, sweetheart?'
Her voice is calculating.
'Board and bed, I think you said?
Yes, dear. Do you mind waiting?'

A gilt and pimply mirror
Flaps with a distant glitter.
Somewhere, far off, there sounds a cough,
And somewhere close, a titter.

Cucumber Kitty

When Cucumber Kitty comes mocking the city,
   The boulevards burst into bud,
The dusty old alleys breathe Roger and Gallet's
   And daffodils blaze in the mud.
We dodder and damn on the back of a tram,
   Or burn off the skin from our noses —
But Cucumber Kitty, without any pity,
   Goes flagrantly,
   Vagrantly,
      Floating so fragrantly,
   Cooler than Eskimo roses.

And why does she never get sunstroke
   In such an inadequate hat?
If you beg for advice, she will recommend ice,
   But you know very well it's not THAT!

Oh, pull up the shutters, there's tar in the gutters!
   Oh, turn on the punkahs, and doze;
We're stupid and sticky with heat and gin-rickey,
   But look! I'll be hanged! There she goes!

Let the westerlies roar, they afflict her no more
   Than a bath-heater worries a plumber —
It's Cucumber Kitty, so cool and so pretty,
   So airily,
      Warily,
         Lightly and merrily,
   Snapping her fingers at summer!

Don't bother to ask me the secret,
   The answer is buried in heat —

I'm satisfied now to sit dabbing my brow
While she ices my side of the street!

The Beauty Parlor!

She has Venus in a bottle, and beauty in a jar,
She can turn a little typist to a motion-picture star,
She can dazzle with her science
All varieties of clients
From the semi-Oriental to the elegant bizarre.

Does your boy-friend love to touch you? Let us have a little chat.
Is your chin, alas, too plural? She can give you things for that,
Or a recipe for henna
From a 'countess in Vienna',
Or a course of 15 treatments for the discontented fat.

She can tell you full particulars of Mr Cohen's yacht,
Why he went to Middle Harbor, whom he took with him and what;
All the interesting orgies
Of the Johnnies and the Georgies,
She will hand you with the cold cream in a whisper or a pot.

She's got 'secrets of society' displayed upon the shelf,
All the beautifying balms of Lady Angelina Guelph —
Though she has them by the gallon,
Madame Sophie of 'The Salon'
(You will notice from the picture) doesn't use them on herself.

Underground Roses

You can talk of botanical gardens,
   Where roses are commonly found,
But the kind that I mean are less frequently seen —
   They're the roses that grow underground.
In the caverns of thundering marble,
   They bloom at 8.30 a.m.,
Or they hang by a door to the 5.44
   As a tiger-rose hangs to the stem.

Underground Roses, powdering noses, down where the sirens
   moo,
Cherubs in chokers, clinging to smokers, rushing the Rockdale
   Through;
Giggles and kisses and Black Narcissus, gurgles and gossip and
   glee,
Like buried canaries, the underground fairies go carolling
   home to tea!

'Museum! Museum! Museum!'
   The passionate porter exclaims —
At a smile from a Rose he forgets all he knows,
   And goes mixing it up with St James.
The Queen is aghast on her statue
   At such a delectable view,
But the Saint, with a sigh, turns away from the sky,
   And would like to go underground too!

Who wouldn't suffer a ride on a buffer to talk to an
   Underground Rose?
Clerks without pity embark for the city and trample all over
   her toes;

Underground ladies, like angels in Hades, the Roses that
Never Sit Down,
With pink little faces and vanity cases, go scampering back
into town!

The Gunman's Girl

The gunman's girl wears mother-of-pearl
And a coat of real opossum;
With a face like stone she walks alone
In a land where the Snowdrops blossom.
There's a kiss of a knife on her neck for life,
And a diamond (the latest fashion).
For bruises and bangles are mixed in tangles
When a gunman bends to passion.

And, O, beware when she takes the air,
Take care in the streets at night —
Cross over and hide on the opposite side
To Dangerous Dan's delight —
So give her a cautious peep, my lad,
From the edge of a hang-dog eye
When a Smith & Wesson delicatessen
Gunman's girl goes by!

O, what are they at in the gunman's flat?
My friend you are quite mistaken.
One peep behind, and you'll probably find
She's cooking him eggs and bacon.
Professional hours in bad men's bowers
Are all very well for rookery,
But a gunman's wife in private life
Is more concerned with cookery.

And, O, beware when she takes the air,
   Take care in the streets at night —
She's wheeling a pram with a pound of ham
   For a bad man's appetite
She's carrying butter and eggs, my lad,
   There's bacon at home to fry,
When the Smith & Wesson delicatessen
   Gunman's girl goes by!

The Girl at the Wheel

What petrifies the city,
   What dislocates the view?
It's Park-a-Moment Kitty
   And Back-in-a-Second Sue.
But, oh, what British jury
   Could blight them with its damn?
When traffic foams in fury,
   They're the sugar in the jam!

Behold the dreadful vision
   Of Law Incarnate reel;
He can't escape collision
   With the angel at the wheel.
Though his forehead needs a foment,
What can duty say to this:
'May I park a weeny moment?'
'Why,
Certainly,
Miss!'
Says Constable Alfred Montgomery Pye,
Pride of the Traffic Department's eye.

They laugh at regulations
While bearded chauffeurs blanch
Before the proclamations
Of the King's Own Traffic Branch.
But don't unless you're pretty,
Expect that YOU can do
Like Park-a-Moment Kitty
And Back-in-a-Second Sue.

In vain, to shake a spanner
When cops in anger scream;
You've got to have a manner,
A sort of wireless beam.
When constables are beckoned,
What can duty say to this:
'I'll be back in half a second!'
'Don't you
Worry
Miss!'
Says Constable Alfred Montgomery Pye,
Pride of the Traffic Department's eye.

Going Home

It's nice to know a fellow with a fancy for a Yellow;
It's nice and all, I quite agree,
For them with diamond brooches to ride in Marmon coaches,
But what I says is,
Trams
Do
Me.

It don't take a brush like Orpen's
   To depict the dashing scene
When I pays me frugal fourpence
   On the 5.15,
It don't need a Michael Arlen
   To describe it if he could —
But it's trams, me little darlin',
   Keep a
      GOOD
         girl
            GOOD.

It's easy to disparage the discomfort of the carriage,
   And the fare may be accounted as a loss,
But I'd sooner sit and suffer on a footboard or a buffer
   Than risk it in a taxi
      with
         the
            boss.

There are blondes who pass St Mary's
In a manner that is free,
But I don't believe in fairies,
   And a tram does me;
So I stands and holds me money
   Where I've very often stood,
For it's trams, believe me, honey,
   Keep a
      GOOD
         girl
            GOOD.

Tête-à-Tête

Signora Del Underwood, greeting!
   Behold me, a ninepenny host!
Forget this inferno of eating,
   These gluttons of hot-buttered toast;
They gabble and gobble and garble,
   But we're in a world of our own —
This table, observe, is real marble,
   This chair — pray be seated — a throne.

   Some chicken in curry, Contessa?
   Ho, garçon, là! Hurry! A plate!
   I'm a hell of a sheik, I get £5 a week,
   But who thinks of that, tête-à-tête,
      Tête-à-Tête,
   Side by side, cheek by cheek,
      Tête-à-Tête?

Oh, please don't address me as 'Horace',
   It's something I want to forget —
Imagine you're dining with MAURICE,
   And you (let us say) are JEANNETTE.
And Pitt Street is part of the Lido
   Where princes eat partridge and ham,
And 95 miles on the speedo
   Is better than taking a tram.

   A trifle more truffle, Marchesa?
   The waiters all scuffle to wait;
   They're dukes in disguise, rolling Romanoff eyes,
   But what do we care, tête-à-tête,
      Tête-à-Tête?
   (Cup of tea and two pies,
      Tête-à-Tête.)

Romano himself comes appealing
(Two pies, cup of tea, deener each),
The moon kind of drips through the ceiling,
The waves are like wine on the beach.
Behold my Hispano-Suiza!
Would Madam come out for a dance?
Then pick up your diamonds, Teresa,
And give Mr Menjou a chance!

Some more Maraschino, Princessa?
Allow me! Casinos can wait;
They can charge one and three for a third cup of tea,
But damn the expense, tête-à-tête,
Tête-à-Tête,
(Let's walk to the Quay
Tête-à-Tête)!

Serenade

Oh, virgins in tropical villas,
Come hark to my Spanish guitar;
You ladies with tango mantillas
Who dwell in the flats 'Alcazar',
Those pretty pink sarsaparillary
Concoctions of dreams and distillery
With fountains and fishponds and frillery
And tiles more bizonk than bizarre.

Plink-a-plink, plink-a-plink,
Bits of glass, bits of zinc,
And tiles more bizonk than bizarre.

Though Carmens incessantly vanish,
And damsels with hurricane-hair
Are not necessarily Spanish —
At least, be as daft as you dare.
Fair blossoms who scorn macaroni — oh
Ye that adorn 'San Antonio'
Disguise your connection with Roneo
When taking up residence there.

Plink-a-plank, plink-a-plank,
You may work in a bank,
But please not to mention it there.

Can this be El Duque who proposes?
Imagine it is, if you can —
But you should be firing down roses
Or bashfully biting a fan,
And I should be christened Ignacio
Fernando Come-into-the-Patio
Porfirio Flor del Moustachio
de las Cruzes y Jaime Esteban.

Plink-a-plonk, plink-a-plonk,
This may sound pretty cronk,
But it's better than HECTOR or DAN.

And do you adore 'La Paloma',
Wear roses behind the left ear
Or dote in a species of coma
At solos on bones? No damn fear.
You turn with a sneer to your savoury,
Adjusting your permanent wavery,
And nobody thinks of my bravery
In singing a serenade here.

Plink-a-plunk, plink-a-plunk,
'What a nuisance! He's drunk.
But he will insist on coming round here!'

The Night Express

Out of the night, immense and shrill,
   It comes with cloudy fire
To curse a girl at Bogan's Hill
   With torments of desire.
A string of golden window-lights,
   A rope of flame — they've gone.
Over the windy mountain-heights,
   The night-express flies on.

Drowned in the silent loneliness,
   The lantern's ruby dies.
A girl looks at the night-express
   With bright and wistful eyes.
The night-express, with panther grace,
   On reaching Bogan's Hill,
Shows its opinion of the place
   By going faster still.

O, to be on the night-express
   O, to be there some day,
Miles to go with a port-mant-eau
   And a ticket for far away!

The Pullman cars are full of light,
   And lurching corridors,
And swagmen huddled out of sight,
   And cigarettes and snores,

The atmosphere you find on trains,
  And fat men playing cards,
And tumbling jugs and rattling panes
  And honeymoons and guards.

The engine roars, the whistle cries,
  The echoes follow shrill;
A girl sits on her berth, and sighs,
  And stares at Bogan's Hill.
Pulling the window-blind, she sees
  A moment into space —
A shed, a flash of moonlit trees,
  Some milk tins and a face.

And, O, to be in Bogan's Hill,
  O, to be there some day,
Cows and peace — release, release,
  And the night-express far away!

The Vestibule

In caverns of marble
  With candle and bell,
Its gossip to garble,
  Its tattle to tell,
Its trouble to cheer,
  Its hurry to cool,
The world waits here
  In the Vest-i-bule.

With fortunes and fables
  And pageboys and plots,

And luggage with labels
   From Shepheard's to Scott's,
Adventurer, spy,
   Madonna and fool,
They all pass by
   In the Vest-i-bule.

Fairy princesses
   With cherry pink lips,
And trunks full of dresses
   And hands full of tips,
And angels and thieves,
   And blossoms from school,
Brushing their sleeves
   In the Vest-i-bule.

But someday they'll muffle
   Their laughter and bells,
For Death doesn't shuffle
   His pick of hotels;
The waiters don't know,
   They're dumb as a rule —
BUT WHERE DO WE GO
   FROM THE VEST-I-BULE?

Miss Pillion

When curls were done in a golden bun
   And whiskers grew by the million,
You'd frequently find a girl behind
   On the good old country pillion.
With a blush and a murmur, she'd wriggle up firmer

(Which some thought grounds for divorce),
'There's What's-His-Name! I shall die of shame!'
Said the Girl
On the Back
Of the Horse.

Where Uncle James with his bygone flames
On a bob-tailed nag would canter,
His niece goes out on an Indian Scout
In a lavender tam-o'-shanter.
There's a bang and a scatter and a headlong clatter
And a roar in the middle of the track —
'Oh, scowl if you must, but pardon our dust!'
Says the Girl
On the Bike
At the Back.

Let Pa explode on the Canterbury Road
And Grandpa write to the paper,
She'll sit all day on a B.S.A.
In the usual cloud of vapor.
You can gaze at her giddily from your Armstrong-Siddeley.
You can frown at the hussy if you like.
'Let her out, old fruit! Cheerio, toot-toot!'
Says the Girl
On the Back
Of the Bike.

Snowdrops

The Snowdrop Girl in fields of snowdrops walks,
Whiter than foam, deeper than waters flowing,

Flakes of wild milk gone blowing,
Snowing on cloudy stalks.
The Snowdrop Girl goes picking flowers of snow,
Blossoms of darkness bubbling into dreams,
In a strange country, by the shadowy streams
Where the cruel petals of the Coke-Tree grow.

From the smoke and the fume of a backyard room,
Where poverty sits and gloats,
On runaway feet from a dirty street
To a field of snow she floats;
And tickets to hell have a curious smell
And a dangerous crystal whiff,
Where men hawk Death in a snowdrop's breath
At a couple of shillings a sniff.

The Snowdrop Girl in fields of snowdrops dwells,
Whiter than graveyard stones, whiter than crosses;
Over her sleep there tosses
A wilderness of bells.
Oh, Snowdrop Girl, picking your blossoms here,
The road grows dark and bitter further on
Where other, lonelier Snowdrop Girls have gone,
Lost in the poisoned snows of yesteryear.
Beware, beware, those petals of air —
There's never a flower in slums.
You're caught in a cage on the basic wage,
But wait till the Snowman comes!
Then the arclights blaze as you walk in a daze,
And the hags of the pavement grin,
And Snow, no doubt, may let you out,
But the grave will suck you in!

The Road to Mandolin

Once in the heyday of ringlets,
  Cupid was frequently seen
Trying on calico singlets,
  Out of regard for the Queen.
Lutes were no longer in fashion,
  Kisses were numbered with sins,
Cupid, when bending to passion,
  Always preferred mandolins,
    Plink-a-plink,
  Always preferred mandolins.

Maidens adored mandolins then,
  Teaching their lovers to strum.
But now they demand a saxophone band,
  Five trumpets, a trombone and drum.

Parlors with bursts of Disraeli
  Echoed that wistful refrain,
Notes that the cheap ukulele
  Hopelessly seeks to regain.
Grandpa, most patient of students,
  Sat with his hand on his chin,
Preening his whiskers while Prudence
  Played him the gay mandolin,
    Prink-a-prink,
  Played him the gay mandolin.

But maidens don't strum mandolins now,
  And lovers don't listen in bliss.
All they play, with a laugh, is a tin phonograph,
  And it doesn't take much to play this.

Damsels, to gladden a hero,
   Gorgeous in trousers of plaid,
Played him 'The Gay Bandolero' —
   'Devilish fetching, by gad!' —
But flappers prefer the piano,
   And dancers insist on a din,
And down in the vaults of Romano
   You won't hear the gay mandolin,
      Plink-a-plonk,
   You won't hear the gay mandolin.

No, maidens don't do it like that now,
   The mandolin's fallen asleep.
It's Lot 34 in a furniture store —
   'This Musical Instrument, Cheap.'

In A/C with Ghosts

You can shuffle and scuffle and scold,
   You can rattle the knockers and knobs,
Or batter the doorsteps with buckets of gold
   Till the Deputy-Governor sobs.
You can sneak up a suitable plank
   In a frantic endeavor to see —
But what do they do in the Commonwealth Bank
   When the Big Door bangs at Three?

Listen in the cellars, listen in the vaults,
Can't you hear the tellers turning somersaults?
Can't you hear the spectres of inspectors and directors
Dancing with the phantoms in a Dead Man's Waltz?

Some are ghosts of nabobs, poverty and stray bobs,
Midas and his mistress, Mammon and his wife;
Other ones are sentries, guarding double entries,
Long-forgotten, double-dealing, troubled double-life.
Down among the pass-books, money lent and spent,
Down among the forests of the Four Per Cent.,
Where the ledgers meet and moulder, and the overdrafts grow older,
And the phantoms shrug a shoulder when you ask 'em for the rent.

They are bogies of Grandfather's cheques,
They are spectres of buried accounts,
They are crinoline sweethearts with pearls on their necks,
Demanding enormous amounts.
They are payment for suppers and flowers,
For diamonds to banish a tear,
For sweet, pretty ladies in opulent hours . . .
And tombstones . . . and bailiffs . . . and beer . . .

Down in the bowels of the bank, the ledgers lie rank upon rank,
The debts of the ages come out of their pages,
The bones of old loans creak and clank —
Oh, if you could peep through the door
To-day at a Quarter Past Four,
You'd find all the ghosts at their usual posts,
And you wouldn't sign cheques any more!

Mademoiselle — All of Them

She's blonde and petite, she's dark and discreet,
  She's plump, and uncommonly slender.
Her eyes get you down, they're purple — no, brown.
  Her smile is both mocking and tender.
She's frozen and fair, with buttercup hair;
  She's brown as a berry, and shingled.
I can picture her yet, just a red-haired brunette,
  With a touch of the Orient mingled.

  Mademoiselle from Armentières,
  The Diggers will argue about her for years.
  If you trust them all, and you haven't gone deaf,
  She was kissed by the whole flaming A.I.F.

According to Jim, she's remarkable slim;
  According to Steve she is tubby.
Both Henry and Dick thought she looked rather sick,
  But William describes her as chubby.
She changes her face to accord with each case,
  She matches the fancy of Nigger —
In fact, it would seem, she was only a dream,
  But a dream that was dear to the Digger.

Mademoiselle from Armentières,
Pride of the tanks and the engineers,
  — and the pioneers,
  — and the brigadiers,
  — and the grenadiers,
  — and the fusiliers,
  — and the bombardiers,
  — and the volunteers,
Mademoiselle from Armentières!

Lonely

I'd like to buy some singing-birds,
    And strings of golden jade,
And floppy books with tender words
    In sentimental suede,
I'd like to buy some roller skates,
    I'd like to buy some cartridges,
And piles of willow-pattern plates,
    And half-a-dozen partridges.

I would love to send a guinea to my little sister Winnie,
If I had a little Winnie, BUT I'M LONELY!
And a rustless steel stiletto to my uncle in the Ghetto,
    If I had a sort of uncle, BUT I'M LONELY!
I would give my cousin Gerald a subscription to the 'Herald'
Or a model of a schooner, or a little thing by Gruner
And a step-sister at Pymble an electroplated thimble
And devoted Great-aunt Dinah, doing uplift work in China,
I'd remember with some kisses, and a pot of Black Narcissus,
Or a bangle, or a ribbon, or the works of Edward Gibbon,
            IF I'D ONLY
Got a cousin or a great-aunt, or a pal at Parramatta,
Or a lubra at Maroubra, or a boy in Wangaratta,
But I'm lonely,
                lonely,
                        lonely!

The papers bang their tambourine:
    'Give Him a trouser-press!'
'Give Them a poker-work machine!'
    'Give Her a satin dress!'
I feel I'd like to please the whim,
    And buy a pretty fur,

But, oh, I don't possess a Him,
   I haven't got a Her!

Coty's crystals, water-pistols, mandolins, and mercery,
Something for the motor car and something for the nursery,
Cigarettes and novelettes and phonographs and tricycles,
Yards and yards of Christmas cards with mistletoe and icicles,
All the girls are buying them, and wrapping them, and sending
    them,
Every girl has got her friends, but never thinks of lending
    them,
All the windows shine with things for Other People Only,
All the world is kissing, and I'm lonely,
                                        lonely,
                                              lonely!

Evolution

Oh, barbarous, beautiful girl
   Carousing to 'Little White Lies',
With a wave in each flyaway curl
   And a beckon in both of your eyes,
Do you think you're so frightfully slinky,
   So timed-to-the-tick '31,
Because, little monkey, your furs are so minky,
Your drinks are so pinky, your coupe so dinky,
   And dancing such fun?

The dinosaur's den you forget,
   Romano's gay caverns you crave;
But it isn't so long since we met
   In another description of cave.
Your chin had a chic Talgai angle,

You didn't wear very much less —
It's rather a bungle to put on a bangle,
Two shoes and a spangle, where leaves used to dangle
Instead of a dress.

And years before THAT, we had swung
Through jungles long crumbled to shale,
While you, perhaps, girlishly hung
By the tip of your sweet pretty tail;
And years before THAT, we were fishes
In some sort of primitive bog;
Or, bounding in dishes, I carried choice dishes
To you — a capricious, entirely delicious
Young womanly frog.

Ah, let us not mention it here,
Nor follow the trail any more,
When you were a tadpole, my dear,
And I was a toad on the shore.
Give thanks to the queer bit of jelly
That swam in a far-away sea,
And turned willy-nilly to Nancy and Nelly
And Marie Corelli and Lang and Ned Kelly and YOU,
Yes, and ME!

The Snow Maiden

Down where the ducks wear gaiters,
Down where the icebergs clink,
Colder than Kelvinators,
Bleak as a barmaid's wink,
Iced like an iceman's daughter,
Laughing at five degrees,

Daphne goes down to the water,
   Bidding the sea-gulls freeze.

If you don't believe it, you've only got to wait,
Peep through the window at half-past eight;
The ice goes clink, but she doesn't give a rap,
In her cherry-pink costume with the Little Green Cap.

Far from the surf-club hero
   Hugging his knees in bed,
Down in the depths of Zero,
   Daphne is miles ahead,
Dodging a deep-sea breaker,
   Perched on a frozen shoot,
Cold as an undertaker
   Firing a funeral mute.

If you don't believe it, blow away the dew,
Peer through the window, shudder at the view;
Pull down the bed-clothes, take another nap —
Far away out bobs the little Green Cap.

Show her an ocean chillier,
   Cooled by a Frigidaire,
Stern as the ice of Hillier,
   Daphne would dive in there,
Frisk with a frozen dumper,
   Follow the penguins through —
If only below her jumper
   Her blood were not frozen too!

If you don't believe it, and you won't be told,
Have a conversation. Boy, this girl is cold!
Your heart might break, and she wouldn't care a scrap,
In her cherry-pink costume with the little Green Cap.

The Ballad of the Knee

When Cupid was coy and complacent,
And garters were harder to see,
We guessed you were somewhere adjacent,
But didn't confess it, O Knee!
With many a bombazine button,
With many a taffeta pleat,
In sleeves of historical mutton,
Our mothers were born without feet.

Oh, come back to black satin bustles,
And whiskers where sparrows laid eggs,
When Pa tried to smarten his trousers with tartan,
And ladies walked out without legs!

To-day they possess no objection
To flaunting patellas at men,
And knees are as free for inspection
As antimacassars were then.
But somehow the magic has faded,
The glamour has gone from the air,
And critics are almost persuaded
That knees aren't as good as they were.

Oh, come back to parrots and peignoirs,
And petticoats buried from view,
When men in Dundrearies were tortured with queries
At seeing a little pink shoe.

When fugitive ankles of Phoebes
Were bared in the wicked gavotte,
Our fathers contracted the Jeebies,
And some would go blind on the spot.

But where is that simple emotion,
   And where have the Jeebies gone now,
When knees are like fish in the ocean
   And garters hang wild on the bough?

   Oh, come back to nightcaps and flannel,
      Come back to the flounce and the frill,
   When flappers in satin consumed no Manhattan,
      And knees could still give us a thrill!

The All-Night Taxi Stand

Behold the brave fellow who sits in his Yellow,
   Attending a ball — or a hearse;
At midnight, like thunder, you'll hear him down under,
   Persuading his cab to reverse.
Like a king in a carriage, he'll drive to a marriage,
   Or drop you at Usher's in style.
From here to Glengarriff, it's all the same tariff —
         ONE
         SHILLING
         A MILE.

From midnight to morrow, he sits in dumb sorrow,
   Expecting a constant appeal;
If you peep through your curtain, you'll see him for
    certain,
   Asleep with his head on the wheel.
Mysterious creatures with shadowy features
   Steal past him, and drown in the night —
Black Jacks in a flutter, and flowers of the gutter,
   They slink out of sight.

In friendly adjacence, with similar patience,
Through blizzards and earthquakes and fogs,
Another lone toiler broods over a boiler —
His comrade, the Count of Hot Dogs.
From twelve to four-thirty, on nights dark and dirty,
They wink at each other a while —
One sells his regard at a
SHILLING
A YARD,
The other
ONE
SHILLING
A MILE!

Good-bye — Chorus Lady!

Ankles that answered our clapping,
Limbs that rotated like one,
Where do your slippers go tapping
Now that the chorus is done?
Nobody waits in a Yellow,
Bribing the doorkeeper's growls —
Only the Vitaphones bellow,
Only the Magnavox howls.

Daisy who danced for us, danced for us,
Danced in her cherry-pink tights;
Rosie who sang for us, sang for us,
Sang like a bird from the heights;
And Susie (ah, Susie!) who didn't do nothing
But walk up a staircase on Saturday nights . . .

Never again will the love-stricken super
Gloat from the wings in beatified stupor,
Never again will the pink feet whirl . . .
And you can't make dates with a Paramount girl!

Daisy de Vere (née Maloney),
   Rosie, the poet's delight,
Susie, my pantomime pony —
   Where are you dancing to-night?
Shadows have plundered your flattery,
   Phantoms have stolen your hire —
Legs that come out of a battery,
   Voices that cry through a wire.

Daisy is dancing, is dancing
   Attendance while shop-walkers sign,
A kind of unwilling, thirty-five shilling,
   Corset-department's Columbine;
Rosie is singing, is singing
   Out orders from seven to nine,
Wasting her legs on bacon and eggs,
   And buckets of soup and bottles of wine;
And Susie (ah, Susie!) is acting
   As though she had money to dine,
Feasting on air with water-waved hair
   And nails there is plenty of leisure to shine.

But nobody waits in Chrysanthemum Alley
For the Western Electric corps-de-ballet,
And nobody listens, and nobody knocks,
With a bunch of flowers for a Magnavox!

Up in Mabel's Room

The stairs are dark, the steps are high —
Too dark and high for YOU —
Where Mabel's living in the sky
And feeding on the view;
Five stories down, a fiery hedge,
The lights of Sydney loom,
But the stars burn on the window-ledge
Up in Mabel's room.

A burning sword, a blazing spear,
Go floating down the night,
And flagons of electric beer
And alphabets of light —
The moon and stars of Choker's Lane,
Like planets lost in fume,
They roost upon the window-pane
Up in Mabel's room.

And you with fifty-shilling pride
Might scorn the top-floor back,
But, flaming on the walls outside,
Behold a golden track!
Oh, bed and board you well may hire
To save the weary hoof,
But not the men of dancing fire
Up on Mabel's roof.

There Mr Neon's nebulae
Are constantly on view,
The starlight falls entirely free,
The moon is always blue,

The clouds are full of shining wings,
   The flowers of carbon bloom —
But you — YOU'LL never see these things
   Up in Mabel's room.

The clouds are full of shining wings
The flowers of carbon bloom —
But you — YOU'LL never see these things
Up in Mabel's room.

Backless Betty from Bondi

ed. Julian Croft (1983)

The Man Who Came Back

Smith's *has received a letter from Papakura, Auckland (N.Z.), as follows: 'Circumstances prevented me from getting my* Smith's *since last March. The last one I had, Oigle had grown up. I have now got a job, and am getting* Smith's *again . . . It is difficult to explain how you miss* Smith's . . . *The paper never lost its brightness in our time of trouble . . .'*

'You can wander the streets without weeping,
Do without butter on bread,
Blankets aren't needed for sleeping,
Beer only goes to your head,
Pinching a belt with a buckle
Is only a kind of a knack —
But fighting bare-knuckle with never a chuckle
Is Hell!'
Said the Man Who Came Back.

'When you choke in the bogs of dejection
Up to your sorrowful chin,
Stiff at the end of the section,
That's when you ache for a grin;
That's when you wail at the winter,
Hearing the icicles crack;
But let 'em all splinter — thank God for a printer
And 4d
To bring the sun back!

'All you far-away men in the city
Jesting with Indian ink,
Drawing me jokes out of pity,
Pause for a moment and think —
What do I care about money?
Blankets and butter may lack,

But life is still sunny as long as YOU'RE funny —
KEEP ON!'
Said the Man Who Came Back.

Night of Romance

Let Banks and Bailiffs rule the land —
Oh, what do lovers care?
The tide still floats upon the sand,
The moon still rules the air.

The sky is still with magic blent,
The heart still cries a tune —
Who'll cut the night by Ten Per Cent,
And who can tax the moon?

A tram is cheap, a kiss is free,
Whate'er the bank proposes;
We'll swap your Otto L.S.D.
For Otto made from roses!

Mademoiselle from Everywhere

To the Digger — Memories

The girl that you kissed at Putney,
O, what is she doing to-day?
She's married to Somebody's chutney
And living out Beckenham way.
You called her your daffodil fairy
(She threw you a flower on a punt),

But those were the days, O, the magical days,
When the real Tipperary
Was far from the Front.

And you have gone over the water —
Behold, you've an office and phone! —
And she has a grown-up daughter
Who weighs about seventeen stone.
But sometimes a touch of the liver
In suburbs where aldermen dwell,
Will bring back the days (ah, the far-away days!)
When you kissed on the river
A. W. L.

The girl that you kissed at Calais,
Or pledged at Beersheba with beer,
Or danced with all night at a Palais,
Or lied to all night on a pier,
Is older and staider and fatter,
She's vanished with vanishing cream —
But those were the days, those miraculous days,
And what does it matter,
You've still got your dream!

In a life of brick bungs. and De Sotos
And pansies — if such is your life —
You can turn out your postcards and photos,
Retaining one eye on the wife.
She's gone with her daffodil kisses,
She's floated away into air,
And oh, the old days, the incredible days,
Are what SHE never misses
And YOU never dare!

Nocturne

The Daily Telegraph Pictorial *and the* Sun *have been printing vile slurs on our Australian girlhood — allowing them to be called, without exception, 'clandestine prostitutes'.*

Darkness; a cloud of lace;
  Shines in the quiet air
Barbara's pale and lovely face
  In a rain of yellow hair.
Moonlight smoking below . . .
  Barbara lazily blinks —
Barbara, evening papers know,
  Is a shameless minx.

Smear her! Slime her!
  Cover her with scum!
Shrilly from the toadstools
  the little voices hum.

Night like a golden dust
  Trembles upon the trees;
Caught in a strayed September gust,
  Marjory hugs her knees.
Silence across the bay . . .
  Only the cry of a gull . . .
Marjory, evening papers say,
  Is a brazen trull.

Daub her! Foul her!
  Dirty her with mud!
Shrilly from the quagmire
  the little voices flood.

Under a sleeping tree,
  Water and stars and night,
Dorothy looks at the running sea;
  Eyes that are crystal bright;
Fingers that fairies kiss,
  Powder and puff to dab —
Dorothy, evening papers hiss,
  Is a heartless drab.

Smirch her! Soil her!
  Drag her in the gutter!
Shrilly from the midden
  the little voices mutter.

The Girl at the Gate

Out of the bush behind her,
  You come in your scornful car;
There on the gate you'll find her,
  Looking for Lochinvar.
But sentiment rarely rankles,
  And nobody wishes to wait,
When she dances on little brown ankles
  To open —
          how very obliging! —
To open the Nine Mile Gate.

Open and shut, open and shut —
  Lochinvar scorns to wait.
He's vanished, alas, in a cloud of gas,
  Poor little Girl at the Gate!

Cars that go past in thunder,
   How can they understand?
Open the gate, and wonder —
   Close it, and wave your hand.
Can you pin your heart to a placard,
   Or wish that he struck you dead,
When a Prince in a fairy Packard
   Throws you a coin —
                 how generous! —
Throws you a coin instead?

Open and shut, open and shut,
   Nobody wants to wait,
You're a speck on the track, and they never look back,
   Poor little Girl at the Gate.

Firefly

Dedicated to the usherettes of the picture palaces of Australia and their torchlights.

I've fallen in love with a firefly,
   Two legs and a flambeau complete,
A heavenly smile as she runs down the aisle,
   And a laugh as she bangs down the seat.

Don't tell me she lives at Clovelly,
   Don't say that she catches a tram,
Or dotes on 'Vendetta' by Marie Corelli,
   And loves to eat pickles and ham.
She comes as a comet to Halley,
   Assisting a duke to his place —
A cloud of gold fire, like a star in the valley,

Two legs and a dim, little face.
I don't adore Mae or Dolores,
Or give Greta Garbo my heart,
Nor yet the particular glories
American pictures impart.
The statues can rust in a thicket,
The Wurlitzer gives me a pain;
If it wasn't a firefly who gazed on my ticket,
I wouldn't have come here again.

And I know when I go to St Peter,
He'll call out his staff with a grin —
A Devil, no doubt, to show the Way Out,
But a firefly to light the Way In!

As We Pine in a Line

Half-an-inch, half-an-inch, lumbering near,
Over the landscape and down to the punt,
Austins are squealing with rage in the rear,
Packards are roaring in front;
Buicks are braying, Hupmobiles neighing,
Sirens are playing, toot, toot;
Horace and Doris, asleep in their Morris —
Frankly they don't give a hoot,
WHILE,
With many a grumble and grunt,
We slumber and shuffle and shunt,
We rattle and curse like a slow-motion hearse,
As we pine
in
a

line
for
the
PUNT.

Oh, well for the rollicking medico's boy,
   Dashing so carelessly down to the front.
Well for the bicyclist, beaming with joy,
   Bouncing his bike on the punt;
The doctor's pal cadges his B.M.A. badges
For Maudies and Madges en route,
And girls riding pillion whizz past by the million,
In clouds of face powder, toot, toot!
                                        But,
One-eighth of an inch to the front,
We grumble and rumble and shunt,
We brood in a trance, or destroy the white ants,
As we pine
   in
   a
   line
   for
   the
   PUNT.

Come Aboard

When Someone in Yellow
   Comes over the side,
The officers bellow,
   The bo'suns collide,
The boilers can blister,
   The stokers don't care,

If Somebody's Sister
    Comes visiting there.

She's full of inquiries,
    Instruction she begs:
Do captains write diaries?
    And what are sea-legs?
And who is Blue Peter?
    And how many tons?
And isn't it neater
    To Duco the guns?

But nobody's able
    To fidget or frown,
With 'Really, Miss Mabel?'
    And 'Won't you sit down?'
And everyone's 'Mr',
    I'm glad to confide,
When Somebody's Sister
    Comes over the side.

The Admiral pauses,
    The sailors all sigh,
She probably causes
    The compass to lie —
And O, what a glister
    Of manners there'd be
If Somebody's Sister
    Were always at sea!

Butterflies

If anyone's looking for Mary,
   She's fallen in love with a star —
You'll have to employ a canary
   To go so impossibly far.
In vain do the cabarets thunder,
   In vain does the Burgundy froth,
She'll never be happy Down Under —
   A Butterfly up in a Moth.

The engine's too loud for entreaty,
   Your signals excite her disdain,
You'll have to produce a Wapiti,
   Or shout from a neighbouring 'plane.
She sneers at the heartbroken caller
   Who comes in a Marmon or Hup,
And Packards look very much smaller
   From Five Thousand Feet Farther Up!

No doubt she resembles a fairy —
   I always knew fairies could fly —
But I didn't expect to find Mary
   So very disturbingly high!

Permit me to borrow a Widgeon,
   Or climb up and wave from a bough,
Or bribe a compassionate pigeon —
   She's got her certificate now!

Underwood Ann

To a Secretary

Her fingers to sell,
Her patience to loan,
A slave of the bell,
She kneels by the throne;
You people who wait
May pester and plan,
Your ultimate Fate
Is Underwood Ann.

Underwood Ann, Underwood Ann,
She talks like a fairy and acts like a man;
The voice that arranges and chooses and changes,
It isn't the boss, but it's Underwood Ann.

You wait on the mat,
She taps on her keys —
Don't frown about that,
Sit down, if you please —
The will that you cross,
The face that you scan,
It isn't the boss,
It's Underwood Ann.

Underwood Ann, Underwood Ann,
You'd like to get past her, but nobody can;
It's easy to hector a common director,
But what about hectoring Underwood Ann?

One blink of her eye,
The boss mutters 'No';

He utters a sigh,
  She runs the whole show.
The smile that rewards,
  That blesses or bans,
It isn't the Board's
  It's Underwood Ann's.

Underwood Ann, Underwood Ann;
Underwood, underworld, underclothes Ann,
Grimness and graces, Napoleon in laces,
General Manager Underwood Ann!

Skis and Shes

I sing about Women and Winter,
  The rapture of 30 degrees,
The damsel who waits with a bundle of skates
  And the girl who goes riding on skis;
And, oh for the flight of an eagle
  To see where she happens to go —
But waving a wing is a difficult thing
  When you lie with your face in the snow.

Poo-pooh to your ice, Kosciusko,
  A fig for your cucumber air,
Your peaks, I'm informed, are sufficiently warmed
  By the presence of Annabel there;
But this I'm unable to warrant,
  The fact is, I really don't know —
Wherever I climb I spend most of my time
  With my face in a puddle of snow.

I know she has wings on her ankles,
   I know she can leap like a trout,
The hoi-polloï thrill when she whistles downhill
   And the guides find their eyes popping out;
For this I'll accept without question
   The word of the Tourist Bureau —
My personal view is a trifle askew
   Due to banging my face in the snow.

If only my skis wouldn't wobble,
   If only my feet would go straight,
I'd chase her with hope down a nursery slope
   And leave introductions to Fate;
But something has doomed me to grovel,
   I crawl on all fours down below,
She catapults by like a bird in the sky,
   And I lie with my face in the snow.

She Keeps on Walking

When Helen goes hiking
You'll have to provide
The heels of a Viking
To walk at her side;
At such a fierce canter
She chooses to tread,
Her blue tam-o'-shanter
Is always ahead.

You mumble and grumble,
She burns up the dust,
Her feet never stumble,
Her boots never bust;

With cramp in each muscle,
By moonlight you'll find,
In spite of all bustle,
You're mountains behind.

In haunts far and hilly
Where centipedes play,
She brings out a billy
To round off the day;
Disdainfully humming,
She waits for a man,
But nobody's coming,
For nobody can.

The knights of the dryad,
So deep their despair,
With harsh jeremiad
Embitter the air,
With groans beyond measure
They fall by the track —
SHE lolls at her leisure,
Her suitors walk back!

She Shoots to Conquer

When Kitty 'shoots' to conquer,
Like wings her ankles beat,
A golden whirl engulfs the girl
And bubbles drown her feet.
A thousand waves attend her,
With foam and passion quaking,
And the gulls ride on the warm tide
Like a white flower breaking.

To brave the deepest breaker
Or don the belt for Beauty,
The beach-patrols would sell their souls,
As is, indeed, their duty.
But, mocked by hopeless fancy,
They pine ashore, disputing;
And the sun burns and the tide turns
And she keeps on shooting!

Nightingale — 1930

The music that warmed Asia Minor
When nightingale perched on the bough
Was certainly never diviner
Than nightingales give to us now.
In corridors dismal and dirty,
A Lady went forth with a Lamp —
To-day, Nineteen Hundred and Thirty,
It's Jones —
Little Jones —
Florence Nightingale Jones —
With Röntgen and radium, wireless and phones,
Who walks in the ward, 1930,
As Nightingale walked in the camp.

Her name is most probably Mary,
Though Sisters address her as 'Jones' —
A kind of iodoform fairy,
The Board in its majesty owns.
She sets all the Fahrenheit foaming —
Behold our thermometer-charts —
And pulses go faster than Gloaming

When Jones —
   Mary Jones —
   The girl they call 'Jones' —
With murder for microbes and magic for moans,
Down rows of white pillows goes roaming,
Severely affecting our hearts.

Oh, bring out your wogs in a wagon,
Wherever bacteria stir,
St George and his twopenny dragon
Had nothing whatever on her.
She doesn't do much, but it's plenty;
She doesn't say much, but it sings —
And, Oh! the effect on Ward Twenty
When Jones —
   You know Jones —
   Probationer Jones —
A smile on her face and an ache in her bones,
Comes floating along to Ward Twenty,
This Nightingale minus the wings!

The Girl on the Corner

Oh, what does she wait for,
   The girl over there,
And who could be late for
   A creature so fair?
Forlorn and forlorner,
   One eye on the clock,
She stands on a corner,
   Bewitching the block.

Who made the appointment,
And what does he mean,
This fly in the ointment
So late on the scene?
Displaying his label,
She waits on the spot —
It must be CLARK GABLE
Or someone like SCOTT!

She stands there, half-smiling,
Half-biting her nails,
Completely beguiling
An army of males;
Though someone forgot her
For several hours,
The moment THEY spot her,
They rush to buy flowers.

They plunder the florist's
They ogle and surge,
While scampering forests
Of roses converge,
But deaf to each greeting
And blind to each beam,
The girl No One's meeting
Waits on in a dream.

Well, have a good snigger,
Then ponder on this —
A little old figure
Limps up with a kiss;
A smile and a chiding,
A tram for the Quay —
Away they go riding
To grandmother's tea!

Little Theatre Girl

Oh, magic patch of Culture
   Where foreheads mount so high
They rise above the vulture
   And bid the skylark fly,
Your brows are not so dizzy
   But SHE can make them whirl —
That pretty little busy little
   Little Theatre Girl!

Not hers the sordid scramble
   Of dancing for a wage —
Like Mrs Patrick Campbell
   She stalks another stage,
Where men of perfect breeding
   Do all the Walking On,
And all the parts are 'leading',
   And all the cares have gone.

On plays by Pirandello
   She sprinkles sex-appeal,
And titbits from *Othello*
   And trifles by O'Neill.

The works of D. H. Lawrence
   She talks about all night —
In private with abhorrence,
   In public with delight.

What if she thinks that Strindberg
   Is just a kind of cheese,
Or mixes him with Lindbergh —
   Who cares for things like these?
We love her willy-nilly,

We listen in a whirl —
That silly little frilly little
Little
Theatre
Girl!

Streamer's End

Roses all over the steamer,
Paper all over the sky,
And You at the end of a streamer
Smiling goodbye, goodbye.
It isn't to me you dangle,
It isn't to me you smile,
But out of the rainbow tangle
Our lines have crossed for a while.

Somebody's benediction
Pitches a streamer — whizz! —
Under the firm conviction
You're on the end of his.
Others may claim attention,
Rolling away to sea,
But nobody's there to mention
The cove at this end is ME!

Don't you consider the danger
Of setting a heart on fire
By tossing a perfect stranger
Your 10,000 volt live-wire?
I'm only a face on the skyline,
Something the wharf obscures —

But you're on the end of my line,
   And I'm on the end of yours!

Off in the vast *Orsova*,
   Soon you will wave in vain;
I could be Casanova,
   You could be Queen of Spain —
I must go back to the city,
   You must go back to the King.
Blow me a kiss for pity,
   Girl at the end of the string!

Spring

Treetops crying, pipits in the creek,
Flowers go flying in a blackbird's beak,
Peach-boughs whirl, hens count eggs,
And a girl comes running like a flower on legs.

There she walks, where the cherry-boughs blow,
Lighting up their stalks with a sweet pink snow,
Strawberries to toss, lavender to fling,
This blue-eyed blossom by the name of Spring!

Spring with her fiddles and her fair, blue skies —
Ask no riddles and she'll tell no lies;
Take her at her word, kiss her when she comes,
Act like a bird and pick up crumbs!

Joy goes jigging — hey, for the guitar! —
Don't go digging underneath too far;
Down below the sunlight, playing hide-and-seek;
Misery and hunger, wait another week!

Great-grandmother Speaks

Pause, child, and stare me in the face
  Before you dare to pass —
Forget the falling shoulder-lace,
  And hear me in the glass!
My pretty mouth you surely know;
  It shouldn't cause dismay —
I am Yourself two lives ago,
  Ten thousand miles away.

My petticoats were just as few,
  My lips were just as red,
I came as lightly home as you,
  And just as late to bed,
All pink above and silk below,
  As bad, as mad, as gay —
But that was ninety years ago,
  Ten thousand miles away.

We didn't sing what RUDY sings
  Nor Mr CRUMMIT croons,
But simple songs of downright things
  With honest, dancing tunes;
We sang 'The Gals of Buffalo',
  'The Thorn' and 'Duncan Gray'
But that was ninety years ago,
  Ten thousand miles away.

The polka came, the polka went,
  And who can dance it still,
Or that divine accomplishment,
  The Ginger Blue quadrille?
With portly men on courtly toe

We ran to meet the day —
But that was ninety years ago,
Ten thousand miles away.

We'd see the lights of morning break
And candles burn the wick,
While still a fist was left awake
To shake a fiddlestick;
And, oh, the fiddle and the bow,
They didn't beg for pay —
But that was ninety years ago,
Ten thousand miles away.

And is your heart as light, as light
As mine was happy then,
Before the gossips learned to write
With such a spiteful pen,
Before the bitters learned to flow,
The saxophone to play —
As mine was ninety years ago,
Ten thousand miles away?

And do you feel the joys we felt
When Captains held our waist?
I fear those faery pleasures melt
Before the fox trot's haste;
A rumba on the radio
Is all you hear today —
And THAT was half-an-hour ago,
And half-a-mile away!

'THE GIRL' REPLIES:

Great-grandmother, there's no defence

For half the things I do,
But (pardon the impertinence)
You weren't so dusty, too;
It's just as well for all, you know,
The papers never say
What happened ninety years ago,
Ten thousand miles away!

Moving Day

When it's Moving Day at midnight,
And the boarders bolt their doors,
When the watchmen blink and the gunmen wink,
And the furious landlord snores,
Oh, it's then that we climb from windows
To take the moon for a ride,
Or fumble and drag at a Gladstone bag
With a couple of shirts inside.

There's a rope from the second storey,
There's a phantom hand below,
But little of ghosts who slide down posts
Does the soul of a landlord know;
Oh, little he thinks of moonlight,
And little he recks of rent,
But he mutters and moans as he dreams of loans
At a hundred and five per cent.

All the mugs and jugs go walking,
All the fruits of bygone debt
We can manage to jam in a broken-down pram
With a second-hand radio set.

Then hey for the moonlight alleys,
Yo-ho for the Bourke Street Main!
When janitors yawn in the fogs of dawn,
They'll bang at our doors in vain.

They'll bang at our doors like thunder
Ere they woefully find us gone,
And we have no need for a prancing steed
Or a big pan-
tech-
ni-
con,
But we go like the ancient Arabs
Whenever the mood invites;
We haven't a tent, but we don't pay rent —
Hooray for Arabian Nights!

The Girl in the Gods

All the din of Donizetti,
All the singers, high and low,
They are merely there for Betty,
Upper Circle, second row;
They are merely there to thunder
(Even Mr ROSSI nods)
For a girl with eyes of wonder
In the twilight of the gods.

Like the damsel of Rossetti,
She is leaning from the sky,
And her name it may be Betty,
But there's Carmen in her eye.

Boom your mellowest, APOLLO,
  Till the prima donna purrs —
She may grab the flowers that follow,
  But the magic isn't hers.

All the dainty allegrettos,
  Airs that ripple, notes that foam,
Full of passion and stilettos,
  Turning Roseville into Rome,
All the altos and contraltos,
  All the beauty and the pain,
Leave her dreaming in Rialtos
  When she's really in the train.

Then the night is full of daggers
  And a thousand torches glow,
And the Prince of Parma swaggers
  Down the path to 'Mon Repos' —
Oh, it's hard to face Artarmon,
  Bricks and mortar, tiles and stones,
When a girl who should be Carmen
  Has to act like Betty Jones!

My Lady's Maid

The girl who stands
  Behind a chair
With prinking hands
  To comb your hair —
Can Age efface
  Without a qualm
So fair a grace
  As this, Madame?

The curls one craves
  Reflected here
(More lasting waves
  Than yours, my dear)
They get no aid,
  They want no skill —
My Lady's Maid
  Adorns them still.

The golden glass
  Floats bright with curls,
Her fingers pass
  Like dancing girls
With crystal dews
  And magic balm,
Not hers to use,
  But YOURS, Madame!

Your flowers and flasks,
  — A.M., P.M.
Her beauty asks
  No help from them.
A Midas paid
  Your modiste's bill?
My Lady's Maid
  Is richer still.

'So slow to-night!
  Not ready yet!'
With icy spite
  You rage and fret;
You fret and rage —
  She keeps her calm.

The pangs of age
Are yours, Madame!

A fruitless plaint,
The mirror mocks —
Put back your paint
And close the box;
Your lips must fade,
Your flesh grow chill —
My Lady's Maid
Is younger still!

Passers-By

Dedicated to the girl in the Centre of Australia.

What do you see from the window?
Torrents of runaway feet,
Ribbons and laces, a whirlpool of faces,
And eyes floating past in the street;
Derricks and dogmen and cranes,
Traffic that darkens the sky,
Daphne and Doris in somebody's Morris,
And tramcars and trains
Passing by.

What do you see from the window?
Furies of blistering sand;
Endless and level, the plains of the devil
Where only the camels dare stand.
No one to hear or to speak,
Telegraph-poles in the sky,

Packhorse and boulders, a skyline that smoulders,
   And teams once a week
      Passing by.

And when I look out of the window,
   Granite and brick fade unseen —
Everything changes to thundering ranges,
   Camels and sand — and Doreen.
Bravely they ride down the years,
   Greeting their God with a cry —
Battered and bleeding, unconquered, unheeding,
   The old pioneers
      Passing by.

Wild Grapes

The old orchard, full of smoking air,
Full of sour marsh and broken boughs, is there,
But kept no more by vanished Mulligans,
Or Hartigans long drowned in earth themselves,
Who gave this bitter fruit their care.

Here's where the cherries grew that birds forgot,
And apples bright as dogstars; now there is not
An apple or a cherry; only grapes,
But wild ones, Isabella grapes they're called,
Small, pointed, black, like boughs of musket-shot.

Eating their flesh, half-savage with black fur,
Acid and gipsy-sweet, I thought of her,
Isabella, the dead girl, who has lingered on
Mutinously when all have gone away,
In an old orchard where swallows never stir.

Isabella grapes, outlaws of a strange bough,
That in their harsh sweetness remind me somehow
Of dark hair swinging and silver ear-rings,
A girl half-fierce, half-melting, as these grapes,
Kissed here and killed here — but who remembers now?

Silence

There aren't any banjos here,
There aren't any ocarinas,
There's no riff-raff with a phonograph
Performing on concertinas;
There's only a million gum-trees
And nothing much else to mention,
And trees don't speak more than once a week
And nobody pays attention.

Only the bush by night
With Jupiter shining clear;
You can listen with all your might,
This is all you'll hear —
Silence.

There aren't any mandolins,
You'll never detect harmoniums,
Nor parties in cars, nor steel guitars,
And certainly not euphoniums;
There's only the cold Antarctic,
Penguins and desolation;
The residents muse in their little igloos,
But they don't make conversation.

Only a polar bear,
Only the icebergs round,
Listen as hard as you care,
This is the only sound —
Silence.

There aren't any women here,
They never take tea at eleven,
There's nobody there in the empty chair,
There's nobody humming 'Blue Heaven',
There's nobody frying potatoes,
There's nobody making toast,
The laughter's all gone, and the lights aren't on,
And you're standing alone with a ghost.

Only a scent is there still,
Only a note on the wall,
'Forgive me. I've gone with Bill.'
What's that in the hall?
Silence.

The Girl in the Window

It's harder than it seems, my dear
   To catch the smiles you drop;
I've stood here dreaming dreams for hours,
   For hours without a stop.
Your fragrance flutters by,
   A flower in every whiff —
But all you deign to signify
   Is: HIM? Pooh! Sniff!

You could stun me with a wink, you could blind me with a
    blink,
You could blow my heart to heaven like a bird,
You could blast me with a 'Bah!' in your Mousseline-de-soir —
But what do you say? Not a word.

Oh, every time I pass, my dear,
    I lose a night's repose.
I rub against the glass my coarse,
    My coarse, adoring nose.
You turn your pretty face,
    You toss your golden head —
You wouldn't care in any case
    If I dropped dead.

You could look at me and sneer, you could kill me with a jeer,
You could drag me round Australia on a string,
You could knock a fellow flat in your saucy little hat —
But what do you do? Not a thing.

Such frenzy, I confide, my dear,
    With hopeless passion cursed —
You're colder in your pride than snow,
    Than snow in Darlinghurst.
You're prouder than a queen,
    Your silence I adore,
But, oh, your price is plainly seen:
    It's Nine Pounds Four!

Though you pout at me and mock, I could buy your silly frock,
I could grab you by the ankles and elope;
I could purchase with a cheque all the sawdust in your neck —
Could I buy you back to life? Not a hope.

Eve — of Ottawa

A NEW DREAM OF FAIR WOMEN

'Eve of Ottawa — Empire Delegates Gather.'
— *Sydney Morning Herald* headline

1

I dream of torches that have flickered out,
Of eyes that men have worshipped for a while,
Of lips that toppled kingdoms with a pout,
And built them with a smile.

2

A girl there was whose face was like a flame,
Her mouth a flower, her voice a chime of joy;
'Men saw me, loved, and died. This is my name —
HELEN. I come from Troy.'

3

And one there was who told of broken years,
Of guns and moonlight, kisses long betrayed,
Some half-remembered girl from Armentières,
Clasping another Maid,

4

That other Mam'selle from an older war,
Girt with a broadsword, blazing in the dark,
Who marched with men five hundred years before,
Immortal JOAN of Arc.

5

And one there was who whispered with a pang:
'I am that phantom of a minstrel-show,
That LILY of Laguna, whom you sang
And dreamt of long ago.'

6

And other ghosts, whose merest dancing smile
Had made a million hearts beat pit-a-pat —
The MAID of Athens, MARY of Argyle,
ELAINE of Astolat,

7

ROSE of Tralee, and ROSE of No Man's Land,
TILLY of Bloomsbury, old Drury's NELL,
And SALLY of Our Alley — hand in hand
They passed. Farewell, farewell!

8

And then you came, mysterious, last of all,
Named EVE of Ottawa, a fountain-pen
Perched on one ear, an Empire in your thrall
And fifty million men —

9

And then YOU came, with Hansards in your lap
And tariffs like tiaras in your hair,
Bidding us read the news, consult the map
And banish our despair.

10

Who are you, Eve? What apples do you bring?
What happiness, what sorrow? Who can say?
Bound to a new divinity, we sing,
Adams to Eve — ten thousand miles away!

Eating by Yourself

Let aristocratic heroes
Boast the platters of the Guelph,
You can dream of Trocaderos
When you're dining by yourself;
You can hover like a glutton,
You can order what you choose,
Try the fricassee of mutton,
Toy with terrapin ragouts,
All the claret of Lugano,
All the fairy teas-and-toasts,
Brought by Ferdinand Romano
And a staff of lovely ghosts.

First the oysters, round and juicy,
Served by some delightful girl —
Call her Nancy, call her Lucy,
She may fetch perhaps a pearl;
Next the soup of tender turtle
From a nymph with yellow hair —
Call her Mabel, call her Myrtle,
She can spice it with a stare;
Then the fowl on gleaming china
That a pretty creature brings —
Call her Dulcie, call her Dinah,
You may find a pair of wings.

For a moment they will glimmer,
For a twinkle they will gleam —
Then the kettle starts to simmer
And they vanish like a dream;
You can whistle for them vainly,
You may call in tender tones,

But the soup is printed plainly
With the name of Foggitt, Jones;
Then you suddenly awaken —
There's a sausage on the shelf,
And the bacon looks like bacon,
And you're eating by yourself!

The Moth and the Candle

O, dear little girl in the Gypsy,
So very disturbingly high,
No doubt you consider them tipsy,
The people you see from the sky.
You frown at the words of a Vandal,
You laugh your contempt of a Goth —
But please to beware of the candle,
O, dear little girl in the Moth,
Little Girl in the Moth!

You float like a runaway fairy
Where only a fairy could swoop;
It's all so delightfully airy,
A sideslip, a dive, and a loop.
Let Mercury lend you a sandal,
Or Pegasus give you a flight,
But don't go too close to the candle
Like Moths that get burnt in the night,
Little Girl in the Moth.
We're down in our boots on the level,
You're up in the sky like a speck —
But aeroplanes burn like the devil,
No matter how dainty the wreck.
For danger has torches to dandle

And Moths are too fond of the flame,
And frequently bother a candle
By burning their wings in the same,
  Little Girl in the Moth.

Leave Waghorn the glories of Schneider,
And Hinkler the frenzied Hooray —
A coroner's verdict and rider
Are very dull reading to-day.
The wine that the Jaguars handle
Has funerals under the froth —
So please to take care of the candle,
O, dear little girl in the Moth,
  Little Girl in the Moth!

Lucky Dogs

Where pink-and-crystal windows burst
  With bottled things to eat,
The lucky dogs of Darlinghurst
  Go dancing down the street;
Each dainty neck involves a string,
  Each string includes a girl —
Two hundred tails in rapture swing,
  Two hundred noses curl.

From shop to shop with Marianne,
  From side to side they tug,
A Sealyham, a black-and-tan,
  A poodle and a pug;
And some are lacquered tooth-and-nail,
  And some have scarlet coats,

Whilst like a flail the splendid tail
Of Cochin China floats.

And is it merely puppy-love
That moves us in despair
To bend from balconies above
So bitterly to stare?
Alas, our blighted bosoms burst —
Where WE beseech in vain,
The lucky dogs of Darlinghurst
Drag Beauty by a chain!

Pantette

Pantette, with her little pink trousers
A sort of silk silhouette,
So Garbo-and-gartery, fire in the artery,
Stopped-for-inspection Pantette —

Pantette has no place in the annals
That echo the deeds of the race,
But who prefers turkey-red flannels
To fringes of unabashed lace?
The kilt still adorns Caledonia,
Pyjamas excite no regret,
And no one considers pneumonia
The logical end of Pantette.

Pantette, so entirely transparent,
A riot of rose and rosette —
Oh, fairy geography, shadow-photography,
Magical-lantern Pantette!

And have we so lightly forgotten
Those garments our grandparents had —
Unthinkable inches of cotton,
Unspeakable objects of plaid?
No longer such heirlooms astonish,
We shudder or smile, and forget,
And nobody tries to admonish
The impudent frills of Pantette.

Pantette, with her pert little ruffles,
Her flutters of cherry georgette,
All pink electricity, pants-and-publicity,
Pooh-to-your-peeping Pantette.

Where ladies in lavender bloomers
Were sold to the devil on bikes,
Pantette is impartial to rumours
And wears what she jolly well likes;
But let her go round as she chooses,
The fact is, we really don't mind,
And nobody's jugular fuses
And no one goes suddenly blind.

Pantette likes the sunlight behind her,
But nobody's died of it yet —
A fig for propriety, into society,
X-ray and all, goes Pantette.

Backless Betty from Bondi

The beach is not entirely free,
The sands are far from trackless,
When Betty dances to the sea,
So rapturously backless;
By this, we don't impute a lack
In one whose back is peerless —

FOR WHO,
POSSESSING SUCH A BACK,
COULD BE DESCRIBED
AS REARLESS?

And, oh, the Euclid of her spine,
The trills, divine and deathless,
That ripple down a magic line
And leave the watcher breathless!
A thousand feet her feet pursue,
With hopeless tread and tireless —

HER BACK IS FULL
OF POOH-FOR-YOU,
HER EYES ARE FULL
OF WIRELESS.

You aldermen who thunder out
Damnation for the Backless,
Your waists, no doubt, are rather stout,
Which makes you somewhat tactless;
And you, arch-bulldogs of the sand,
So big and brown and artless,

WHO PUT THE BELLOW
IN THE BANNED —
INSPECTORS,
DON'T BE HEARTLESS!

Oh, make the great Pacific dry,
And drive the council speechless,
Remove the breakers from Bondi —
The beach, and leave us beachless,
The fair, the bare, the naked-backed,
The beer, the pier, the jetty —

TAKE ANYTHING AT ALL,
IN FACT,
BUT LEAVE,
OH LEAVE US BETTY!

Extra Hand

'To cope with the rush of Christmas business, most of the big city emporiums have put on extra hands . . .'

In the halls of the Ninepenny Bargain,
    In the caves of the great god Cash,
Where the jungle is filled with jargon,
    And the counters are filled with trash,
Where the arc-lights flare and flicker,
    In a storm of string you stand,
With a permanent stack of things to pack,
    An aching wrist and a breaking back,
Little Extra Hand.

In the vaults of the Fourpenny Docket,
    In the teeth of a raving mob,
Where the change comes out of a rocket
    With a hoarse, pneumatic sob,
Like a kind of a kidnapped fairy
    In a strange and sunless land,
You struggle and strap and wrestle and wrap,
    Paper to fold and string to snap,
Little Extra Hand.

Do you hark to the merry gabble
    Or dance to the far-off sound
Of a Christmas that doesn't mean babble
    In a dungeon underground?
But that is a dream of sunshine
    It's harder to understand
When you're doomed to stop in a roaring shop,
    With a pain beneath and an ache on top,
As a little Extra Hand!

Poor Little Rich Girl

Your table is dainty with damask,
You dine upon delicate fare,
And four gold tapers with frosty vapors
Flash in the Dresden ware;

But why do you sit so silent,
And why do you turn so pale,
And why does the ghost of cocoa-and-toast
Trouble your cakes-and-ale?

Your gown is the glory of Lanvin,
Your pearls are a pleasure to see,
Your wine-glass glitters with sherry-and-bitters
Or Pommery '23;

But why do you think of onions,
And why do you sigh for stew
On a plate with a crack in a third-floor-back
Somewhere in Woolloomooloo?

Your fingers are hard with diamonds,
They gleam on a crystal cup;
Their wealth you'd scatter to stand and chatter
Back there — washing up;

But the man who stood at the gas-ring
Belongs to a buried life
And there you are with your caviare,
Poor little rich man's wife!

Uncollected Poems

Jerusalem Set Free

I — The Crusaders Retreating

A.D. 1192

The Crusaders rode home from the siege on the horse-beaten track
Where the Lion-Heart led them to glory, and now led them back.
Then they paused in retreat on the hills, where below the long line
Lay Jerusalem, noiseless, and white as their half-forgot snow;
Where a bell sounded distant and shrill from a Saracen shrine —
Such a bell as they heard with light hearts, when they struck the first blow,
There they prayed for a final and splendid Crusade yet to be,
Which would come there with pomp, and with triumph would set the land free.

II — The Crusaders Advancing

A.D. 1917

Not with echoing outburst of cannon and splendid array,
Not with solemn procession and pomp did the conquerors come;
For they flourished no banners, and stepped without martial display,
And their trumpeters sounded no fanfare, nor loud was their drum —
But they straggled the streets, and they spoke in a casual drawl,
With no prayer, but a jest, on their lips as they surged through the Wall.

Yet, if Spirit, and Manhood, and Deeds be the actual test,
Who shall say that this last and most splendid Crusade was not best?

Goin'

Ain't I got no hope, Nurse? Garn, tell a feller straight!
I'd jest as soon be goin' now I 'aven't got me mate.
The doctor bloke, I bet he knows
'Nd if 'e says I goes, I goes . . .
The others went at Anzac, 'nd I kinder guess I'm late.

But tell us 'onest, Miss, ain't y'never some time been
'Round Sydney, down Australia way — what! ain't y'never seen
The buildings, harbor, steamers, all
The places where the ferries call —
Manly! Mosman! Middle 'Arbor! Them's the ones I mean.

Manly! Gawd, it fairly makes me funny in the throat —
The kiddies! 'Nd bananas! 'Nd the music on the boat!
The ferries flitting all about —
They cock-a-doodle-dooed us out . . .
Fort Denison! It seemed to *smile* the day we went about.

Old Sydney never was as good as on that sunny day —
Aw . . . I'm gettin' sentimental . . . an' the light is goin' grey . . .
That's the surf at Manly drummin' . . .
Hold on, cobber, I am comin' . . .
Well . . . so long, nurse . . . I must be a-gettin' . . . on . . . my way.

Southern Song

My minstrels sing ballads of daring deeds,
  Of armoured knights and their curvetting steeds,
They sing me of Lovers the whole day long,
  When I'd sell my soul for one Southern Song.

Oh, play me the beat of a brumbie's heels,
  On the sun-baked grassless ground;
The thud of his heels like a drum tattoo,
And the ring of the steel in your own mount's shoe,
  As you beat the stragglers round.

Nay, sing not, O Minstrels, of maiden's gage,
  Of jousting monarch or amorous page;
Strike not thy harps to a chivalrous tune,
  But sing me the surf on a low sand dune.

The boom of the surf on Australian shores,
  Its wash over green capped rocks,
The Pacific kissed surge on a windless day,
Its swirl over sand on its rippling way,
  Like the rustle of silken frocks.

Thy Knights and thy Ladies, Good Minstrel, are dead;
  They lived but in Song, and the years have fled,
But the rustle of leaves on a restless gum,
  Will stir and will thrill our descendants to come.

France — 1918

The tangled smoke-wreaths grovel on the plain;
They weave fantastic patterns in the rain,
And ever seem to hurry in their train

Faint echoes of a distant convent bell,
Where some old priest, made bolder with the night,
Crawls slowly from his devastated cell,
   And keeps an only half-remembered rite,
With eye cocked wary for an errant shell,
   And cassock girded for an instant flight.

The bell tolls slowly, in a sober vein,
And yet it rings a message through the rain
Which half blots out grey Death upon the plain.

Some say it rings the end of Wrong and Sin,
Some say it is the Herald of God's War;
To me it sends no thoughts but those of kin . . .
   A station on the Darling, through the door
The mellow beat of horse-bells drifting in,
   Which, hearing once, I did not think of more.

The convent bells have ceased their solemn strain;
The priest has scuttled to his lair again . . .
But still the horse-bells murmur in the rain.

Ophelia

So still she floats, so still and clear,
The river-lilies straggle near,
   And tangle with her tresses;
Their wary cups, their waxen green,
Enclasp her, and she slides between,
   White in the water-cresses.

So will she drift upon her way,
Beneath the leaf-strained sun by day,

The far, cold stars at even;
And mourn her not, nor call her dead,
For even ere her soul hath sped,
She is herself in Heaven.

Untitled

Have you ever noticed the pediment of the Emden gun in Hyde Park? If so you will doubtless have perceived the entire front of the obelisk is dedicated to the glory of Mr Richard Denis Meagher, and such officials as the Town Clerk, the Deputy Town Clerk, and the Architect and City Building Surveyor! A list of the killed etc., of the mere nobodies who took the gun is reserved (as a happy afterthought) for the extreme back of the monument, where only one passer-by in five thinks of looking.

I sing the Epic of those valiant souls
Whose dignities we honour, and whose name
Is writ (in six-inch gilt) upon the scrolls
Of Harbour City fame.

Above the plinth they run in chiselled rows,
About the base the gilt reflections fleet,
Below, the Gun, that tips a pretty nose
South-east to Oxford-street.

And these are they who fought the glorious fight,
Who ran the rakish Emden to the reef —
These warriors, whose titles stun the sight,
In blatant bas-relief.

Whose carven names scream fiercely to the eye,
Whose dignities assault the atmosphere —
Hats off, and read them, you who hurry by,

And pause to cheer!
(Space here for a little silent applause.)

So these are they who died for you and me,
Fallen, alas! in all their pristine pride —
Cut short — (but wait a moment, let me see —
I don't think any died:

However, it was glorious, all the same)
And now they gleam emblazoned on the Gun —
Hats off, once more to each immortal name,
And mark them, one by one:

First, MICHAEL MEAGHER (THE RIGHT HON. M.L.C.);
Next, MR LAYTON (DEPUTY TOWN CLERK),
And R. H. BRODRICK (LAND SURVEYOR, he)
These names illume Hyde Park.

The deeds of THOMAS NESBITT, too shall ring
Illustrious with reverent renown,
And skeely singers, yet unborn, shall sing
The CLERK of Sydney Town.

And down in Song and Story they shall go —
They'll shine in legend to our grandson's son —
(Though nobody who reads them then shall know
Just how the thing was done!)

To a Forgotten Portrait

Wind in the corridor, wailing in sniffle and eddy and gust,
Whose is this face that looms pale through the skin of a
century's dust?

Admiral, general, murderer, merchant or duke — who can say?
Crony of Georgie the Third, or a tourist to Botany Bay?

Prelate or dandy or rogue? And the narrow or primrosy path?
Droning sad sermons or ogling the belles in the Pump Room at Bath?

Tremulous high lights, that shake on the damp of his lip, seem to swell;
Surely he breathes, is awake, and can see, and can hear, and can tell

All that he knows (and so wise is he now with his bundle of years,
Watching the world with those eyes, and hearing it spin with those ears)!

Speak to me, Painted One! . . . What is it stirs on his lips? Is it dust?
But what shall become of you, knotted old face, when the picture-cords rust?

The Uncharted

'Full many a flower is born to blush unseen
And waste its sweetness on the desert air.'

All emerald writhes the uncharted Pacific, where, under the moon,
Beachward it beats to the furze on the dune,
Bursting to foam-crust and breaking in spindrift rain
That chequers the sea-paths mosaic, green cobble and ivory vein.

Unkempt is the couche on the dunes, and the white of the sand is untrod.
So was it ever since Nature began.
So may it be even *after* the Kingdom of Man!
Can nought possess Beauty unless *he* be present to patronise God?

There's never an island uncharted, whose loveliness mariners seek,
But the seagull can reach in a week;
For Nature built shrines ere she fashioned your jellyfish sire,
And always the sun shall rise splendidly over *your* funeral pyre!

The Buccaneers

When Doris and I, and Peggy and Sim,
Went by water to Watson's Bay,
The night shone blue on the harbor-rim,
And the hills ran gold, with liquid day;
For this was the hour of interlude,
When the sunlight thins, and the shadows brood,
And the sea-mist smokes away.

'We'll steer by the stars,' I cried, for the stars
Beat milkily over the yacht,
And the moon lay netted among the spars
Like the slice of an apricot;
'We'll steer by the Cross to Caribbee,
One thousand leagues from Circular Quay,
And east-nor'-south, I wot!'

Doris danced round, and she made a mouth,
And she wrinkled her nose in scorn:

'O silly, to talk of your east-nor'-south!
  And is Caribbee near Cremorne?'
'Cremorne, do you say? Indeed, and indeed.
I'll swear that this yacht is a dolphin steed
  In a faëry land forlorn!'

The sun swam down, and the darkness fell,
  All olive it dripped in the skies;
And the ferry-light fires in the glinting swell
  Were like deep-sea fishes' eyes.
But Sim cried: 'Ho, for the Spanish Main!
I smell red gold on galleons twain —
  Ho, ho for the pirates' prize!'

O you who gape from the ferry-decks
  At the lunatic yacht below,
Do you ken, as you sluggishly loll your necks,
  You were slaughtered an age ago?
Plundered and put to the plank and the sharks,
You factory-hands and insurance-clerks,
  In a stolidly staring row?

Poetic Licence

WHEREAS apprenticeship to Verse
  Is at its best a ticklish venture,
I'll take a tolerant Muse to nurse,
  As herein witness the *Indenture*:-

INDENTURE

I, KENNETH SLESSOR, of uncertain mind,
  And hereinafter named as the CONTRACTOR,

Having this moment duly sealed and signed
   High bond with my Parnassian benefactor,

Do vow to keep (for some convenient time)
   All Items of the MUSE'S stipulation,
PROVIDED ALWAYS that to wrench a rhyme
   I may employ my own interpretation.

The MUSE in turn (as will by this transpire)
   Doth vow by all the Gods and Little Fishes
To help the said CONTRACTOR twang the Lyre,
   PROVIDED he respects her stated wishes.

IN PROOF WHEREOF these presents do appear,
   (Signed) KENNETH SLESSOR and (by proxy) THALIA,
This 1st of April, goodness knows the year,
   At Kirribilli, New South Wales, Australia.

. . . .

ITEM. —
The said CONTRACTOR shall, on no excuse,
Write *anything* without he introduce
Upon a most precarious verbal stilt
The world 'Lilt'.
As, for example, the following sample:

   'The loving *lilt* of laughing life
      And the laughing *lilt* of living love,
   All with alliteration rife,
      I could permute as the above,
   And lilt them round about again,
   To the lilting last of factorial *n*.'

ITEM. —
The said CONTRACTOR shall at every chance
Delight in such Poetic Elegance,
Such Nice embodiment of the Genteel,
And such *reel*
Extravaganza, as in the stanza:

'Oh, the balmy wet dewdrops bespangled the sward,
And an odorous zephyr breathed over the dale,
And the reeds of the meads danced about in the ford,
To the prance of the prawns (circumstantially stale)
And the smells of bluebells in the sweet balmy dells
Were wafted like onions and tripe in the gale.
(Though exactly *what* 'dales', 'meads', and so on may be
I have no more idea than a petrified flea.)'

ITEM. —
The said CONTRACTOR shall in every case
Pen bilious lyrics to the Populace,
And preach the (Copyright) Doctrine of the Smile
On each dial,
As you may see in the following paean:

'Keep a smiling face, lad, whatever be the sky,
Sme-ile about the place, lad, and never murmur Die,
Whatever be the weather, let us all, sme-ile together,
Let us all sme-ile together, with a (Copyright) Smile.
In the callow, hollow, Ella Wheeler Wilcox style.'

Civilisation

From the Chinese of Yuan Chieh — 8th Century A.D.

South-east a thousand leagues and more,
Where the Yuan and Hsiang roar
　To seethe in a giant lake as one,
Sheer passes twist above the shore,
　Where only the wild men run;

Wild men of very simple mind,
　Who bask on tree-tops in the sun,
And prehistoric pleasures find
Where the silent mountain-valleys wind;

Restrained by neither law nor man,
Content with the primeval plan.

Preening upon our cultured age,
The Nine Lands sneer and scoff —
And yet (for all this talk of saint and sage)
Are we much better off?

Songs from the Chinese

From poets who died before the Danes took England.

I　The Scarlet Cockatoo

Out of Annam came
　The scarlet cockatoo;
All peach-blossom and flame
　He seemed in hue;
And the ways of woman, and the speech of man,
　He knew.

And they did what they always do
To the poet and the sage —
For they all admired the cockatoo,
And shut him in a cage.

II The Birth of His Son

Because I knew too much,
And shattered my career,
I wish the boy no wit —

But hope to see him such
A beetle-headed cit
That he will batten here
With snug and corpulent cheer
Upon plump revenues,
In a Cabinet Minister's shoes.

III Cockcrow Song

Now that it's morning the stars flicker pale in the east,
The cock of the dawning at Ju-nan has crowed and awoke,
The clocks have run dry, and the singers have sung at the feast,
Till the moon blurs the sky, and the stars gutter dim, and the morning has broke.

They are turning a thousand fish-shaped keys, and a thousand hinges are crying,
And round by the Palace, and up through the trees of the Castle, the magpies are flying.

IV In Protest

O you who made your battlefields upon
The pleasant country of the lowland plains —
How shall the peasant that you trampled on
Keep the thin blood a-circle in his veins?

Let me not hear you mouth your soapy jests:
  Prate not of booty, ranks, and spoil again —
The reputation of a Marshal rests
  Upon the corpses of a million men!

Youth

From the Chinese

The careless gallants of Ooling
Ride forth caparisoned at Spring
  With silver saddles, horses white,
And dainty garments fluttering.

Soon in the golden market places,
They crush the flowers with heedless paces,
  And pledge in ardent wine the eyes
Of Tartar girls with merry faces.

The Drunken Poet

Because he lurched down Castlereagh-Street, thrilled
  By potent wines of witchery, they laughed
  In sleek battalions, leering as he quaffed
Strange amber brews, or vintages distilled
From old Thessalian grapes. (*They* said he swilled
  Stale dregs of beer. How might they know that draught
  Of heather-ale, which turns the drinker daft,
All thinking on high visions unfulfilled?)

O blind! The little people snigger by,
More sunk in daily dirt than he in drink,
Some to sell boots, and some to traffic butter,
And all of them to moulder till they die
Respectably; and better it is, I think,
To see the poet belching in the gutter!

In an Old Book Shop

Here are the clocks all conjur'd lunatic:
Here do their cogs dawdle, and their pinions rust;
Here dozes Father Time, his hour-glass thick
With fallen dust.

Here is no dial to mark the minutes' flight —
Save that the motey sun-shaft further falls,
In one great gilt diagonal of light,
Across the walls.

Here are old ivory chessmen, beaten brass,
Great platters from Japan, bespotted shells,
Cups cleft from onyx, bowls of frosted glass,
And temple bells.

Breastplates and rapiers of Damascene,
Boule cabinets, and copper-panelled chairs,
Buddhas in jade, old bronzes tawny-green,
And Dresden wares.

Here, too, are stowed in shambling stack and tier
The myriad million thoughts of buried men,
Whose bodies rot; but they are risen here,
And speak again.

Their voices whisper querulous along
  The sombre aisles; they mumble in the gloom
From shelf to shelf; those muffled voices throng
  The darkling room.

Broadsheets there are, of horrid hangman's tales;
  Yellow-stained maps from some forgotten book;
Journals of convict years in New South Wales,
  And Captain Cook.

Mottled monastic tomes of Cicero;
  Ballads of murder, testaments of thieves;
Shakespeares in brindled duodecimo,
  With rusty leaves.

Long forgot, relics of a dead decade:
  All that is old, and nothing that is new —
Here, in the shadows, half an earth has made
  Last rendezvous.

A Chaplet

I treasure the faery phrases that unchain
  The ivory-fretted doors of fantasy —
Words to be strung upon a silver skein,
  As carven beads upon a rosary;
And there, as beads upon the silk are told,
With sound-approving relish to be rolled
  In sonorous refrain.

And mostly I adventure on the sea
  That sings about a Caribbean bay;
For 'Caribbean' is the Devil's key

To Treasure Island, and the roaring way
Down pirate paths; and many a pig-tailed horde,
Most swart disciples of the bloody sword,
I hear in 'Caribbee'.

'Haroun Alraschid' — words of potent thrall:
Singing of Eastern moonshine, and the spark
Of rosy lanterns on the Sultan's wall,
Where looms the purple palace, shadowed stark
Against the spinning stars and silver-grey
Of lustrous minarets, where moon-fires play
About each tapered ball.

And 'Pompadour' is lit with memories —
Blue evenings at Versailles; the olive box;
Green-bronze of Tritons, through the cone-cut trees,
And slender swords a-tilt to scented frocks;
The stone canal, with sleepy carp a-swim,
And patch and powder by the fountain rim —
Forgotten ghosts of these.

The ghostly gallants of the 'Forty-four
That linger in the sound of 'Holyrood';
And 'Araby' and 'Bath', and many more,
Brave cobwebs of a wistful minor mood —
Oh, these are Devil's cabala to me,
And every letter is a magic key,
And every word a door.

Magnanimous Manly

'The Mayor of Manly said that certainly he would invite the Prince of Wales to come to Manly on the occasion of his visit to Australia.'
— Sydney Pickles

Cover the Corso with confetti, sweep the beaches, paint the jetty,
Decorate with flags prolific half a mile of the Pacific,
Whilst above the festal main Sydney Pickles' aeroplane,
Strung with bunting, madly stunting, loops wild loops across the Steyne.

Let the Surf Club, bare of torso, prance in posses down the Corso,
Or, arrayed as gladiators, quell innocuous spectators!
Let the sirens of the board dance in frolicsome accord
With the Pierrots and surf-heroes of a masquerading horde!

Let the Doges of the city meet in dignified committee,
And adjourn, upon a motion, to a banquet by the Ocean,
Where the Mayor, by lure of wine and mock-turtle by the brine,
May inveigle a Vice-Regal representative to dine!

Then, by municipal bounty, unsurpassed within the county,
Let the meeting, in addition, post a ticket of admission
To the Prince (complete with Crown) in the solitude of town,
Or the gloom of his room on the H.M.S. Renown.

Wayside Pipers

'The charm of open-air dancing has not been fully recognised here, though in America it is greatly in vogue. Some exponents are allowed to exercise their grace and agility in Central Park, New York, but here the officials . . . do not let their imaginations soar any higher than grass-plots . . . and band-stands.' The *Sun*, in an account of a dancing performance called 'The Wayside Piper', Ascham Girls' School.

Oh, you sordid city-planners, with your narrow-minded manners,
Whose confined imagination knows no further inspiration
Than another railway station for a paralytic train,
Mark the high aesthetic way of the cultured U.S.A.,
And be influenced, I pray, to remodel the Domain!

Then no more shall Sunday quiet be disturbed by rant and riot,
By the Bolshevik and traitor, by the long-haired agitator,
By the loud-mouthed legislator, by the prophets and the quacks,
By esoteric Hindus, or by Ryan or by Hughes,
Or the Rabelaisian views of the mystic maniacs.

But instead the town shall rally in a Brobdingnagian ballet,
When, on lively legs and nimble, to the blare of brass and cymbal,
It shall whirl the girls from Pymble and from Ascham to and fro;
While each typiste, navvy, clerk, shall assemble in Hyde Park,
And proceed from dawn to dark on the light fantastic toe.

The patricians of the peerage, and the Pommies from the steerage,

They shall foot it willy-nilly, from the Rocks to Kirribilli,
Nor carouse one half so shrilly as the city oligarchs,
Who, from office-boy to mayor, gambol gaily, pair and pair,
In the classic open air of the Great Australian Parks.

Stanzas Written by a Bard who is Morbidly Anxious to Know Exactly What *Professor Einstein Discovered about Newton*

Pray tell me, ye professors of the higher mathematics,
Ye 'Varsity disciples at the feet of Mr Wellisch,
Who ogle the parabola, philander with quadratics,
And dissect the harmless cycloid with a scientific relish.
Pray tell me, all ye pundits of collegiate renown,
Did what went Up come Down?

Surely somebody was chosen in that 'Varsity election
Who can put the matter clearly to his fellows on the Senate;
What the Hades is the good of all this stuff about 'deflection'
And its horrible effect upon the great Newtonian tenet?
What *I* should like to know at once, and know for once and all,
Is *do* or *don't* things fall?

Don't leave me in this flutter of suspense and agitation,
But tell me, tell me quickly, *what the devil is the matter?*
Forget the fevered formula, relinquish the equation,
And (for the sake of Michael) cut the scientific patter;
Is Newtown squashed? *Has* Cambridge come an academic flop?
And *did* (ah, DID) the Apple drop?

Blind

It's all smoke in the town,
    All smoke round Cockatoo,
And over Balmain the star-showered night sifts down,
    Smoking with powdered-blue.

Clean yellow lights
    That wink to the men-of-war,
Strung in the velvet of the Greenwich heights
    Like golden louis d'or.

Smeared in the haze,
    A barge with steam-white hair,
Towing to Pyrmont and the darker ways
    Its blood-lit Temeraire.

The peacock-green
    Of night on the moonstone hills —
The painter wipes his twilight canvas clean,
    But half his palette spills.

Beyond the flood,
    That wine-red ship, the sun,
Careened in molten lakes of dragon's-blood,
    Whose rims have overrun.

All these, all these,
    Can shout their organ-sound,
But those who wait in blindness on the quays
    Blink agate eyes around.

He dreams aside,
    And, burning through his mind,
Go giant sunsets in a scarlet tide
    Of light. Men call him blind.

Ave!

Our sun-fermented seas run sweet as wine
   To welcome thee, O Viscount of the Pen,
Who swung for us those gateways that confine
   Romance and magic from the world of men.
Here, in an older land than mortals know,
Australians greet thee, poet of the Hoe;
   Whilst men in London talk of 'colonies' —
Ten thousand miles away from us Below!

Not in this island of unconjur'd stars
   And mountain-peaks contemptuous of man
May custom web our springtime calendars
   With old traditions or a mouldered plan —
Here are no fumbling barons of decay
To croak philosophies of Yesterday,
   Here are no ghosts of feudal centuries
For you and your sons of ink to blast away!

And yet, because your eyes outfly the sun,
   You'll pass beyond these towers and smoky domes,
And crowded men, to bush where brumbies run
   And only unknown wild things make their homes —
Ah, then in lands that modern folk ignore
You'll see futurity as once before
   It lit you, when our guns were one to nine,
And every town in Belgium spouted war!

The Ego of Aaron

To those who hold decomposed souls in abhorrence,
This wink should be almost as good as a nod —
Look out for the frightfully deep Mr Lawrence,
And likewise avoid *Aaron's Rod*.
No babble of flappers in moonlight assuages
This great psychological porridge of brains —
Its author dissects them in three hundred pages
And burrows with gusto amongst the remains.

Our hero is prompted by various 'urges'
To 'cast off the chains' of his daughters and wife,
Turns flautist in London, talks art, and emerges
With dogmas on love and a grudge against life;
And ev'ryone gabbles and jabbers and chatters
Of 'will-power' and 'egg-cells' and topics like those —
But what is its meaning, and whether it matters,
The present reviewer is darned if he knows!

Henley on Crayfish Swamp

Oh you that float in cushioned ease,
With parasols and pedigrees,
And footmen punting at the rear —
Oh mariners of Yarra banks,
Don't think because of empty tanks
We can't have Henley here!

Our punts, except at picnic races,
Consist of old piano-cases,
And all our poles are tad.
But what about those cauliflowers?

And have you whiskers quite like ours?
And don't you wish you had?

Bogged animals emerge with pomp
When Henley comes to Crayfish Swamp —
The landscape oozes cows.
The concertina's honeyed squeal
Resounds like mad from eel to eel,
And lizards bend the boughs.

Would WE touch champagne cup? No fear.
We sink our teeth in honest beer,
Watching goannas romp.
Is there a Thames? We scratch our head.
Dunno. But we've got this instead —
'Henley — on Crayfish Swamp'.

Passenger by Greycliffe

Who sits beside you in the empty seat,
Staring, most strange of passengers?
Who reads your paper, moves his bony feet?
Who bends across your shoulder! Who is there?
Who stirs?

Sometimes he lights a lantern far below;
The cloudy waters melt, the shadows pass,
Foam turns to crystal; down a tunnel of glass,
We gaze at things forgotten long ago.

The Harbour opens like a sepulchre
Its golden trap-door, air and birds one side,

And on the other, sea-flowers in the tide,
And white, dead bodies; and the Passenger.

Who is it rides beside you in still air?
Who sits between your fellow-travellers?
Who blows his frozen breath? Who's there?
Who's there?
Who stirs?

The Office Lunch

I met a little maiden like a melody from Haydn,
With her arms completely laden, she was dancing down the street;
She had parcels tied together, and a suitcase on a tether,
Made of imitation leather, getting tangled in her feet.
With her pretty elbows swaying, I distinctly heard her saying:
'Pork and pickles,
Beef for Betty,
Sardine Sandwiches,
Spaghetti,
Pies and rissoles,
Apple custard,
Ham — and don't forget the
MUSTARD.'

'Have you robbed,' I asked, 'a draper?' as I sidestepped to escape her,
'Why this quantity of paper, why these bundles in a bunch?'
But she murmured in a flurry, 'Please, I'm in an awful hurry,
All the office, they will worry, they are waiting for their lunch.'
'Saveloys and peanut butter,' I distinctly heard her mutter,

'Tongue and salad,
Tea for Tony,
German sausage,
Macaroni,
Two of biscuits,
Cakes and custard,
And I MUST remember
MUSTARD!'

Hinkler Picks the Lorry

'The Mayor of Bundaberg phoned Hinkler asking him if he would prefer a limousine or a lorry to bring him home in triumph. Hinkler picked the lorry.' — News Item

No, I don't want a chariot to greet the proletariat,
  I don't want a Cadillac with silver on the door,
You can keep your cabs and carriages for funerals and
    marriages,
  I don't wish to see them any more —
But give me a lorry and I won't be sorry,
  An ordinary lorry that they use for carting beer,
A simple motor lorry from the brickyard or the quarry,
  An ordinary lorry, and
                they'll
                    know
                        Bert's
                            here!

Where my caravan reposes I don't bother about roses,
  You can take away your Hudson and your big Rolls-Royce,
Keep your Packards for an actor, all I ask for is a tractor,
  Or a wagon with a butter-box for choice.

But give me a lorry, a downright lorry,
A busted, rusted lorry on the old home-track,
A truck, by gorry, or a one-ton lorry,
A Bundaberg lorry, and
they'll
know
Bert's
back!

With Regrets

If waiters were stricken with blindness,
And taxis were cheaper than trams,
If Joan wanted nothing but kindness,
And all Mary wanted was lambs,
If florists would listen to reason,
And prices of suppers came down,
And theatres were free for the season,
I'd probably still be in town.

But Moët costs too much a bottle,
And chickens cost too much a bite,
And orchids are dearer than wattle,
And diamonds are Dulcie's delight,
And Fifi is mad about pheasant,
And Lulu is keen on champagne,
Which explains where you find me at present —
I'm back on the land once again.

from *Heine*

Well, the bottles are finished, the meal's a delight,
The damsels are gay as the deuce —
They have drunk just a drop more Chablis than is right,
And their camisoles hang rather loose.

That their shoulders and breasts are both rosy and white
I observe, with a desperate eye,
As they curl themselves up on the couch out of sight,
And the counterpane shakes where they lie.

They have drawn the curtain — what happens beyond
Is a secret concealed from my view;
For I stand like an idiot, foolish and fond,
And I'm damned if I know what I do!

The Vanishing Army

'Every year about 2000 members of the A.I.F. go to join their cobbers who were killed in the war. The A.I.F. is a vanishing army.' — Captain C. Is. A. Abbott, M.H.R., Minister for Home Affairs

The army marches, marches on,
  To strange campaigns and starrier wars,
Climbing across the sky, they've gone,
  The old familiar column of fours.

The sergeants bawl, the drums begin,
  The bayonets toss, the bugles blast;
The pale centurions fall in,
  The army marches, marches past.

They go, the careless brotherhood,
  Sailing again for darker shores,
We stand and watch, as others stood
  And watched, in other, dirtier wars.

And soldiers who have waited long
  Will greet their brothers in mid-air,
Almost as if, ten thousand strong,
  They kept an old appointment there.

Economics

'Unemployment?' The professor cocked one ear,
  Plunged into rich, good-humoured explanation.
'Undoubtedly exceptional . . . this time of year . . .
  Local depression . . . foreign importation . . .
Prohibitive tariff urged . . . competition severe . . .'
Really, he solved it all so splendidly, made it all so clear,
  Brought it all down to the simplest calculation.

Out in the night, men stumbled on burnt feet,
The river to drink, stars to eat.

No doubt, x and y feel the same in an equation.

Sally in Our Alley

Words by 'Mo'
Music by 'Whatsisname'
Sung with very little success by 'Cressy' O'Reilly

With nasal organ accompaniment
Latest song hit. On sale at all undertakers.

PASSED BY MR CRESSWELL O'REILLY

Songs in Neck-to-Knee Costumes

MAY BE SUNG WITHOUT FEE OR LICENCE
IN ANY SOUNDPROOF CELLAR

In the exercise of his functions as Commonwealth Film Censor, Mr Cresswell O'Reilly 'cut' the song 'I Wonder What Is Really On His Mind' from the talkie Paris. *To give producers of future talkies a line on what's wanted,* Smith's *submits herewith certain song-classics, in their original naked and unashamed state, and as likely to be passed by Mr O'Reilly. The cotton stockings, Jemima boots, red Turkey twill, flannelette, hair nets, and other vegetarian effects are by that well-known clothier poet, Mr Kenneth Slessor.*

'Take a Pair of Sparkling Eyes'

Take a pair of sparkling eyes
Hidden ever and anon
In a merciful eclipse;
Do not heed their mild surprise,
Having passed the Rubicon;
Take a pair of ruby lips,
Take a figure neatly planned
Such as admiration whets,
Be particular in this.

Take a pretty little cot
Quite a miniature affair,
Hung around with trellised vine.

Take all these, you lucky man,
Take and keep them if you can,
Happy man, happy man,
Take and keep them if you can,
Happy man, happy man.

Take a pair of horn-rimmed specs,
Hidden ever and anon
By a high and bulging brow;
Make a mystery of sex,
Having passed no picture on
That contains a naked cow.
Take a pair of paintless lips,
Take a chaste, hygienic kiss —
Be particular in this.
Don't permit an infant's cot
To be photographed, far less
An immodest double-bed.
Take all three, O saintly man,
They'll receive no censor's ban;
Saintly man, saintly man.
Sit them out then, if you can,
Righteous man, righteous man.

'Hallelujah, I'm a Bum'

Hallelujah, I'm a bum,
Hallelujah, bum again,
Hallelujah, give us a hand-out
To revive us again.

Hallelujah, I'm a Christian young man,
Hallelujah, I'm still a Christian young man,

Hallelujah, if you can't be as virtuous as me,
For goodness' sake, be as virtuous as you can.

'At Seventeen'

At seventeen, he falls in love quite madly
With eyes of tender blue;
At twenty-five he gets it rather badly
With eyes of a different hue;
At thirty-five, you'll find him flirting madly
With two or three or more —
And when he thinks he's past love, it is then he meets his last love,
And he loves her as he never loved before.

At seventeen he goes to night-school dully,
And studies ancient Greek;
At twenty-one, he spurns the ukulele
For a business-college twice a week;
At forty-five, he takes to bowls quite gaily,
As a Man of Forty-five Should Know;
When he has no other pastime, there is ludo for the last time,
And he plays it till they plank him down below.

'Come Into the Garden, Maud'

Come into the garden, Maud,
For the black bat, night, has flown.
Come into the garden, Maud,
I am here at the gate alone . . .
There has fallen a splendid tear
From the passion-flower at the gate . . .
The red rose cries 'She is near! She is near!'
And the white rose weeps 'She is late'.

Come into the vicarage, Sephonisba,
For the chiropterous mammal, night, has flown.
Come into the vicarage, Sephonisba,
I am here with a chaperone.
There has fallen a splendid tear
From the pumpkin-vine at the gate:
The cauliflowers cry 'She is here! She is here!'
And the cabbages weep 'She is late'.

'Gin a Body Meet a Body'

Gin a body meet a body
Comin' through the rye,
Gin a body kiss a body,
Need a body cry?
Ilka lassie has her laddie,
Nane, they say, have I;
But all the lads, they look at me
Comin' through the rye.

Gyx a physical organism meet a physical organism
Comin' through the O.T.,
Spa a physical etc. shake hands with a physical etc.,
Need a physical etc. flee?
Ilka (a) young gentleman has a young lady,
In buttermilk they toast 'em —
But all the young gentlemen raise their hats,
Comin' through the Postum.

Footnote (a): Change here for Ilka, Bilka, Milparinka, and Onkaparinga.

'Drink to Me Only'

Drink to me only with thine eyes
And I will pledge with mine;
Or leave a kiss but in the cup
And I'll not look for wine.
The thirst that from the soul does rise
Doth ask a drink divine;
But might I of Jove's nectar sup,
I would not change for thine.

Drink (gg) to me only with thine eyes,
I'll sign the pledge instanter —
Or leave some Flytox in the cup
And poison my decanter.
The thirst that from the soul doth rise
Demands a drink of Kola,
But might I of Schweppe's Sarte sup,
I'd still eat Gorgonzola.

Footnote (gg): Stops only to set down.

'I Wonder Who's Kissing Her Now'

I wonder who's kissing her now,
I wonder who's teaching her how,
I wonder who's gazing into her eyes,
Breathing sighs, telling lies.
I wonder who's buying the wine
For the lips that I used to call mine,
I wonder if ever she tells him of me,
I wonder who's kissing her now!

I wonder who's her Sunday-school superintendent now,
I'll bet he regrets it, poor cow.
I wonder who's gazing into her pince-nez
    As she stands at bay all through the day.
I wonder who now cocoa stirs
    For lips irreproachably hers.
I wonder if ever she gives him a tract,
    I wonder who's taking off his hat to her now!

'Mademoiselle from Armentieres'

Mademoiselle from Armentières,
    Parlez-vous,
Mademoiselle from Armentières,
    Parlez-vous,
Mademoiselle from Armentières,
Hasn't been kissed for 40 years,
    Inky, pinky, parlez-vous.

Mademoiselle from Armentières,
    Parlez-vous,
Mademoiselle from Armentières,
    Parlez-vous,
Mademoiselle from Armentières,
Hasn't had a conversation-lolly for 40 years,
    Inky, Vino Gattino, parlez-vous.

Virgil and Slessor Throw a Party on the Strength of the Lang Party's Return to Office

On a Bottle of Indian Ink

Imagine that bankers were banished,
 Imagine that prices are down;
Depression has utterly vanished,
 We're all of us dining in town;
Endeavour to keep up your pecker
 By copious draughts of champagne —
We'll go to the Ritz in a Checker
 And fare back to foxtrots again.

And fare back to foxtrots again —
 Hurrah for the pop of champagne!
 A trifle informal,
 Ferociously normal,
We'll fare back to foxtrots again!

Let 'Merry and Bright' be our motto,
 Forget the financier's price;
If gloom be the ransom of Otto,
 Good God, we ha' purchased him twice.
And why should we groan for 'em doubly,
 Those faults of our palmier days!
Go, pour us a pint of the bubbly,
 And bring out the prawn mayonnaise!

And bring out the prawn mayonnaise,
We're back to the happy old days;
There's time to be solemn

In some other column,
But bring out the prawn mayonnaise!
Imagine there's no more privation,
No matter what pay you may draw,
And people who mention taxation
Are straightway strangled by law,
And no one goes round with a chopper
To sack or reduce or revise,
And (this is a bit of a whopper),
WE'VE ALL GOT A TEN PER CENT RISE!

We've all got a Ten Per Cent rise!
Oh, shake out the woe from your eyes,
And sing like a linnet
With joy for a minute,
Before we return to meat pies!

Earth Speaks

New Zealand, February 2, 1931

Do you forget me? I have slept so long,
Asked for no payment, begged no thought or thanks,
But you have climbed, and found my body strong,
And crawled upon my huge and patient flanks.
Think of me now; for though I slumber deep,
Stretched on the stony pinions of my rack,
Sometimes, between two centuries of sleep,
I shake my back.

I shake my back, and you that walk thereon,
Your shells of brick, your little beds of men,
Your kennels and cathedrals — all have gone,

And I, dumb Earth, take back my dust again.
Think of me now, and though my teeth devour,
Know that in common men, that ecstasy,
The immortal blood of heroes, waits its hour,
Sleeping like me.

Once a Year

A fig for the proximity
Of doldrums on the dole,
When ladies dress in dimity
And Spring is in the soul,
And moths are in the money-box
And music in the air,
And girls with merry faces and little laughing noses
By merely shaking laces turn races into roses,
Flowing lightly,
Blowing brightly,
Growing there!

Who cares about economy
When unexpected skies
Are full of mad astronomy
And moons of monster size,
When Venus walks in organdi,
A blossom in her gown,
While flowers go floating, fleeting, like flakes of petals flying
And birds go round repeating the sighs of angels crying,
Frisking sweetly,
Whisking fleetly,
Up and down?

Vicar of Wakefield, M.H.R.

RICHARD FOSTER LOOMING LARGE AT CANBERRA

When Stanley Melbourne stoops to folly,
And dooms the House to sit all night,
Dick Foster conquers melancholy
With blasts of verbal dynamite.

Down bangs his fist, loud booms his bellow,
Curls tremble on the Speaker's wig,
While Dick, in tones more hoarse than mellow,
Roars at the Federal whirligig.

Goldsmith at this alarming Vicar,
Would turn his head, and faint away —
The beadle take in tears to liquor,
And Wakefield take to church, and pray.

But let him spout his fiery dictums;
When fifteen hours the House has sat,
You'll find, surrounded by his victims,
Dick Foster shouting For, not At.

She'll Say:–

When a lady wants the moon,
You must hurry to assist —
It's a pony to a prune
She will hang it on her wrist;
When her mind is in the sky,
Don't offend her with a frown,

If you think a moon too high,
   Someone else will pull it down.

You can bully all the day,
   You can argue till you're blind,
But no matter what you say
   She will never change her mind,
And she doesn't care a dump
   What you try to get it WITH —
You can take a flying jump
   Or apply to Kingsford Smith.

Hire a ladder and a rope,
   Buy a telescope and chain,
Bring a quantity of hope
   And a pilot in a 'plane;
You must climb the Milky Way,
   Hop the planets in the blue,
And persuade the moon to stray
   By the use of a lasso.

Having towed it down to ground
   With a star or two for fun,
You can bet an even pound
   She'll be yearning for the sun —
She will make you want to swoon,
   With a scornful sort of laugh:
'But I wanted a FULL moon,
   Not this miserable half!'

Birds of a Feather

Out of the subways teeming
    Back to the twilight flats,
Millions of quills go streaming
    Stuck on a million hats —
What do the redheads carry,
    Doing the eyesight good?
It's either a bold Glengarry
    Or a swaggering Robin Hood.

Sue from the wintergardens,
    Lil from the kitchen sink —
Once they wore Dolly Vardons,
    Floppy and pale and pink;
Now from the cash-and-carry,
    As elegant ladies should,
They come in a new Glengarry
    Or a little red Robin Hood.

All of them girls together,
    Office and lounge and shop,
Linked by a single feather,
    Wearing the same on top;
Somebody's bound to marry
    Somebody else for good —
A girl in a Scotch Glengarry
    Or a girl in a Robin Hood.

Nine o'clock beauties from Burwood
    (Such are the hats they wear)
Walk in the forest of Sherwood,
    Going to Wynyard Square,
Pirates who hunt and harry

As never a bandit could —
The girl in the cocked Glengarry
And the girl in the Robin Hood!

Jack-in-the-box

Come to Court and take the stand,
Jack-in-the-box,
Hold the Bible in your hand,
Jack-in-the-box.
Take the book and swear the vow,
Wipe the glory from your brow,
You're a human being now,
Jack-in-the-box.

Bid your Cabinets adieu,
Jack-in-the-box,
Say good-bye and let them stew,
Jack-in-the-box,
Take your freedom off the chain,
Mow the lawn and catch the train,
Be a common bloke again,
Jack-in-the-box.

Raise your pumpkins, feed your mares,
Jack-in-the-box,
They're your only sort of cares,
Jack-in-the-box.
Let the Parliaments go hang,
Turn your back without a pang,
Just become 'a Mr Lang',
Jack-in-the-box.

Sugar Daddy

Sugar-Daddy dotes
    Fondly on brunettes,
Buys 'em coney coats,
    Fixes up their debts;
Sugar-Daddy gloats
    Blissfully at blondes,
Gives 'em little notes,
    Not to mention bonds.

DEAR Sugar-Daddy, SWEET Sugar-Daddy (hear the flappers coo),
What's a teeny million to a
                    MAN
                        LIKE
                            YOU?

Sugar-Daddy thrills
    When a lady speaks,
Pays her little bills,
    Pecks her little cheeks.
What the flappers bid,
    Sugar-Daddies do —
'Want a million quid?
    Bless you, child, take two!'

NICE Sugar-Daddy, DEAR Sugar-Daddy, all the flappers purr,
Gimme, gimme, gimme what you
                    GAVE
                        TO
                            HER!

Sugar-Daddy frets,
    Sugar-Daddy's kind,

Sugar-Daddy's pets
   Hypnotise his mind —
'Come, my dear, and sit
   On the Old Man's knee;
Wheedle him a bit —
   You'll have jam for tea!'

NICE Sir Robert, DEAR Sir Robert, hear the
   Premiers coo:
What's another million to a
                                        MAN
                                           LIKE
                                              YOU?

Camille

The lady who writes to Camille
   On paper so mauve and so musky
May try, if she cares, to conceal
   A past that is possibly dusky,
But let her beware of the ink
   Ere seizing her little Onoto,
There's more in a 'nib' than you think,
   Your fist is as good as a photo.

Consider, I beg you, the danger
   Of posting a letter to-day —
Camille or some positive stranger
   May use an invisible ray;
Those little pink, panting epistles —
   Each page is a picture in ink,
The back of the envelope bristles,
   The Face on the stamp has a wink.

Your manner of dotting an i,
Your habit of signing a flourish,
May lead a professor to pry
His nasty suspicion to nourish,
And even the gum on the flap
So recently kissed by Estella
May babble all over the map
As loud as the vulgar rosella.

Camille has a mind like a dagger,
Camille has an eye like a hawk,
She causes the postman to stagger,
She teaches the pot-hook to talk,
The loop of the D in 'Dear Mabel',
The curl of a lavender seal —
They mightn't look much of a label,
But, oh, what they mean to Camille!

And That's That

The bailiff came, and he was fat,
And he was hard as frozen suet;
He bade us change our habitat:
We did it, for we had to do it.
Living on doles and Irish Stew,
Australia of the brave and free! —
That was in Nineteen-Thirty-Two
BUT THIS IS NINETEEN-THIRTY-THREE!

We backed a horse, and it was dead,
And if it won we paid the tax;
The sun burned savage overhead,

And scorpions frolicked on our backs;
Down on the rocks our basking crew
Tried roasted limpets for their tea;
That was in Nineteen-Thirty-Two
BUT THIS IS NINETEEN-THIRTY-THREE!

With knocks and jolts and bumps and ruts
Right through a dismal year we came;
Hope springs eternal in the . . .
The place that Scotchmen call the wame;
The sun is gold, the sky is blue,
So come and have a pint with me:
For that was Nineteen-Thirty-Two,
BUT THIS IS NINETEEN-THIRTY-THREE.

Oh Brother, on the ration track
Don't sit upon a rail and grizzle,
Look-Forward's better than Look-Back,
And Man was never made to mizzle;
Come shower or shine, we'll all get through,
There's yet good fish in every sea;
Good-bye to Nineteen-Thirty-Two,
WHAT-HO FOR NINETEEN-THIRTY-THREE!

Epitaph for a Dead Dog

'During the recent storms in Sydney, the body of a dead mongrel dog was discovered. It had scratched a hole in the ground, where it had lain over its four newly-born puppies in an endeavor to protect them from the wind and rain. Though it managed by this means to keep two of them alive, the dog when found had died from exposure.' — News Item

Small breeding in your mongrel blood
And little pride were yours,
To lie down dumbly in the mud
As men have died in wars.

Few laws you had to comprehend,
Few rules you understood —
So utterly as this to spend
The only thing you could.

We do not know what came about
In your queer, dog-dark mind,
Nor how the spark was beaten out
That left such flame behind.

We do not know what Master flung
His blows upon your head,
Nor how you lifted once your tongue,
Stirred quietly, and were dead.

'Blind instinct' — so professors' lore
Invents a name to give;
But surely it is something more
That's more than will-to-live.

We cheat the heart and check the mind
And choke them at the spring —
But in our country of the blind
You do a simple thing.

An Australian Spring Song that is Different

Oh, fold your cold umbrellas
   And put your burdens by —
A rainbow of rosellas
   Is bursting in the sky;
A burning town of berries
   Is blazing on the bough,
The wind is full of cherries,
   Here
      In Australia
         NOW!

No gods on mouldy leopards,
   No myths of old are ours;
We mock the piping shepherds,
   But keep the pagan flowers.
Our Pan's a trifle fleeter,
   The fastest thing alive —
His other name is Peter,
   He carries 9 stone 5.

The blossoms on our altars
   Would make a Roman stare,
Our Strephons all are Walters,
   Our Helens bob their hair;
But all the Greeks in Hades
   Would pawn their gods for speech
To greet those golden ladies,
   Our naiads of the beach.

We ride the great Merino
   In triumph to the Spring;
Our songs are andantino
   Because we like to sing.
We take what Fortune offers,
   Nor puzzle Why nor How —
When spring unlocks her coffers
   Here
      In Australia
         NOW!

Melinda in a Hurry

Oh, bang the door and jump the stairs
   And fling the flapjack down,
Put off your hat, put off your cares —
   Melinda's back from town!
The mirror shakes, the curtains rock,
   The candles quake, and then —
This hurricane at six o'clock
   Goes dancing at 6.10!

6.1, she's in a whirl of shoes,
   6.2 . . . pantette . . . georgette . . .
6.3, she's pink in various views,
   6.4, she's pink and wet,
6.5, she's glowing like a rose,
   6.6 — a frock to wear! —
6.7, she adorns her nose,
   6.8, enchants her hair!

O lucky man Melinda meets
   At some disdainful Ritz,

You'll never know the magic feats
   A working-girl commits;
She floats to greet you at the door,
   A mist of silver foam —
But, oh, you ought to see the floor
   Melinda leaves at home!

Not Understood

Presented by Smith's, *with apologies to Thomas Bracken, as a national anthem for those members of the Federal Parliament who voted for a salary-increase.*

Not understood, while half the world retrenches,
   Bloated with vows we never meant to keep,
Year after year we scramble to our benches,
   Bang the front door — and then we fall asleep
Not understood.

Not understood, we clutch our paltry splendours,
   Hugging them closer as the years go by,
Till booty that the common herd surrenders
   Seems ours, divinely ours, to justify
Not understood.

Not understood! Poor souls with petty 'slander'
   Oft pester giants with their vulgar 'spite';
The hateful shafts of Daylight, bright with candour,
   Are oft impelled 'gainst those who grab by night
Not understood.

Not understood! How trifles often harm us!
   The thoughtless sentence and the fancied jeer

Destroy long years of comfort, and alarm us,
And on our souls there falls a freezing fear;
Not understood.

Not understood! How many hungry fillings
Our bellies bluster from the public pay!
How many noble hearts, for thirty shillings,
Are bought and sold, and slowly pine away
Not understood.

Ye Gods! that we could hide the gruesome spectres
That vex the conscience and affright the soul
When next we have to bow to the electors
And face the final judgement of the poll
Well understood!

Armistice Day — Military Hospital

The dumb November air takes tongue,
The bells ring out, the bugle cries,
The volleys of the dead are flung
From rifles aimed at empty skies;
A pomp of banners cloaks our eyes,
We pave with Stones the old Abyss —
But quietly in his bed he lies,
The man without an Armistice.

Two Minutes' pause! The glories wane;
His Silence is a longer kind,
A Silence measured out by pain,
Bitter with dreams that mock the mind,
A world of shadows left behind,
A buried life, a phantom's kiss —

He waits a Peace we never signed,
The man without an Armistice.

Triumphal Ode

(WITH PLENTY STILL OWING)
ON THE AUSPICIOUS OCCASION OF THE
TWENTY-FIRST ANNIVERSARY OF THE
FOUNDATION OF CANBERRA

Dedicated to That Enlightened Patron of the Bathetic Muse,
the Honorable Thomas White, Esq.

O, Heavens! O, Canberra! Majestic zone
Of plush upholsteries and purest bone,
Twaddle's last fortress, babble's dearest nest,
Where bombast burgeons in the boiling breast —
Hail, CANBERRA! Thy festal banners fly,
We greet thee with an apprehensive eye,
With shudd'ring fingers turn another page
Whilst CANBERRA, sweet bumpkin, comes of age.

Lo! As the news is cried, the message spread,
Mixed metaphor unfurls his gorgeous head,
Shy Platitudes fly slipslop down the breeze,
And the King's English trembles as it flees.

Call for the stricken tourist but to peep,
And lo! the House will waken out of sleep,
Wit flop cadaverous from slab to slab
At the mere beck of Mr MOSES GABB,
Thunder and lightning sizzle in the ink
And PERKINS' eye blaze forth its ghoulish blink,

GANDER warn Rome of that thing and of this,
Dazzling his list'ners with a venomed hiss
That, heard but once, brings on paralysis.

SEE, see the legions of the storied Great,
HOLMAN and HUGHES, those Daniels of debate,
PARKHILL and CHARLIE MARR and WHITE and GREEN,
Casting their lustre on the radiant scene —
And see! He comes, with patriarchal smile,
The arch-Malthusian of the Apple Isle.

O, CANBERRA! O, heavens! Snore thy snore,
Immortal Flatulence, bewitching Bore!
Curl-papers cut from Hansard deck thy head,
And tape incarnadined Morocco-red.
Boldly thou waddlest on thy destined way,
Begging for nothing but a pass and pay.
This be the nature of thy last reward —
The right to ev'rything we can't afford.
O, CANBERRA! O, heavens! Oh, my gord!

God Save the Duke of Gloucester

From the cannon's fearful bang,
From *The Herald* and *The Star*,
From the jaws of Mr Lang,
And the might of Mr Marr,
From the mumble of the mayors,
From the rattle of the roads,
From the speeches and the prayers

And illuminated odes —
Save the Duke!

From the little busy lens,
From Associated News,
From the poets and the pens,
From the parsons and the pews,
From the municipal port,
From political intrigues,
From the curtsey and the court
And the ladies of the Leagues —
Save the Duke!

From the colic after meals,
From the shivers in the hand,
From the concertina's peals,
And the Parramatta band,
From the festival and fete,
From the swallowtails and spats,
From the mothballs of the Great
And 2000 grey top hats —
Save the Duke!

From the crowding and the crush,
And the Band of Social Hope,
From the litanies of gush
And the symphonies of soap,
From the things we have to bear
And the bores we can't rebuke —
Save the Duke, we make our prayer,
Save the Duke!

Body-Line!

Sweet Miss Prue, in a crinoline frock,
Was a hot performer at postman's-knock;
In the ding-dong days of '94,
She banged the devilish battledore —
Sweet Miss Prudence, sweet Miss Prue,
Why do you hesitate, what would you do,
Where would you wander, and how would you frown,
If YOU went in First Wicket Down?

Dear Miss Lilia, Tennyson's pride,
Was a first-class fiend on a croquet-side;
The 'Nineties thrilled as they watched her stoop
With a deadshot eye on a little white hoop —
Dear Miss Lilia, dear Miss Lil,
What would they meditate, how would they thrill,
What would they think, those goggle-eyed lads,
If YOU walked out in a pair of pads!

Little Miss Peggy is frequently found
With an autographed bat at the Cricket Ground;
She fields square-leg, but I'm willing to swear,
Her legs are anything else but square.
Little Miss Peggy, little Miss Peg,
Ours is the theory, yours is the leg —
How can we barrack you, how can we frown,
When YOU go in First Wicket Down?

Dad's Toast

(I)

Ladies and gents, I begs leave to perpose
The 'ealth of a party which all of us knows —
THE KING ('Eaven bless 'im), what started 'is reign
When me whiskers was black and me 'abits was vain,
When the crows 'adn't trod (stone the cows!) on me face,
And the world, yer might add, was a rum kind er place —

(II)

When a pub was a pub, not a six-o'clock gaol,
With schooners for threepence, AND turkeys AND quail,
And me and nine cobbers could 'ave a night out,
Drinking Franz Josef lager and Red Anchor stout,
Play 'ell at the Troc. (which we frequently did),
With a peep at West's Pitchers — fer under a quid;

(III)

When 'Ughes and his views was regarded as strange,
And WIMMEN, sweet wimmen, worked Central
    exchange,
And H.M.S *Powerful* 'ung smoke in the sky,
And Signor Gasparri sung Tosti's 'Good-Bye',
And Mr Mark Foy 'ad a new kind er car,
And trams was a penny, and so was *The Star* —

(IV)

But, bless yer, no matter what changes they ring,
I'm still the same Dad, and 'e's still the same King —
In spite of all crazes and phases we've 'ad,
'E's still the same King and I'm still the same Dad.
What's twenty-five years to a bloke who's alive?
I'll give yer a toast — to the NEXT twenty-five!

The Taxpayers' Marseillaise

To be sung, with passionate feeling, to the same tune

Come all you poor dumb goats with votes, with votes,
  Form 92 falls due to-day —
Can't you feel the cold steel at your thro-oats,
  Can't you hear the cashier on his way?
Can't you hear the cashier on his way?
  Hear the croaks of the blokes in the backblocks,
Hear the sobs of the nobs in the towns!
  They are coming for your last half-crowns,
They are pouncing like a panther on its prey-ay!

Fork out, and face the axe!
Bail up, and bare your backs!
Tax on! (tut-tut-tut-ta-a) Tax on! (tut-tut-tut-ta-a)
Stones bleed with groans,
But we-e-e-e bleed income-tax!

The system never fails on sales, on sales,
  We pay in Blue Gum Creek on beer,
And in case any place ever sca-hales,
  There's a toll on your roll all the year!
There's a toll on your roll all the year!
  There's a sting on the wing for amusement,
There's a thug with a slug for a wage,
  There's a duty upon dying of old age,
And a surreptitious tax upon the mai-hails!

Fork out, and face the axe!
Bail up, and bare your backs!
Tax on! Tax on!
Stones bleed with groans,
But we-e-e-e bleed income tax!

primage
probate
wages
sales
tobacco
amusement
etc., etc.

The world has all been wrong so long, so long,
There's not an ear will deign to hear —
But we wait for our fate with a song-ong,
That is more like a roar than a cheer,
That is more like a roar than a cheer!
Oh, beware on the Treas-ury benches,
When we swarm in a storm, Mr Sikes —
We'll impale a few heads on our pikes,
As we thunder along in a throng-ong!

Come forth, and face the axe!
Walk out! (Hark, hark, the whacks!)
Tax on! Tax on!
Stones bleed with groans,
But WE'LL pay no more tax!

THIS BATTLE HYMN OF THE REPUBLIC OF THE LEGION OF THE LOST, MAY BE SUNG WITHOUT FEE OR LICENCE AT ANY PUBLIC MEETING OF TAX-PAYERS. IN FACT WE'D ASK YOU TO SING IT: SING IT WHENEVER YOU PAY 2D ON A TWO BOB TICKET TO THE PICTURES, WHENEVER THEY SOCK YOU FIFTY QUID ON THE PRICE OF A CAR, AND, IMITATING PAT MALONE ON A FAMOUS OCCASION WHEN HE FORGOT THAT HE WAS DEAD, SIT UP IN YOUR COFFIN AND SING IT TO THE PROBATE OFFICIALS. THE LINES OF WORDS ARE A BIT BENT, BECAUSE THE METAL FROM WHICH THIS PAGE WAS PRINTED STOOD UP ON ITS HIND FEET AND JOINED IN THE CHORUS.

Lady Spider

To the wooing of Arachne
In a cosy little flat,
They arrive by cab and hackney
On the mat, mat, mat,
And their arms are full of roses,
And their faces full of care,
And they stick their silly noses
In the snare, snare, snare!

There's a person with a Humber,
Fifteen colonels and a king,
And a corresponding number
With a ring, ring, ring.
Night and morning, Claude and Clarence
In a tide without an ebb
See the beauties of transparence
In a web, web, web.

Such a pretty little spider,
So particularly bright
(And their eyelids open wider),
Can it bite, bite, bite?
But they very soon discover,
As philosophers declare,
That the lady eats the lover —
So beware, ware, ware!

Slow Coach

No proper girls would think to run
Along the Road to Twenty-one;

With soft, reluctant feet they go,
And all the Coaches there are Slow.

The piping countrysides of Youth
Are hard to leave, and that's the truth —
So many birds disturb the mind
Or whistle from the boughs behind.

So many poppies wake from sleep,
So many painted daisies peep,
So many kisses to pursue,
So much to say, so much to do.

But when at last the fearful Post
Goes past, as it must go with most,
Though steep the hills we still must climb,
How fast the trolley-bus of Time!

Outboard

Pass the cushion, drop the rudder,
   Let the outboard take its head,
Let the horsepower shake and shudder,
   We shall dream of oars instead,
When I touched the concertina
   Where to-day they pluck the uke —
You were once a signorina,
   I was once a flaming duke.

You were once a Doge's daughter,
   And the street was bright with fins,
And we rowed upon the water
   In a world of mandolins,

And there might have been a basso,
    Like an angel in the door,
Singing tender bits from Tasso,
    Pushing moonlight with an oar.

Such engaging gondolieri,
    Floating stars and golden keels,
May be Paradise in theory,
    But our world is full of wheels,
Full of tea-cups, full of tennis,
    And the surf is our canal,
And we've never gone to Venice,
    And we never, never shall.

But I'm not inclined to quarrel,
    For the water's just as fair,
And the moon that mocks Balmoral
    Is the moon that glitters there;
If we haven't got the gala,
    Here's a ferry just as snug —
And I wouldn't change La Scala
    For our chug
        chug
        chug!

Hands

Beryl sells bottles of beauty,
    Magic of mystical brands,
Babe has a craving for permanent waving,
    But Manicure Mabel 'does hands'.
Life may be roses for someone,

Love is a wine to be sipped,
But hands on a table keep floating past Mabel,
Pale hands
Pink-tipped.

Hands that may dangle with diamonds,
Hands that may dip into dirt,
Hands that may flutter like flowers in a gutter
Or fumble, or flourish, or flirt;
Fingers as light as a feather,
Kissed by impertinent males,
Painted & varnished and otherwise garnished —
And nails —
Pink nails.

Nails that are bright as a cherry,
Nails that are Burgundy red,
Fingers that copy the dyes of the poppy
Or vie with a bushfire instead;
Coral and powder and lacquer,
Lacquer and powder and lace,
Cover the tables — but what about Mabel's
Pink hands,
Pale face?

King's Cross Gardens

Where the flats are crowded flatter,
She was floating down the street —
There was music in her chatter,
There was magic on her feet,
But I hadn't got a notion,

Till she hastened to convey,
With a flutter of emotion —
She was 'gardening' to-day.

Then I said: 'I beg your pardon,
There's a thing I'd like to know —
If you've really got a garden,
Where the devil does it grow?
Though we lunch upon a lotus,
Not a blossom ever falls,
And the only beds I notice
Are the beds that fold in walls.'

But she took a sudden turning,
Paused a while to pluck a rose,
And the window blurred with yearning
Where she pressed her pretty nose,
And she smelt a bunch of crocus,
Pulled a lily from its moss,
And the shop flew out of focus —
There were gardens at the Cross!

To a Town Hall Pigeon

'A contractor is at present being paid £10 to eradicate the pigeons which nest on the roof of the Sydney Town Hall.' — News item

The mayors go in, the mayors go out,
With golden chains and vanity;
You perch on some convenient spout
And contemplate humanity.
Who cares if some be pink or pale,

And some be wise or wordy?
You preen your disrespectful tail,
And wink at Dr Purdy.

Here, where the city's conscience rests
And Sydney's bells go pealing,
A hundred mayors have made their nests,
But yours is past the ceiling;
And some had wit and some had words
And numbers had religion —
But, choosing between mayors and birds,
My vote is for the pigeon!

The pigeon that with dauntless plumes
Defies a Works Committee,
That mocks the clerk in office-rooms
Five floors above the city;
No passions fill you as you fly,
Nor envy as you flutter —
You ask a bedroom in the sky,
A breakfast from the gutter.

But when you scorn to play the lark,
Descending from your mountain
To pick a living from the Park
By Archibald, his Fountain,
There, where the misty water whirls
And gravel crunches, crunches,
You watch the little office-girls
A-munching of their lunches;

Or note, perhaps, how mayors and knights
And such important people,
Are mere perambulating mites

Below St Andrew's steeple.
So, when you scour this building, sir,
That braves a hundred weathers,
Eradicate the rabbit's fur,
But spare the pigeon's feathers!

When I Was King

'You know,' said Mr Hughes last week, 'I had more power in the war-days than an Australian politician has ever had. Sometimes I sigh for the halcyon period when I took out my fountain-pen, the ink flowed and a law was made.'

With apologies to W. E. Henley

Or ever the War Precautions Act
Was given a pauper's grave,
I was a kind of a King, in fact,
And you were a blithering Slave.

I huffed and I puffed, and I blew my cheeks,
I shivered the bones of men —
And there weren't any constitutional shrieks
Or High Court flummery then,
But I upped and scuppered a million squeaks
With a little black fountain pen.

But many a winter and many a spring
Have covered the old Act's grave
Since I was a regular blazing King
And you were a blithering Slave.

The pride and the glory have passed away,
The pomp and the power have gone,

And babble is all you'll hear to-day
   In Canberra's Babylon,
And nobody's bones reveal dismay
   Whenever I wave my Swan.

Yet I often think of the vanished joys
   And the pen that nobody waves,
When I was the King of the Castle, boys,
   And you were the blooming slaves.

Come to Sydney!

'The opening day of Sydney's Sesquicentenary Celebrations will be packed with spectacle and atmosphere. There will be an historical pageant through the city . . . and a host of professional events. Days and nights of festival will follow, with band-championships, the National Eisteddfod, sports championships and a week of juvenile show and pageantry. Other items include the National Rifle Association's meeting, an angling-competition, a Chinese festival, and a commercial and industrial pageant. This is a programme which does not depend on night-life for its attractiveness.' — J. M. Dunningham, Minister in charge of Sydney Celebrations

Oh, the scurry and rush of excitement,
   The scenes of hysterical fun,
When Sydney goes gay in a devilish way
   On a diet of biscuit-and-bun!
There'll be spelling-bees, also eisteddfods —
   Imagine the hubbub and din! —
And hectic debates on colonial dates
   With a lantern-slide lecture chucked in.
There'll be dozens of bands tooting tubas,
   And riflemen banging like mad;

And Scotsmen, by cripes, playing tunes on the pipes,
    In the Highland Society's plaid.
There'll be thousands of tots around maypoles,
    Wherever you happen to look,
And picnics and jaunts to historical haunts,
    With a series of talks about Cook.
There'll be Japanese crackers and lanterns
    To light up the beautiful dark,
And fishing, by Jove, off the wharf at Lane Cove,
    With a prize for the best-looking shark.
So come to the circus in Sydney —
    The programme's a positive gem —
Where bottles go pop till festivities stop
    At 5.57 p.m.!

Truthful Bob

With apologies to Bret Harte

'He's such a good type of man. He doesn't know a crooked way. I suppose that's the trouble, he's a bit too straight for some of them.'
— Mrs James Menzies, mother of the Prime Minister

I reside at Kew in Melbourne, and my name is Truthful Bob,
Which I draws the line at arson, and I never learned to rob;
There's a beam of blazing virtue like a lighthouse in my eye —
I have never picked a pocket, and I cannot tell a lie.

I was never one for murder — and they call me Truthful Bob —
Which I dunno how I done it, in my present kind of job;
Why, the mere idea of slander gives me pimples on the skin,
And in 40 years, so help me, I have never been put in.

I have never forged a fiver — and my name is Truthful Bob —
When I think of common larceny, I nearly gives a sob;
I've a nervous kind of horror when I kick a referee,
And I've never earned my living with a thimble and a pea.

I have never been corrupted — and they call me Truthful Bob —
Which they takes away their money, and they curse me for a snob.
I'm so pitifully honest that it fills me full of gall
When I wonder what the blazes I am doing here at all!

Second-Class Ballad of the North Shore First

With apologies to 'The Gondoliers'

There lived a king — a kind of czar —
Who governed like a guiding star
The N.S.W.G.R.
With wisdom none could alter.
In first-class carriages he'd stick
A seat according to their pick,
For Hawkins, Jorkins, Mr Crick,
Sir Marcus and Sir Walter.

But such, of course, did not pertain
To lowlier portions of the train
With placards on the window-pane
Emblazoned 'Second Smoking'.
Here — filled with pitying scorn, perhaps,
For Potts and Watts and suchlike chaps —

He thoughtfully provided straps
    Which looked (and were) provoking.

Alas, what change is here to day!
That ordered state, that extra trey,
Have all, it seems, been swept away,
    And Potts with Hawkins reckoned!
O, faces brazener than brass!
That such a thing should come to pass
And men so utterly first-class
    Be forced to travel second!

It makes a decent person sick
To see Sir Alf, and Mr Crick
Compelled to shuffle, scuffle, kick,
    And join the vulgar hubbub,
While in that seat — for 50 year
Sir Arthur's own — with frigid sneer
The homeward plumber rests his rear,
    Returning to his subbub!

An Inscription for the Graves at Bergoulive

Maximus Martius is the greatest and most enlightened of
    generals.
For his deeds, look around you on this coast —
Here is his name cut next to Ashur Bani Pal's,
Nebuchadnezzar and the Roman host;
And, though it is true that we whose identities have been lost
Lack the validity of stone or metal,
We, too, are part of his memorial,
Having been put in for the cost.

Not That There Here

'Mr Wells, SM: Mr Claux and Mrs Crick object to the surroundings of Forbes-street, Woolloomooloo, but bad as it may be, one would never see people walking about in that street in the nude.'

You'd be surprised by what goes on,
At Narrabeen and Avalon,
And things that happen after dark
Make burglars blush at Hurlstone Park.
In Pymble, Hornsby and St Ives,
They stone the crows and beat their wives,
Whilst at Palm Beach and Collaroy
Gin-rummy is their only joy,
And, oh, the frightful words they use
At Chowder Bay and La Perouse!

But let them keep their sin and drinks,
Their frolics, orgies and high jinks —
Thank heaven for this rectitude:
We never walk here in the nude!
A thing like that would never do
For us in Forbes-street, Woolloomooloo!

Lovett Bay

After looking at the Admiralty Chart made
by Captain F.W. Sidney R.N., 1868–72

This bay was full of drowning light
   While morning lit the other bay,
So Captain Sidney called one Night
   And named the other after Day.

A bay all phosphorus and shine,
A bay of burning gold, perhaps —
Or so it seemed in '69
To Captain Sidney making maps.

NIGHT BAY and MORNING BAY
He wrote them on the survey then,
But someone took their names away
And called them after aldermen.

A curse be on the cuckoo clerk
And all the stolen fame he covets,
May he go down into the dark
With 50 million lousy Lovetts,

May councils love him less and less
Till, wheresoever he may dwell,
The Devil changes *his* address
To 'Emoh Ruo', Smith Street, Hell!

A Short History of K. Slessor

K. Slessor was born at Orange in Nineteen-Hundred-and-One,
He went to Shore for a number of years and then he went to *The Sun*.
In 1925 he switched to the *Melbourne Herald* and *Punch*
And 2 years later he worked on *Smith's* (with Stan Cross, Joe Jonsson, George Finey & all that bunch).
In 1940, for some quaint reason or other, the stars in their courses

Turned him into an Official War Correspondent
with the Australian military forces
And for the next 4 years he experienced a variety
of unenjoyable emotions
In places such as New Guinea, Great Britain,
Greece, Egypt and the Atlantic and Pacific
oceans.
Now back with *The Sun*, where he first begun, he
has no more use for the Muse,
Spending most of his time writing leading articles
about Tito and SEATO and tiny little book-
reviews.
His hair comes out, he suffers from gout, his
physical charms are small,
But he manages to live at Elizabeth Bay with a
wife, 3 cats, 2 goldfish and one little boy
called Paul.

Lines Written on the Occasion of the Transposition of the Ladies' and Gents' Lavatories on the 9th Floor

How beautiful it is to know,
Whatever else our notions,
Some Higher Power than us below
Controls our daily motions.
High at his lonely desk enshrined,
Where no one dares to wander,

Some far, mysterious Mastermind
On privvies deigns to ponder.

Oft had he passed the humble door,
And thought that 'ME' disgraced it
('ME' which was written 'MEN' before
Some egotist defaced it).
'The job will call for tact,' he mused,
'And some would say they dare not —
But I, for one, am not confused,
And as for them, I care not.'

(For he, unlike the vulgar herds
Who think that crowds are funny,
Dropped only rich, superior turds
In some exclusive dunny,
Some private, padlocked, holy nest
Reserved for Lord and Master,
Where none but Sacred Bums may rest
On thrones of alabaster.)

'All those who flout my will,' he swore,
'May pull the chain in Hades!'
Twas done. They painted on the door,
And 'Gents' was turned to 'Ladies'.
Now what befalls? The die is cast,
The 'Ladies' blush and flutter,
And 'Men' flee forth, with eyes aghast,
Who button as they mutter.

With flies agape, they flee the place,
Their very language blisters —
And who can tell the redder face,
The Miss's or the Mr's?

'What miracle,' they cry, 'is this,
And who can solve the riddle?
Where Gentlemen once stood to piss,
Now Ladies sit to piddle!'

I Wish I Were . . .

I wish I were in Orange
Which I left at the age of two,
Sitting in the 5A classroom
With the summertime bursting through.

Hearing a thousand cicadas,
Piping in the white hot air
And the tree my mother planted
In the schoolyard over there.

But here I am in Sydney
At the age of sixty-one
With the clock at a quarter to bedtime
And my homework still not done.

The Peep-hole

Unmasked behind the willow-tree,
Eyes, bold before, grew shy to see . . .
What happy chance
Of revel and of dance
Rhymed me to you and you to me.

(Sweet silver girl, with turn and twist,
Our rondeau twine: first, down the list,
With cadenced beat
Our pretty theme repeat:
Thus ending, in my arms and kisst.)

The willow-tree above our head
Bars out the lantern-moon of red . . .
One ray strikes through
To show, slipped round a shoe,
Pearl-garters on a grassy bed.

Young Death

One love I ask, and one alone
Yet may it be
Such magic mystery
That charms the clocks, until a second, even, has grown
Into a rimless eternity.
This is a love the gods, I think, have never known.

For O! This is no marble idyll . . . this
No casual traffic in a frozen kiss . . .
This
Is quintessential human; and it thrills
With very earthy joys and ills.

A day to live in the great blaze of youth
That knows not law nor God, nor fear nor ruth
And then . . .
Quick speeding from the minds of men;

Save that they say:
'These two were lovers yesterday,
And lovers still,
Together probe the dark, unfathomed deep,
Call it eternal life, immortal sleep,
Or what you will.'

Ode
on
The Enlightened & Liberal Patronage Bestowed on the Arts
by
Their Majesties, The King and Queen of Great Britain

Dedicated with Humble Refpect to that Maecenas of
the Mufical Halls, His Majefty the Late King Edward VII

Thrice-bleffėd MONARCHS who, with princely parts,
Conduct the Mufes and inform the Arts,
Who, with fuch gen'rous geftures of the Soul,
The Laureate Pen, the Phidian Clay, controul!

Attend, ye Mufes, whilft with duteous Heart
I celebrate Q---n M--y's love for Art,
Who, with Herbaceous Borders fondly ftruck,
Quoth 'Gardens!' to that other Raphael, TUCK!

Can this be true? Nay, ftay the fleeting wing
Whilft of great G----e's Patronage I fing,

Who purchafed, though fuch opulence aftounds,
A STAMP COLLECTION for Two Thoufand Pounds!

Thrice-favoured Albion, whofe cultured THRONE
Illuminates the Mufe's lowlier zone,
Where Art & Letters (long may they endure!)
Are fertilifed with fuch a Royal Manure!

Untitled

Oh what a pleasure 'tis to see
Dear Doctor Johnson drinking tea,
Mount Kosciusko come to sup
An Alp descending on a cup,
Above the steam, with solemn grace,
He lifts his round enormous face
Roaring like water in a cave
With sermons, excellent and grave.
In dreadful quiet the guests exhale,
Viewed with a frown by Mrs Thrale,
As one by one across the room
Tremendous cannon-lectures boom.

Thus Dr Johnson graces tea
With virtuous philosophy;
But all the time, in buried cells
He gloats on birds and dancing bells,
His mind a pool of naked rose,
Of girls, and of seraglios . . .

Popular Song

When I get to the homestead of Heaven
They'll fill up my billy with tea,
And a jackeroo cherub with bright golden syrup
Will spread the white damper for me.

I shall lie with my back to a fencepost,
And the blowflies buzz me to sleep,
And I won't have to shrivel my fists on a shovel
Or shoulder an axe for my keep.

And Celestial cooks in the cookhouse
Will give me their leavings to eat
With rum by the dipper to bring a sweet stupor
And Heavenly hounds at my feet.

Explanatory and textual notes

Legend

Works by Slessor:

TOTM: *Thief of the Moon*

E-V: *Earth-Visitors*

CC: Cuckooz Contrey

FB: *Five Bells*

DN: *Darlinghurst Nights*

BBFB: *Backless Betty from Bondi*

UP: Uncollected poems

BW: *Bread and Wine: Selected Prose* (Sydney: Angus & Robertson, 1970)

Works by others:

Dutton: Geoffrey Dutton, *Kenneth Slessor: A Biography* (Ringwood, Vic.: Viking, 1991)

Kiernan: Brian Kiernan, ed., *Considerations: New Essays on Kenneth Slessor, Judith Wright and Douglas Stewart* (Sydney: Angus & Robertson, 1977)

Haskell: Dennis Haskell, ed., *Kenneth Slessor* (St Lucia: University of Queensland Press, 1991)

Stewart: Douglas Stewart, *A Man of Sydney: An Appreciation of Kenneth Slessor* (Melbourne: Nelson, 1977)

Thomson: A.K. Thomson, ed., *Critical Essays on Kenneth Slessor* (Brisbane: Jacaranda, 1968)

S: Southerly

Other references:

ML: Mitchell Library

NLA: National Library of Australia

• Writing dates are as indicated by Slessor and denote completion dates.

• Magazine publication dates are recorded where known. Many of Slessor's poems did not receive magazine publication before book publication.

• Poems selected by Slessor for inclusion in *Poems* (1957) are marked '(P)'.

General note

Many of Slessor's early poems were revised for *One Hundred Poems*. Slessor commented on this in a 1968 letter to Herbert Jaffa (NLA MS 3020/1/711):

> Changes in the text of poems in later editions were caused by a desire to eliminate youthful affectations and mock Elizabethan archaisms (e.g. 'wenches' and 'wenching', 'magick' and 'fantastick'), precious decoration ('sable masks' and 'gules') and special 'poetic' language (e.g. 'fruitage'). I also tried to avoid the 'poetic' spellings imitated from Jack Lindsay in *Vision* (e.g. 'presst' for 'pressed') though I suspect there is perhaps a slight case to be argued for the staccato whip of the 't' ending in past participles where there is a sound-effect that differs (to my ear at least) from the less decisive 'ed' ending . . .
>
> The elimination of words like 'wenches' and 'wenching' arose simply from a desire to cut away the conceits and archaisms, of which I had had a surfeit. And perhaps it might be added that certainly most Australian poetry, and possibly most English poetry, of the period (1918–1925) was stultified by an outworn special 'poetic' language. This is the reason why in later editions I changed as many of the 'thous' and 'thines' as possible to 'yous' and 'yours'.

Thief of the Moon

(Sydney: J.B. Kirtley, 1924)

Incongruity

completed April 1921; first published *Art in Australia*, February 1923

7 *glaives*: swords, especially broadswords (archaic).

10 *Lupus*: the wolf (Latin). Lupus is a star constellation visible in

Australia. 'Lupus' is also the name of a skin disease caused by tuberculosis.

16 *puling*: crying in a high-pitched tone.

21 *nightjar*: a nocturnal, insect-eating bird, found throughout Australia.

Nuremberg

June 1921; *Art in Australia*, February 1922; (P)

A ms. copy held in NLA declares: 'inspired by a picture by Durer'. Albrecht Dürer (1471–1528) was born and brought up in Nuremberg. He is especially admired for his woodcuts and engravings. Slessor's surname was originally 'Schloesser', before it was Anglicised by his father in 1914, and the poem reflects Slessor's interest in his own German background. James McAuley ('An Imprint of Slessor', *Quadrant*, No. 1, 1973, p. 6) noted that Slessor's presentation of Nuremberg's roofs resembled his description of St James's Church, King Street, Sydney (in *Bread and Wine*, p. 9).

4 *clock-jacks*: human figures which strike bells on the outsides of clocks.

7 *horologe*: any instrument which indicates the time; mistakenly printed as 'horologue' in *Poems* and subsequent reprintings.

13 *cowls*: hood-shaped chimney covers, used to increase the draught.

14 *vanes*: weather vanes.

16 *manticores*: fabulous monsters.

20 *intaglios*: engravings.

The Ghost

June 1923; (P)

3 *Music*: 'Musick' in *TOTM*.

9 *you*: 'thou' in *TOTM*.

11 *your*: 'thy' in *TOTM*.

21 *your*: 'thy' in *TOTM*.

25 *pressed*: 'presst' in *TOTM*.

the dark pane: This is the first use in Slessor's poetry of an image that was to recur many times — that of a person kept behind glass, preventing a desired contact.

A Surrender

May 1923; (P)

1 *Venusbergs*: here an extravagant word for 'breasts'. In Wagner's *Tannhauser* the Venusberg is the mountain inhabited by the Goddess of Love. Knights were enticed into and held captive in the Venusberg.

2 *batteries*: artillery.

4 *culverins twain*: two large cannons.

5 *bells*: this imagery in the poem recalls Norman Lindsay's drawings of women's breasts (see Thomson, p. 12).

9 *trow*: believe (archaic).

Mangroves

July 1922; (P)

Mangroves are trees which grow in brackish water on mudflats. They are common in Australian river estuaries.

6 *bubbles*: Slessor's first use of an image which was to recur in many poems.

14 *they*: the leaves of the mangroves.
in vain: also used in the last line of 'The Ghost'.

Thief of the Moon

January 1922; *Vision*, May 1923; (P)

Undine

June 1923; (P)

Undine: in Greek and Roman mythology a female water sprite.

1 *cutpurse*: pickpocket, thief.

2 *magic*: 'magick' in *TOTM*.

5 *gourds*: bowl-like shapes of the candle flames. A gourd is a

fruit whose dried shell can be used for bowls or bottles.

6 *gilt*: a recurrent word in Slessor's early poetry.

10 *Pressed*: 'Presst' in *TOTM*.

Good-Night

July 1923; *Vision*, November 1923

19 *turnpike-boy*: a highwayman.

The Mask

August 1923; *Vision*, November 1923

(To J.L.): To Jack Lindsay. The poem, like many of those Slessor wrote after meeting Norman and Jack Lindsay, presents the Lindsayan doctrine of transcendental experience gained through or imaged by passionate revelry.

1 *rout*: a group of revellers (archaic).

Rubens' Innocents

April 1921; *Vision*, May 1923; (P)

Rubens: Peter Paul Rubens (1577–1640), Flemish painter. Norman Lindsay regarded him as one of the greatest of all artists.

2 *cherubim*: winged child angels.

6 *Ganymedes*: young male figures. In Greek mythology Ganymede was a Trojan youth whom the god Zeus took to be his lover and cupbearer.

11 *to dark-faced clergy*: 'to staid old clergy' in *TOTM*.

17 *trice*: a moment.

18 *ichor*: in Greek mythology an ethereal fluid which flowed through the gods' veins.

20 *pardons*: in past Roman Catholic doctrine, remissions granted by priests of punishments on earth for sins committed.

21 *closes*: (a noun) cathedral precincts.

Adventure Bay

July 1923; *Vision*, November 1923; (P)

An allegory of male sexual exploration. In *Vision* the poem was published with an illustration by Norman Lindsay.

6 *waterspouts*: 'water-spouts' in *TOTM*.

Thieves' Kitchen

April 1923; *Vision*, August 1923; (P)

This poem is based on an etching with the same title by Norman Lindsay.

4 *Canary*: Canary Islands wine similar to sherry.

11 *main*: sea (here used metaphorically).

19 *Cyprian*: relating to Cyprus, famous for the worship of Venus, goddess of sexual love; sometimes a reference to prostitutes.

21 *Tyburn*: a London site, near Marble Arch, used for public hangings. *swart*: dark-complexioned (archaic).

'Quite Modern'

April 1922; *Art in Australia*, December 1924

On his father's side Slessor was descended from some highly regarded composers and musical performers, and he himself had a life-long interest in music.

14 *Stravinsky*: Igor Stravinsky (1882–1971), Soviet composer now regarded as one of the major composers of the twentieth century. In 1922 he was a very controversial avant-garde modernist composer. *'Ah, ma foi, quelle force!'*: literally, 'Ah, my faith, what power!' (French).

22 *Merry Peasant*: a short piece written for piano by Robert Schumann and often used in teaching children music.

23 *squall*: cry or scream.

Secret Pastures

May 1922

January 18, 1922

May 1922; *Vision*, May 1923

3 *shrine*: i.e. enshrine.
13 *Lady Helen*: presumably Helen of Troy.

Two Nocturnes

exact date not known, between 1917 and 1924

1 *magnifico*: a grand person.
2 *catafalque*: a grand bier for holding the body of a deceased person.
3 *Arakoon*: a town north of Kempsey, New South Wales, just south of Trial Bay.
5 *Red in the gums*: In his essay, 'Australian Verse — Light and Bad', Slessor ruefully recalled this phrase:

> I wrote a poem intended to be descriptive of evening in the bush, with the darkness falling, the moon shining through the gumtrees and so on. It was, I am afraid, a particularly bad Bad bit of Verse, and I remember only one line: 'Red in the gums, there floats a smoking moon.' I thought that wasn't a bad line until {a} writer in *Smith's Weekly* said: 'Red in the gums? Obviously gingivitis'. (*BW*, 154; or Haskell, 136–7)

9 *paven*: presumably 'paved', with some suggestion of 'pavé', meaning bejewelled.
10 *oriel-eyed*: having bay windows.
12 *phosphor*: phosphorus (i.e. luminescence).
14 *vermilion*: mistakenly printed as 'vermillion' in *TOTM*.
17 *Doré*: Gustave Doré (1833–83), French artist and illustrator. Slessor admired his work. He refers to it in a newspaper article, 'Storm Winds', written in December 1920 (see Haskell, 205).
18 *Morse*: Morse code.

Threatenings

exact date not known, between 1917 and 1924

3 *panaches*: tufts of feathers, worn in hats.
10 *flumes*: deep, narrow channels.
Kurrajong: type of tree, common in eastern Australia.
23 *opuscules*: short literary or musical works.

28 *sarcenets*: fine silk fabrics.
31 *steppes*: plains.
32 *brasier-dregs*: last pieces of coal, charcoal or other heating fuel.
33 *scrofulous*: diseased, as in tuberculosis.
slag-red: red as the dross created in refining metal from ore.
37 *Murrumbidgee*: a river in New South Wales.

Pan at Lane Cove

December 1920; *Art in Australia*, May 1922; (P)

Pan: Greek god of woods and pastures and of pastoral fertility. He played the Pan-pipes, a kind of flute, and was often associated with sexual frivolity. Pan, fauns and centaurs figured prominently in the art of Norman Lindsay.
Lane Cove: a suburb of Sydney, north-west of the city area.

1 *Scaly with poison, bright with flame*: 'In phosphor-green and gules and flame' in *TOTM*.
5 *pitchy*: dark-coloured; or perhaps, uneven — with some suggestions of musical pitch.
6 *seignior*: a lord of a manor.
9 *faun*: in Roman mythology a pastoral god, lower in stature than Pan.
10 *skies where no Immortals hide*: i.e. Australian skies where the gods of Roman and Greek mythology have never resided.
13 *Your*: 'Thy' in *TOTM*.
Hellas: ancient name for Greece.
14 *Cyclades*: a group of islands off Greece, in the Aegean Sea.
15 *you are*: 'thou art' in *TOTM*.
17 *your*: 'thy' in *TOTM*.
20 *Indiaman*: a merchant ship trading goods obtained in India.
24 *your . . . you*: 'thy . . . thou' in *TOTM*.
25 *Chiron*: one of the leading centaurs
your: 'thy' in *TOTM*.
27 *campanili*: bell towers (Italian).
28 *Clontarf*: a suburb of Sydney, east of Lane Cove.
30 *Paynim*: pagan (archaic).

31 *Samian*: relating to Samos, an island in the Aegean Sea.
32 *your*: 'thy' in *TOTM*.
35 *sandals*: Greek and Roman gods were often depicted wearing sandals.
36 *Ionian*: Ionia was an area of ancient Greece.

Clocks

July 1921

This is the first poem in which Slessor contrasts subjective and objective concepts of time, a major theme in his work, including 'Five Bells', which also uses the image of 'flood'.

1 *trows*: believes (archaic).
6 *doméd citadels*: i.e. observatories.
19 *horology*: the science of measuring time.

New Magic

May 1922; *Vision*, August 1923

14 *Antwerp*: the province or the city in Belgium; Antwerp blue is a well-known artist's colour.
23 *gardens*: mistakenly printed as 'garden' in *TOTM*.
verdigris: green or blue film that forms on copper, bronze or brass.

For Noela

dated by Slessor 25 December 1921, presumably written not long before

Noela: Noela Senior (1905–45), Slessor's first wife.

4 *Noel*: i.e. Noël; Noela Senior was born on Christmas day.
6 *seigniors*: lords of manors; Slessor is punning on Noela's maiden name, 'Senior'.
10 *fairings*: gifts brought from a fair.

Amazement

exact date not known, between 1917 and 1924

The dullness of observation produced by habit was one of Slessor's prominent concerns in his early journalism. (See 'Force of Habit', Haskell, 203–5.)

14 *Nine Lands*: a reference to ancient China, especially used in poetry.

The Hidden Lands

exact date not known, between 1917 and 1924

3 *southing snipe*: snipe birds flying south during the northern hemisphere winter.

6 *cylinders*: i.e. the thousand planes of line 2; the 'nomads of the middle air' in line 5 are their pilots and passengers. This poem was probably written in the early 1920s when aeroplanes were still an unusual sight. Some of Slessor's early journalism, written for the Sydney *Sun*, described the experience of flying and the new perspective on the world which it gave.

7 *Dandaloo*: a town in New South Wales, west of Dubbo.

12 *picaroons*: pirates, rogues.

Before the Rain

exact date not known, between 1917 and 1924

6 *sans*: without (French).

14 *bucklered swarm*: an army carrying shields.

15 *argosy*: a ship or ships carrying valuable cargo.

Marco Polo

October 1920; (P)

Marco Polo: Venetian adventurer (c. 1254–1324) who spent approximately 17 years in China and became an ambassador for Kublai Khan. His experiences are recounted in his book, *The Travels of Marco Polo*, first printed in 1477.

2 *bridle-path*: a path used by riders or walkers of horses.
Kanbalu: a city in present day Burma, north of Mandalay.

3 *Forgotten fibres wake to flame*: 'My fibres wake in writhing flame' in *TOTM*.

4 *And smoke*: 'To smoke' in *TOTM*.

5 *in a bygone life of mine*: an imaginative notion adopted for the sake

of the poem. Slessor did not elsewhere express any belief in reincarnation except in the poem 'Simone', which toys with the idea.

7 *Kublai's*: belonging to Kublai (or Kubla) Khan (1215–94), the first *khan*, or ruler, in the Mongol dynasty of thirteenth-century China.

8 *wyverns*: winged monsters.

11 *verdigris*: see 'New Magic' (*TOTM*), line 23n.

15 *Tree of Life*: God planted the tree of life in the middle of the Garden of Eden. Anyone who ate its fruit would live forever. (See Genesis 2: 9 and 3: 22.)

19 *topaz*: yellow sapphire or quartz, or a mineral of varied colours.

21 *cornelian*: a semi-transparent quartz.

22 *aqueduct*: water channel.

25 *Tartars*: members of Mongolian, Turkish or similar tribes.

26 *balustrades*: railings, as on parapets or stairs.

27 *maces*: war clubs.

28 *turquoise-hafted*: turquoise-handled.

40 *aflare*: 'a-flare' in *TOTM*.

Old Chinese Poem

exact date not known, between 1917 and 1924

Slessor's poem is an adaptation of number 12 of 'Seventeen Old Poems' translated by Arthur Waley in his *One Hundred & Seventy Chinese Poems* (London: Constable, 1918, 45–6). Arthur Waley (1889–1966) was an influential Sinologist whose translations of Chinese poetry influenced Ezra Pound and W.B. Yeats; like Slessor, he experienced a change from a German name during the First World War, his father changing the family name from 'Schloss'. Waley's translation reads:

> I drive my chariot up to the Eastern Gate;
> From afar I see the graveyard north of the Wall.
> The white aspens how they murmur, murmur;
> Pines and cypresses flank the broad paths.

Beneath lie men who died long ago;
Black, black is the long night that holds them.
Deep down beneath the Yellow Springs,
Thousands of years they lie without waking.

In infinite succession light and darkness shift,
And years vanish like the morning dew.
Man's life is like a sojourning,
His longevity lacks the firmness of stone and metal.
For ever it has been that mourners in their turn were
mourned,
Saint and Sage, — all alike are trapped.
Seeking by food to obtain Immortality
Many have been the dupe of strange drugs.
Better far to drink good wine
And clothe our bodies in robes of satin and silk.

Taoist

November 1920; *Art in Australia*, February 1923; (P)

Taoist: A follower of Taoism, an influential ancient Chinese philosophy whose central book is the *Tao-te Ching*, attributed to Lao-Tzu. Taoism is a quietist philosophy which stresses natural action and natural states, and avoidance of possessing or of investing one's ego in things external to the self. It is opposed to all artificial ways and organisations.

1 *Lao-Tzu*: Lao Tan, called 'Lao Tzu' ('Master Lao'), to whom is attributed authorship of the *Tao-te Ching*, the central book of Taoism. Chinese tradition says that he was born c. 600 BC and that Confucius was one of his pupils.

3 *tomes*: large books.

6 *To dog the path*: 'To trace the runes' in *TOTM*.

9 *mandarins*: senior Chinese officials
mages: magicians or astrologers (archaic).

13 *'Repenting always . . .'*: These lines are adapted from a poem, 'Taoist Song', by Chi K'ang (223–262), translated by Arthur Waley in his *One Hundred & Seventy Chinese Poems* (64). Waley's translation reads:

Taoist Song

I will cast out Wisdom and reject Learning.
My thoughts shall wander in the Great Void
Always repenting of wrongs done
Will never bring my heart to rest.
I cast my hook in a single stream;
But my joy is as though I possessed a Kingdom.
I loose my hair and go singing;
To the four frontiers men join in my refrain.
This is the purport of my song:
'My thoughts shall wander in the Great Void.'

19 *Star-Chamber*: tribunal or court which operates by unjust or arbitrary methods, and often secretly.

An Old Harp

exact date not known, between 1917 and 1924; *Bulletin*, 30 October 1919.

Slessor's poem is an adaptation of a poem by Po Chü-I (772–846), a popular poet of lyric clarity who was concerned with the moral dimension of literature. The poem was translated by Arthur Waley and included in his *One Hundred & Seventy Chinese Poems* (125). Waley's translation reads:

The Old Harp

Of cord and cassia-wood is the harp compounded:
Within it lie ancient melodies.
Ancient melodies weak and savourless,
Not appealing to present men's taste.
Light and colour are faded from the jade stops:
Dust has covered the rose-red strings.
Decay and ruin came to it long ago,

But the sound that is left is still cold and clear.
I do not refuse to play it, if you want me to:
But even if I play, people will not listen.
. . . .
How did it come to be neglected so?
Because of the Ch'iang flute and the Ch'in flageolet*.

*Barbarous modern instruments.

1 *cassia*: timber from the cinnamon tree, originally from southern China.
7 *stops*: knobs on the harp frame used to tune the strings.
8 *sorrel*: light reddish brown in colour.
10 *verdigris*: see 'New Magic', line 23n.

Chessmen

November 1920; (P)

Slessor and his father played keen chess matches. Slessor's sister, Maud, was also an enthusiast and married a chess champion, Maurice Goldstein.

2 *paladins*: heroic champions.
6 *tobacco-steam*: 'Latakian steam' in *TOTM*. Latakia is the name of both a city and a region on the west coast of Syria.
13 *counter-plots from old Arabian books*: Chess was introduced into western Europe by the Arabs.

April 25

April 1921; *The Sun*, 25 April 1921

April 25 is Anzac Day, the day on which Australians remember those who served, and particularly those who died, in war. Marches are held throughout the country and it is regarded as one of the most important days in the Australian calendar.

Simone

exact date not known, probably between 1918 and 1919; *Bulletin*, 23 October 1919

This poem seems a forerunner to the light verse which Slessor published in *Smith's Weekly* during the 1920s and 1930s.

10 *a life I forget*: see note to 'Marco Polo', line 5.

Some New Poets

exact date not known, between 1917 and 1924

1 *prate*: speak foolishly.
homunculi: very small people, dwarves.
2 *amain*: vigorously.
5 *reechy*: smoky, dirty, or rancid (archaic).
9 *danse macabre*: dance of death.

The Embarkation for Cythera

September 1923; *Vision*, February 1924

Cythera: Cythera, an island off the southern Peloponnesus, was one of the main centres of the cult of Aphrodite, Greek goddess of love. The poem is an allegory for the experience of sexual love, or, more precisely, of its anticipation. Slessor's poem seems closely related to the painting 'A Pilgrimage to Cythera' (1717), now in the Louvre, by the French painter Jean-Antoine Watteau (1684–1721); it may also be influenced by the poem '*Un Voyage à Cythère*' by the French poet Charles Baudelaire (1821–67).

7 *postillions*: generally horse riders who watch over the horses when they are pulling carriages.
12 *Spanish Main*: seas controlled by the Spanish.
13 *Spars*: masts or yards.
14 *cherubim*: see 'Rubens' Innocents', line 2n.
15 *undines*: see 'Undine'.
19 *Infanta*: a princess, daughter of the king of Spain.
21 *lemans*: lovers, mistresses (archaic).
31 *Cyprian's*: Cyprus was another principal site for the worship of Aphrodite. See 'Thieves' Kitchen', line 19n.

The Man of Sentiment

Part One

March 1923; *Vision*, May 1923; (P)

Sentiment: an eighteenth-century cult of sensibility, concerned with education of the heart and a strong capacity for delicate sympathy with people, creatures, art and nature. *Tristram Shandy* is the prototypical 'Sentimental' novel.

1 *A walled garden of York*: 'SCENE — This is 1759 in a walled garden of York' in *TOTM.*

2 *Laurence Sterne*: 1713–68, author of *Tristram Shandy* and *A Sentimental Journey*.

3 *prebendary*: a clergyman who receives an income from the church. Sterne early in his career became a prebendary of York Minster.
Catherine de Fromantel: Also known as Catherine (or Kitty) de Fourmentelle or Fourmantel. A young woman with whom Sterne had an affair, probably Platonic. She moved from York to London once Sterne was there as a result of the success of *Tristram Shandy*.

4 *Ranelagh*: a fashionable resort by the Thames in Chelsea, London, where concerts were held. Sterne frequented it often and tried to arrange singing engagements there for Catherine de Fromantel.

23 *bergamot*: a type of small citrus tree.

24 *Notaries*: officials, especially solicitors.

26 *Oh*: 'oh' in *TOTM.*

29 *duennas*: chaperones.
Dutch garden: a garden with trees clipped into unusual shapes and with long serpentine or straight walks.

51 *St Michael's*: St Michael-le-Belfrey, a church in York.

52 *prinking*: showy, elaborate.

53 *turnpike*: barrier, toll gate.

56 *ambulation*: walking.

80 *Plato*: Athenian philosopher (c. 427–347 BC); Plato's *Symposium* presents spiritual love as the highest love.

81 *Platonic*: 'Platonick' in *TOTM.*

84 *authentic*: 'authentick' in *TOTM.*

88 *Orris-root*: type of Iris with a root used for fragrance.

95 *taboured*: made music similar to the playing of a tabour, a small drum.

96 Holbein's *Dance*: a book of engravings of the Dance of Death

published 1524–26 by the German artist Hans Holbein the Younger (1497–1543).

98 *Voluptuary*: person given to licentious pleasure.

99 *New-greased*: 'New greased' in *TOTM*.
pomatum: scented fluid used on the scalp or hair.

101 *Yorick*: Parson Yorick is a character in *Tristram Shandy*. Sterne adopted the name of the dead jester in *Hamlet* as a pseudonym, publishing his sermons under the title *The Sermons of Mr Yorick*, and *A Sentimental Journey* as *A Sentimental Journey Through France and Italy, by Mr Yorick*.

103 *Peruked*: wearing a wig.

110 *Like pennies*: 'In sweet bravado' in *TOTM*.
secret breasts: 'breasts' in TOTM.

112 *Janatone*: the beautiful daughter of the innkeeper at Montreuil, France, whom Sterne describes in *Tristram Shandy* (Book VIII, Ch. 9).
apricocks: apricots.

114 *Dimity*: a strong cotton cloth, apparently thought by Slessor to be a light material. In 'Once a Year' (*UP*), the mistake is repeated.

117 *Mechlin lace*: type of lace originally made in Mechlin, Belgium.

119 *Satin*: 'Sattin' in *TOTM*.

121 A stanza break followed 'Sorrows . . .' in *TOTM*.

129 *my Wife*: Elizabeth Lumley, whom Sterne married in l741. With Sterne pursuing various sentimental love affairs, she became mentally unstable. She lived apart from Sterne, in France.

The Man of Sentiment

Part Two

March 1923; *Vision*, August 1923; (P)

In *TOTM* Norman Lindsay provided an illustration of Sterne and Catherine. Slessor's comments on it provide his sense of the characters:

> The girl is captivating, and I can see that she has the right sort of humourous [*sic*] twinkle ambushed in her eyes. Of course, if she hadn't had a sense of the comic, she would either have strangled

Sterne on the spot or locked herself in the pantry. Possessing that delicious bubble of fun which you have caught, she finds herself amused. As for Sterne, the sly female face which you have given him is exactly what I had pictured. (ML MSS 742/14/73b–74)

2–3 Catherine's mother is examining the contents of a chest: *'Catherine's mother at a chest'* in *TOTM*.

5 *Calcavillo*: presumably Calcavellos, sweet white Portuguese wine.

6 *Comfits*: sugar-coated sweets.
Eau de Chypre: perfume from Cyprus.

11 Fête Aqueuse: celebrations to take place upon the water.

12 *mirror*: 'mirrour' in *TOTM*.

13 *Cotillon*: type of lively dance.

14 *Mr Campbell*: Colin Campbell (?–1729), Scottish architect of English country houses who published three volumes of prints of English architectural works.

16 *lacker*: lacquer.

18 *Your*: 'Thy' in *TOTM*.

27 *Satin*: 'Sattin' in *TOTM*.

40 *indites*: composes.

46 *lanthorns*: lanterns.

76 *Ridottos*: public balls, often in masquerade.
Fêtes Champêtres: country parties.

80 *Carlton House*: London home of the Prince of Wales.

89 *Ouse*: river that flows through the city of York.

99 *Platonic*: 'Platonick' in *TOTM*.

120 *your*: 'thy' in *TOTM*.
mechanics: 'mechanicks' in *TOTM*.

123 *rustic*: 'rustick' in *TOTM*.

125 *your*: 'thy' in *TOTM*.

131 *mirror*: 'mirrour' in *TOTM*.

147 *romantic*: 'romantick' in *TOTM*.

151 Left: *'left'* in *TOTM*.

152 *your*: 'thy' in *TOTM*.

153 *You*: 'Thou' in *TOTM*.

157 *clip*: kiss.

169 *Mirror*: 'Mirrour' in *TOTM*.

Slessor wrote about the poem's ending to Norman Lindsay:

> In the second part of the Man of Sentiment, I have carried the contact of the girl and the priest to what seems its only logical conclusion — Sterne's contemptuous rejection [i.e. the rejection of Sterne] on Catherine's discovery that he floated merely in 'sentiment', a word of his own invention. (ML MSS 742/14/73b–74)

Earth-Visitors

(London: Fanfrolico Press, 1926)

The book was dedicated to Noela Slessor, with her name misspelt 'Noella', and included illustrations by Norman Lindsay. *Earth-Visitors* reproduced, unchanged, many poems published in *Thief of the Moon*. The notes that follow cover only poems first collected in *Earth-Visitors*. Altogether *Earth-Visitors* included the following poems, and in this order; those previously published in *Thief of the Moon* are marked '(*TOTM*)':

Winter Dawn
Music
Incongruity (*TOTM*)
Nuremberg (*TOTM*)
Realities
The Ghost (*TOTM*)
Earth-Visitors
A Surrender (*TOTM*)
Next Turn
The Embarkation for Cythera (*TOTM*)

Good-Night (*TOTM*)
The Mask (*TOTM*)
Undine (*TOTM*)
Marco Polo (*TOTM*)
A Sunset
Taoist (*TOTM*)
Heine in Paris
Adventure Bay (*TOTM*)
Stars
Thieves' Kitchen (*TOTM*)
Pan at Lane Cove (*TOTM*)
Rubens' Innocents (*TOTM*)
Mangroves (*TOTM*)
New Magic (*TOTM*)
Chessmen (*TOTM*)
April 25 (*TOTM*)
The Night-Ride
Melbourne
City Nightfall
January 18, 1922 (*TOTM*)
Clocks (*TOTM*)
'Quite Modern' (*TOTM*)
The Man of Sentiment (*TOTM*)

Thus, ten poems in *Thief of the Moon* were not included in *Earth-Visitors*, viz. 'Two Nocturnes', 'Threatenings', 'For Noela', 'Amazement', 'The Hidden Lands', 'Before the Rain', 'Old Chinese Poem', 'An Old Harp', 'Simone' and 'Some New Poets'. None of these ten poems was selected for *One Hundred Poems*.

Winter Dawn

completed July 1924; (P)

35 *morning air*: 'morning-air' in *E-V.*

Music

February 1926; first published *London Aphrodite*, No. 1, 1928; (P)

In *London Aphrodite* the poem had only nine sections. The present IV, V and VII were added in *Earth-Visitors*. Number VII was originally a separate poem.

In a letter to Julian Croft dated 23 April 1966 (NLA MS 3020/1/549) Slessor commented:

> The poems are not strictly tied to particular musical sources but in general they were influenced by certain kinds of music experienced while writing them, roughly as follows:
>
> 1, Wagner. 2, Wagner. 3, Beethoven. 4, Beethoven. 5, Stravinsky. 6, Borodin. 7, Beethoven. 8, Wagner. 9, Wagner. 10, Chopin. 11, Rimsky-Korsakov.

This accords with a copy of *Earth-Visitors* held in NLA where the attributions are in Noela Slessor's handwriting. Slessor's friend Alexander MacDonald, writing in the *Sydney Morning Herald* on 9 December 1967, reported Slessor as giving two different attributions: no. IV to Stravinsky rather than Beethoven, and VII to Mozart rather than Beethoven. It seems certain that MacDonald was mistaken. Some critics have attempted to detail links between the poem 'sequence' (as Slessor described it) and particular pieces of music, especially A.K. Thomson and Bev. Sherry in Thomson, 184–203.

I

1 *Music*: i.e. the god, Music.

4 *Tuscan*: from Tuscany in Italy.

9 *Valkyrs*: an abbreviation for 'Valkyries', warrior maidens in Wagner's opera *The Valkyries*, who took the bodies of fallen heroes to Valhalla, the palace of the gods; there the heroes were given eternal life in the service of Wotan.

15 *Vulcanals*: forges or the blacksmiths who operate them. Vulcan was the Roman god of fire. The allusion here seems to be to the transformation of the fallen heroes into immortal figures.

18 *Tartars*: See 'Marco Polo', line 25n. The Tartars were famous as warriors.

II

21 *unguents*: ointments.

34 Tristan: the hero of Wagner's opera *Tristan and Isolde*. He and his lover Isolde are betrayed and parted, Tristan receiving a fatal wound. A faithful servant carries the dying Tristan to a ship which sets sail for Tristan's castle in Brittany, where Tristan hopes to meet Isolde again. In *E-V* the name was not italicised.

III

51 A stanza break followed the word 'hide . . .' in *E-V*.

52 *Nonie*: a fictional name.

IV

Slessor commented on this poem in his essay, 'Writing Poetry: The Why and the How':

> In another early poem, from the sequence called 'Music', I tried to find a form to express the monotony and the loneliness of a stream of water running through flat, empty, manless, noiseless, enormous plains — and I tried to do this by using a flat monotonous rhythm with a down-fall at the end of each line's last double-syllabled word. (*S*, No. 3, 1948; rpt Thomson, 153)

62 A stanza break followed the word 'grasses' in *E-V*.

V

In 'Writing Poetry: The Why and the How' Slessor said of this poem: 'form can . . . be used to reflect excitement, movement and colour . . . The form here depends on the confections of rhyme with a strong, quick, music-hall beat, and is, in fact, quite traditional in its formality'(*S*, No. 3, 1948; Thomson, 154).

78 A stanza break followed the word 'faces' in *E-V*.

88 *waggon-jacks*: jacks to lift waggons, which were made of wood and therefore squeaked when used.

91 *watch it rise, buy*: 'watch it rise, wise guys, buy' in *E-V*.

99 Petroushka's: 'Petroushka' is the Russian version of Punch. Stravinsky's ballet *Petrouschka* presents a carnival in St Petersburg, with a puppet stall as the central attraction. The puppet master claims to be a magician. (He is actually a charlatan.) The name was not italicised in *E-V*.

VI

103 *Konchak's*: a reference to Khan Konchak, the Tartar leader in the opera *Prince Igor* by Aleksandr Borodin (1834–87). (The opera was actually completed by Rimsky-Korsakov and Glazounov.) Konchak captures the Russian prince, Igor, in battle but treats him with great respect, and entertains him with exotic music and dancing. The name was printed 'Kolchak's' in *E-V*.

107 *mare's milk*: Thomson and Sherry (see introductory note to poem, above) point out that the drinking of mare's milk was a serious Tartar ritual. Konchak's drinking mare's milk with Igor is a sign of his respect for Igor (Thomson, 196–7).

113 *Konchak*: 'Kolchak' in *E-V*.

VII

136 *sentimentalist*: see introductory note to 'The Man of Sentiment, Part One'.

VIII

144 *Juno's*: In Roman mythology Juno was the goddess of marriage and of childbirth. She was associated with the moon.

148 Siegmund: a heroic warrior in *The Valkyries*. The first half of the poem is spoken by Sieglinde, who is attempting to save Siegmund from death at the hands of her husband, Hunding. Siegmund has taken refuge in their house, and Sieglinde wakes him, just before moonlight floods into the room, in order to let him escape. In fact, Siegmund and Sieglinde are twin children of Wotan, king of the gods, but each meets a tragic end. The name *Siegmund* was not italicised in *E-V*.

IX

Thomson and Sherry claim that 'the person addressed in this poem is the moon, symbolizing the passions of earthly lovers' (Thomson, 200).

X

In 'Writing Poetry: The Why and the How' (*S*, No. 3, 1948; Thomson, 155) Slessor said that in this poem 'the remote, unfinished, frustrated feeling of some of Chopin's music is perhaps expressed . . . by means of half-rhymes which echo with their vowels but not their consonants'.

200 *gourds*: see 'Undine', line 5n.

XI

226 *cassia-tree*: The harp in 'An Old Harp' (*TOTM*) is made of cassia.

XII

231 *pressed*: 'presst' in *E-V.*

235 *Orpheus*: in Greek mythology the son of Apollo whose music could charm even the gods. He is the divine archetype of all musicians and poets.

Realities

July 1924; (P)

1 *the statues*: the statues in Norman Lindsay's garden at Springwood, New South Wales.

10 *Mercury*: in Roman mythology the god of merchants and the gods' messenger.

16 *Faun*: see 'Pan at Lane Cove', line 9n.

20 *Tritons*: in Greek mythology sea gods, with merman bodies.

21 *Apollo*: in Greek mythology one of the most important gods; he had many functions, being a sun god, a pastoral god, a god of music and poetry, and a god of prophecy. He was the son of Zeus.

27 *dancers*: 'wenches' in *E-V.*

30 *Life*: In his theorising Norman Lindsay distinguished sharply between 'Life' with a capital 'L', deeply meaningful consciousness and experience, and mere 'Existence'. (See especially *Creative Effort*, Sydney: Art in Australia, 1920.) Lindsay used figures from classical mythology to symbolise 'Life'.

39 *Cythera*: see 'The Embarkation for Cythera', introductory note.

44 *your*: 'thy' in *E-V.*

Earth-Visitors

September 1924; (P)

(*To N.L.*): To Norman Lindsay. In deference to Lindsay, Slessor placed this poem first in editions of his selected poems.

4 *Princes gone feasting, barons with gipsy eyes*: 'Princes gone wenching, barons with sable masks' in *E-V.*

6 *Tartary*: area ruled by the Tartars. See 'Marco Polo', line 25n.

10 *Post-boys*: postillions. See 'The Embarkation for Cythera', line 7n.

28 *Mercury*: see 'Realities', line 10n.

32 *To vex a farm-girl*: 'To clash the wench's mind' in *E-V.*

33 *Cloth of Gold*: a generalised reference, rather than a phrase drawn from any particular myth.

43 *Springwood*: a town in the Blue Mountains, west of Sydney, near which Norman Lindsay lived.

Next Turn

October 1924; (P)

The punning title refers to the next performance in the (allegorical) theatre and to death, and also suggests the colloquial Australian usage of 'turn' to mean sudden illness.

2 *Antic*: clown.

3 *Columbine*: a traditional theatre figure, in Italian comedy the mistress of Harlequin.

8 *Footmen*: servants; here both theatre ushers and undertakers or agents of death.

14 *Plumed with black trees*: horse-drawn carriages used as hearses carried large black feathers.
Post-boys: postillions. See 'The Embarkation for Cythera', line 7n.

A Sunset

February 1926; (P)

5 A stanza break followed the word 'trails' in *E-V*.

Heine in Paris

June 1924; (P)

Heine: Heinrich Heine (1797–1856), generally regarded as the most important nineteenth-century German poet. Heine was born in Düsseldorf, moved to Hamburg in 1816 and to Paris in 1831. In 1848 he suffered a paralysing stroke and was confined to bed until his death. The poem is set at the end of Heine's life.

In a letter written in March 1971 Slessor named Heine as an influence on his work (NLA MS 3020/1/73g). In an article in *Quadrant* in April 1978 (pp. 56–9) Margaret Rose claims verbal links between Slessor's poem and Heine's work.

6 *mail*: armour.

8 *La Mouche*: Elise Krinitz, whom Heine called '*Die Mouche*' (The Fly) after the fly on her crest. She visited Heine regularly during the last months of his life and one of his last poems is titled '*La Mouche*'.

10 *Mercutio*: a name for a clown.
Miss Nellie: a fictional name for a circus horse rider.

12 'Mon dieu, quelle cirque!': literally, 'My god, what a circle [of friends]!' (French). The words were not italicised in *E-V*.
Madame Stephanie: a fictional name.

20 'Eighteen Twenty-Nine': Heine actually left Hamburg for Paris in 1831. Letters of 1829 reveal that Heine thought he had dried up as a poet and began writing prose.

25 *Uncle Solomon*: Heine's uncle, Salomon, was a Hamburg merchant

who gave Heine employment, accommodation and money in Heine's early years. Nevertheless Heine was very unhappy in his uncle's house, and while on his sickbed in Paris wrote a poem, '*Affrontenburg*' ('Château Affronteries') recounting his hatred of the experience.

29 *Amalie*: Heine's cousin, the daughter of Uncle Salomon, with whom he fell in love; his feelings were not reciprocated. In his early poetry Heine often depicted himself as standing longingly below her window.

36 *Louise, Diana, and Jenny*: probably fictional names, although Heine in 1832 did write a poem 'To Jenny', a girl who was fifteen, twenty years younger than Heine.

60 *Meyerbeer*: Giacomo Meyerbeer (1791–1864), German operatic composer of Jewish descent.
Borne: Ludwig Börne (1786–1837), German political satirist of Jewish descent who settled in Paris in 1830.
Klopstock: Friedrich Gottlieb Klopstock (1724–1803), German poet who worked in Hamburg. Heine often visited his grave while dreaming of fame as a poet.

93 Christ Jesus: Heine was a Jew but became a Protestant in 1825, at least partly in order to graduate from the University of Göttingen. Slessor was of Jewish descent on his father's side.

Stars

June 1924; (P)

2 *drop their harvest*: 'blow their fruitage' in *E-V.*

7 *Cyprian*: see 'Thieves' Kitchen', line 19n.

11 *link-boys*: servants, like Cupids, linked to Venus.

15 *romantic*: 'romantick' in *E-V.*

21 *Cross*: the Southern Cross, the star constellation; but the Christian cross may also be inferred by many readers.

The Night-Ride

August 1924; (P)

Night-Ride: a train ride at night, but here also an allegory for dying.

10 *Fates*: in Greek and Roman mythology, the three daughters of Night who represented destiny. Atropos, the third of the Fates, could not be appealed to; she cut the thread of life.

17 *Rapptown*:'Bargo' in *E-V*. Slessor wrote to Herbert Jaffa (NLA MS 3020/1/711) that:

'Bargo' was changed to 'Rapptown' to avoid identification with the near-Sydney town of Bargo, once a small country district, now almost a metropolitan suburb. 'Rapptown' is an invented general name, in the spirit of small Australian (and American) town-names and cannot be identified with any specific place.

Melbourne

March 1926

Slessor lived in Melbourne from late 1924 to early 1926.

1 *mastodon*: a large extinct animal related to the elephant.

City Nightfall

March 1926; (P)

5 *lazar*: a diseased person, especially a leper; the word derives from Lazarus whom Jesus raised from the dead. (See Luke 16.) Dutton (107) draws a link with Christopher Brennan's *Poems (1913)*.

7 *Infanta's*: see 'The Embarkation for Cythera', line 19n.

13 *limed*: cemented, or caught. Birds were trapped by using lime.

Cuckooz Contrey

(Sydney: Frank C. Johnson, 1932)

The Atlas

completed December 1930; (P)

In *CC* Slessor included a note which read: 'For much of the information concerning the subjects of these poems, also the prefatory quotation [*sic*], the author is indebted to the catalogue, "Old Maps of the World", published by Francis Edwards Ltd., of London'. In a 1966 letter to Julian Croft, Slessor said of 'The Atlas': 'I derived the ideas of these poems from a catalogue of *Old Maps of the World* . . . The prefatory quotations describing the maps come from the catalogue' (NLA MS 3020/1/549). Slessor also comments in the letter: 'My interest in the sea and seafarers certainly increased greatly because of the stimulus and information given by Captain Bayldon and his library'. Francis Bayldon (1872–1948), a retired sea captain, was an uncle of Slessor's first wife, Noela; Slessor and Noela visited him weekly in the 1920s (see Dutton, 142–4). For more on Bayldon see Slessor's comments in 'Five Visions of Captain Cook', introductory n. Bayldon's library collection is now held in the Mitchell Library, Sydney.

In drafts the poem that was to become 'Lesbia's Daughter' was section 3 of 'The Atlas' and was titled 'Lost Lands'.

In the diary which he used for drafting poems, Slessor wrote on the page dated 5 March 1927: 'If only world c[oul]d be like world of old mapmakers neatly parcelled into known and unknown . . . instead of which it is strange dark confusing baffling currents & whole [of] living is insubstantial' (NLA MS 3020/19/1).

1 *The King of Cuckooz*

Epigraph: The Platt [flat map] of Algiers and the Points adjoining within the view thereof made by Robert Norton the Master Mariner of his Master's Fleet there Anno Domini 1620 and by his own careful and diligent observations then not without danger.

In *CC* Slessor included a note which said: 'Robert Norton probably took part in the English expedition to Algiers sent against the Barbary pirates in 1620. On his manuscript map, the unknown hilly country to the south of the Bay is coloured green, and marked "Part of the King of Cuckooz Contrey". ("Argier", of course, is pronounced with the g soft, as in "Algiers".)' The 'Cuckooz' reference is to unknown country which thus becomes the province of the imagination.

2 *Argier*: Algiers.

3 *Janzaries*: a corruption of 'janizaries', Turkish soldiers composed of tributary children of Christians, persuasively converted to Islam and renowned for their fierce fighting.
Marabutts: jibsails hoisted in bad weather.

7 *basilisks*: brass cannons.

12 *dulcimers*: musical instruments, similar to zithers. The muse who inspired Coleridge's 'Kubla Khan' played one.

23 *curricle*: an open carriage.

31 *that Fowl*: i.e. the falcon of the King of Cuckooz Contrey mentioned in line 33.

34 *limed*: see 'City Nightfall' (*E-V*), line 13n.

36 *King James's*: King James I of England (and James VI of Scotland) (1566–1625).

40 *dainty leg*: i.e. of the falcon.

2 *Post-Roads*

Epigraph: 'Mr. Ogilby' is John Ogilby (1600–76), English author and printer who published many geographical works, including 'An Illustration of the Kingdom of England and Dominion of Wales, by a Geographical and Historical Description of the principal Roads thereof' (1675). 'Mensuration' is measurement.

49 *Post-roads*: roads with stations or inns for the benefit of travellers and horses. The mail was taken along such roads.
tympan: literally a sheet of metal; here, drum-like.

50 *tilburies*: light, open carriages.
spanking: moving vigorously.

54 *Escurials*: palaces; the Escorial or Escurial was the chief palace of Spanish monarchs.

57 *savanna*: grassy plain.
58 *ducts*: i.e. the post-roads.
59 *bastinadoes*: beatings.
61 *phaetons and fiacres, flys and breaks*: types of horse-drawn carriage.
65 *criniers*: armour for war horses.
69 *hackneys*: carriages used for hire.
70 *madeira*: a fortified wine originally from the island of Madeira.
71 *Fares*: people journeying in the carriages who paid to do so.
72 *spatulas*: broad flat implements.
74 *Guildford*: a town south-west of London.
76 *ecstasies*: misspelt as 'ecstacies' in earlier printings.

3 *Dutch Seacoast*

Epigraph: 'Towns of the United Netherlands illustrated and described, published by Joan. Blaeu.'

Johann Blaeu (1571–1638) was a Dutch author, cartographer and publisher of maps; from 1663 to 1667 he published a *Grand Atlas*, subtitled *Theatrum Mundi* (Theatre of the World), in twelve volumes.

In *CC* Slessor included a note which read:

> To see a Dutch town by Blaeu is to see how delightful the art of map-making can be made — little red houses neatly arranged in rows, with blue tiled roofs, churches and public buildings standing out above their neighbours, watermills turning merrily, not only the ocean but rivers and canals filled with shipping, shipbuilding in the yards, soldiers on the fortifications, mynheers walking down shady groves, even the very design of garden-plots being shown— the whole forms an animated scene of infinite brilliance.

4 *Mermaids*

Epigraph: John Speed (1628–1711) was an author, and mayor of Southampton who gathered a manuscript collection there.

In *CC* Slessor's note read: 'Speed's map is filled with pictures of ships at sea, mermaids and sea-monsters'.

118 *Ondines*: undines. See 'Undine' (*TOTM*).
Sirens: in Greek mythology sea nymphs, part-woman and part-bird, whose beautiful singing lured sailors to destruction.
119 *Kraken*: sea-monster.
120 *Firedrake*: dragon.
129 *portulano*: a book describing harbours, coasts and navigation routes.
130 *compass-roses*: illustrations on Speed's map.
134 *Jinns*: in Arabic mythology spirits that could take human or animal form.
135 *Anthropophagi*: cannibals.
136 *Antient*: ancient.
Palanquins: chairs or beds carried by poles resting on the carriers' shoulders.
141 *Harpies*: in Greek mythology, rapacious monsters, part-woman and part-bird.
153 *pisciform*: fish-like.
154 *Doctor Gerbrandus's*: a fictional name.

5 *The Seafight*

Epigraph: '[The] Mexican Archipelago where are the islands of Cuba, Spanish Jamaica etc.' Nicholas Sanson (1600–67) was a French cartographer.

In *CC* Slessor's note read: 'Published by P. Mortier, with a view of the country, natives, buccaneers, seafight, &c., in left-hand corner'.

159 *Tirduf*: a word imitating the sound of the cannons' firing. In *CC* Slessor included a quotation from his source:
Then quhar i sat i hard the cannons and gunnis mak mony hiddeus crak duf, duf, duf, duf, duf, duf, the barsis and falcos cryit tirduf, tirduf, tirduf, tirduf, tirduf, tirduf, than the smal artailye cryit tik tak, tik tak, tik tak, tik tak. — 'The Complaynt of Scotland', Robert Wedderburn (1549).
160 *collop*: cut or slice, especially used in regard to meat.
166 *jacks*: dice, or perhaps a reference to knuckle bones (of sheep) used in the game of 'jacks'.

180 *this dangerous planet*: In a note on 'Beach Burial' first published in the *Daily Telegraph* on 31 July 1967 (rpt *BW*, 200 and Haskell, 154), some forty years later, Slessor repeated the idea and phrasing used here, saying that humankind's 'hatreds, quarrels and wars should be dwarfed by the huger human struggle to survive against disease and cataclysms on this dangerous planet'.

Captain Dobbin

April 1929; (P)

In a 1962 television interview with John Thompson (reproduced in *S*, No. 3, 1966 and in Kiernan, 7) Slessor said: 'I had the fortune and privilege when I was younger of knowing an old, retired seacaptain, who had an astonishing knowledge of nautical things . . . — he'd been an old sailing-ship master, and also he had a magnificent library of nautical books'. Thompson then asked, 'That sounds rather like Captain Dobbin himself, doesn't it?', and Slessor answered, 'Well, yes. In some ways he was Captain Dobbin'. Slessor's reference is to Captain Bayldon (see 'The Atlas', introductory n.)

Slessor's note to the poem in *CC* cryptically says: '"Captain Dobbin's" debt to Herman Melville will be plain'. Slessor's reference is to Melville's *Omoo: A Narrative of Adventures in the South Seas*, first published in 1847. Thomson examines the 'debt' (16–18).

4 *colonial funds*: government bonds.

5 *Laburnum Villa*: a fictional name; a laburnum is a small bush with yellow flowers.

10 *Blue Funnel, Red Funnel, Messageries Maritimes*: the names of well-known shipping lines.

23 Comorin: a well-known ship at the time.

33 *urn-burial*: a vase holding the ashes of the dead.

42 *hydrostatics*: the scientific study of liquids.

43 *dropsy*: a disease involving excessive accumulation of fluids.

45 *quadrants*: navigational instruments.

55 *albicores*: a type of fish; they are mentioned in *Omoo.*

56 *admirals*: a type of fish.

57 *planters*: thieves.

58 *ambergris*: ash-coloured secretion of sperm whales, used in perfumes; it is mentioned in *Omoo.*

63 *marish*: from the sea.

68 *Queen Pomaree*: Queen Pomare of Tahiti (1827–77); in *Omoo* Melville describes her as 'sailing about from one island to another, attended by a licentious court; and wherever she went, all manner of games and festivities celebrated her arrival' (Ch. 80).

69 *Yankee's*: a number of American ships visited Tahiti in this period.

72 *calabashes*: bottles or pipes made from the shells of fruit from calabash trees; the word is used in *Omoo.*

79 *chanty*: shanty, a sailor's song, often sung to accompany work.

80 'Shenandoah': a well-known shanty
mew: a cat's sound.

82 *Neptune*: in Roman mythology the god of the sea.

84 'Stormalong': a well-known shanty, less melodious than 'Shenandoah'.

88 *lap-dogs*: small pet dogs.

91 *Pea-jackets*: a short woollen overcoat worn by sailors.

96 *Port au Prince*: the capital of Haiti.

98 *Captain Baggs*: a fictional name.

100 *cribbage*: a type of card game scored on a cribbage board.

101 *tops'l sheets*: ropes attached to the corners of the upper sails which let the sails in or out according to the direction of the wind.

106 *quarter-decks*: afterdecks or upper decks, sometimes reserved for officers.

112 *Odysseys*: epic voyages, as in that of Odysseus.

114 *lozenges*: diamond shapes.

117 *Merak and Alamak and Alpherat*: the names of stars.

129 *Hotoo*: a type of tree that grows in Tahiti; it is mentioned in *Omoo.*
palmetto: palm tree with fan-shaped leaves.

131 *Magellan*: Ferdinand Magellan (*c.*1480–1521), Portuguese mariner and explorer.

Bougainville: Louis Antoine de Bougainville (1729–1811), French navigator and scientist.

Cook: James Cook (1728–79), English mariner and explorer whose voyage of discovery to Australia in 1770 led to white settlement of the country.

140 *Sebastian Juan del Cano*: Juan Sebastian del Cano (?–1526), Spanish mariner and explorer; second in charge to Magellan, he took command when Magellan was killed in the Philippines (1521) and in 1522 completed the first circumnavigation of the world.

157 *Blue Funnel, Red Funnel*: the names of shipping lines.

160 *stokers*: sailors who loaded and tended the fire in steam ships.

Talbingo

July 1929; (P)

In *CC* Slessor included a note which said: 'This name is used at random, and the poem, of course, bears no geographical veracity'.

9 *Basalt*: a dark, dense rock created by lava flows.

13 *pocks*: literally, small swellings; but here probably an abbreviation for pock-holes, left by miners beside the mounds produced by their digging.

Gulliver

September 1926; (P)

Gulliver: Captain Lemuel Gulliver is the main character in Jonathan Swift's satire, *Gulliver's Travels* (1726). Gulliver voyages to a number of strange countries, the first of which is Lilliput, a nation of people one-twelfth the size of normal human beings. At first frightened of Gulliver, they tie him down with numerous strings and peg down his hair.

21 *turnkey*: main key for a prison, or the person in charge of the key.

Crow Country

November 1930; (P)

1 *station*: proper place or position in which to be found.
3 *nitrous*: containing nitrogen.
6 *riven*: split apart.
9 *abraded*: scraped off or worn away.
10 *graped*: peppered, as in 'grapeshot'.

Glubbdubdrib

August 1927; (P)

The third part of *Gulliver's Travels* (see 'Gulliver'), whose short title is 'A Voyage to Laputa', includes a visit to Glubbdubdrib, 'the Island of *Sorcerers* or *Magicians*'. Gulliver at first is apprehensive about the presence of spirits, but his companions are unconcerned. Gulliver dines with the Governor, who enables him to call up any spirits he wishes.

3 *potagers*: bowls, especially soup bowls.
6 *Lackeys*: servants.
9 *flunkey*: servant, or servile person.
19 *Catullus*: Gaius Valerius Catullus (*c.*84–*c.*54 BC), Roman lyric and satirical poet.
21 *Plato*: See 'The Man of Sentiment, Part One', line 81n. Plato believed in ideal 'forms' as eternal realities which were unattainable on earth.

The Nabob

December 1928; (P)

Nabob: a governor of a town or district in India.

William Hickey: (1749?–1830) was a bon viveur and charming rogue; he travelled many parts of the world but his *Memoirs* are best known for Hickey's period in pre-British Raj India, where he was a drinking companion of Colonel Wellesley (later Duke of Wellington) amongst others.

2 *Faust*: Johann (or Georg) Faust (*c.*1480–*c.*1540), an itinerant German scholar and magician. In the legends built about him he is so curious for learning and experience that he sells his soul to the devil, or to an evil spirit, in order to have more experiences.
4 *Roc's*: in Arabian mythology, an enormous bird.
6 *Yellow Jack*: (slang) yellow fever, a disease of hot climates which results in jaundice.
10 *hirelings*: mercenaries.
11 *Rajah*: Indian prince or dignitary.
12 *Madeira*: see 'Post-Roads' ('The Atlas, 2') line 70n.
13 *Bon de Paris*: best French jacket or coat.
14 *equipage*: a carriage, with servants.
16 *Post-Captains*: naval captains holding commissions, as distinguished from naval officers with 'captain' as a courtesy title.
18 *tureens*: covered dishes.
19 *provender*: food.
20 *pitchcocked*: filleted, cut into pieces and grilled well (archaic).
27 *bussing*: kissing.
36 *damned profession of writing*: In *CC* Slessor included a note which said: 'The phrase "this damned profession of writing" is quoted from Ezra Pound's poem, "The Lake Isle"'. Pound's poem, in part a parody of W.B. Yeats's 'The Lake Isle of Innisfree', ends with an imploring of the gods to 'install me in any profession / Save this damn'd profession of writing, / where one needs one's brains all the time'.

Five Visions of Captain Cook

May 1929; *Trio* [pamphlet with Harley Matthews and Colin Simpson], Sydney: Sunnybrook Press, 1931; (P)

In *CC* Slessor's note said:

> 'Five Visions of Captain Cook' is founded on literal fact, according to the narratives of Cook and the sailors who accompanied him. For an excellent marshalling of these details, the author is indebted to Captain F. J. Bayldon, of Sydney. Part

IV was suggested by an autobiographical verse by Captain Trevenen, who sailed with Cook on his third voyage as a midshipman. Part V was derived from the manuscript journal of Captain Alexander Home, who accompanied Cook on the same cruise, and who later retired totally blind to his home in Berwickshire, on a pension of half-a-crown a day. Captain Home was not an eyewitness of Cook's death, but he obtained details from those who had been ashore, and combined them in his journal into one of the most lucid accounts of the affair that has been preserved.

In a letter (dated only 'June 11') to Norman Lindsay, Slessor wrote:

> I'm enclosing some verses which may interest you, most of them in the rough. I don't know whether the Captain Cook series is successful, but they are an attempt to do something about one of the few figures in Australian history who really has dramatic possibilities, most of them obscured, unfortunately, by the clouds of academic rubbish raised in the school-books. (ML MSS 742 Vol. 14, f. 83; in Haskell, 265–6)

Slessor offered more extensive commentary on the poem in a 1965 lecture, asserting:

> The sequence of poems called 'Five Visions of Captain Cook' is, I think, quite straightforward in its intention and expression. It could be described as a sort of Identikit likeness, made by superimposing a number of aspects of Cook, seen through the eyes of various men who sailed with him, thus approaching perhaps a total portrait.
>
> The first vision of Cook is that of the ordinary seamen who manned his ships on the three great voyages. The second is that of some of the officers who served under him. The third is the view of history (denoted by the time-measuring instruments in Cook's cabin). The fourth is that of some of the midshipmen. The fifth is the vision of Cook which remained in the memory

of one of his companions many years after his death.

The whole work owes a great debt to a remarkable man whom I was once privileged to know and visit, Captain Francis Bayldon, who lived at Darling Point in the '20s and who died in 1948. Captain Bayldon was a sea-captain himself, if not of the 'powder days' at least of the clipper ship days of last century. From sail he transferred to steam in 1901 and commanded many Burns Philp vessels in the Pacific until 1910, charting previously unsurveyed anchorages for the Hydrographic Office. In 1910 he founded the Sydney Nautical School (in which hundreds of Australian merchant service officers have been trained). He was an authority on the history of Pacific navigation, especially on Torres and Cook, and his reconstruction of Cook's *Endeavour* was published as a plate. But above all he had a magnificent nautical library, more than a thousand books about the sea and seamen, logs, journals, learned papers, instruction manuals, maps and charts, many of them exceedingly rare and valuable . . .

Since he was my wife's uncle, I was allowed to browse through this collection on my weekly visits. Over a glass of sherry I was encouraged to ask questions, and his enthusiasm, his scholarly gusto and his astonishing knowledge of unfamiliar details soon infected me with his own worship of Cook. Indeed, all that I have written about Captain Cook I got from Captain Bayldon. The *Five Visions*, rough and incomplete as they seem to me still, are merely fragments of the image he built for me. (rpt in *BW*, 191–6 and Haskell, 144–9)

In a letter dated 10 September 1969 Slessor commented that 'my own notes on Five Visions were purposely simplified for school use' (NLA MS 3020/1/831).

I

This section concerns Cook's first voyage, in the *Endeavour* (1768–71).

In his 1965 lecture Slessor said:

In part 1, there are two principal themes — the contrast between the old kind of sea captain and the modern kind, and the crucial decision which brought Cook to the coast of Australia.

The ship's captain of the days of sail and 'powder' (gunpowder) was required to have some working knowledge of such things as mathematics, astronomy, navigation, chart-reading, sight-taking, foreign languages and elementary medicine, attainments which made him seem an almost supernatural being in the eyes of his crew, most of whom were unable to read or write. The simple sailors under his command did what they were bidden, sailed where they were taken, ate and drank what they were given, blindly confident that the magic of their captain (as it must have seemed to them) would preserve their lives from evil spirits, monsters and spells (some of them still believed in seaserpents) and convey them safely across unmapped seas and unknown lands.

Captains like this were indeed 'daemons in wigs', navigating by signs in the stars which they could read as easily as books, though to ordinary men the sky seemed just a tangle of constellations They gave their crews medicaments and drugs against disease (in Cook's case against scurvy), which seemed nonsense to the sailors but which they swallowed with childish faith. The success of such commanders depended above all on their personal qualities, their individual resources of courage, nerve, imagination, shrewdness and self-confidence.

'No laws of schoolbook steam' expresses this idea. The speed of a passage by sail (and in consequence its profitability to the owners of the ship) were often determined by the captain's daring and skill in such things as putting on full sail in a high wind and knowing when it could be done and at what risk. In modern days of steam and oil, the captain is limited by the purely mechanical factor of the ship's engines and their capacities. The boiler-plates will take just so much pressure before blowing up. There is no call, therefore, for the same kind of personal nerve or judgement in deciding what sails to use or risks to run. The modern skipper is often an 'executive of company rules', bound not to take any undue chances . . .

In the second section, we have Cook coming to the Coral Sea, at the north of the Australian coastline, after his voyage to New Zealand. This was the great turning-point for earlier explorers who depended on sails. If they went west, they turned against the prevailing winds, with no indication of how long their provisions would need to last, or what lay in store for them, or whether indeed they would ever come back. It was in every respect a 'passage into the dark'. But if they turned north, into Torres Strait, the winds would be with them all their way home through the Indian Ocean. It was a fateful decision to have to make, and most of those who confronted it — including Tasman and Bougainville — had chosen the path of prudence by sailing north. Bougainville recorded that he had heard 'the voice of God' advising him to take the safe way home to the north, away from the 'dead lee shore'. But Captain Cook, at these crossroads of navigation and history, determined to sail west instead of north, 'into the devil's mouth', and so came to the coastline of eastern Australia — and so, 160 years later, I was able to write this poem.' (*BW* 192–3; Haskell, 145–6)

3 *krakens*: see 'Mermaids' ('The Atlas, 4'), line ll9n.

4 *nativities*: horoscopes.

8 *companionways*: steps leading from a ship's deck down to a cabin, or the space the steps occupy.

9 *warlocks*: sorcerers, wizards.

11 *horn-eyed sailors*: sailors who imagine that they see the devil.

27 *sortilege*: sorcery.

28 *medicines*: Cook forced his sailors to drink broth made from vegetables and fruit, and so found a cure for scurvy.

31 *the Coral Sea*: part of the southern Pacific Ocean off the coast of Queensland and south of Papua New Guinea. There has been some controversy about the geographical directions referred to in the poem; the debate is summarised and commented on by Gerald

McCallum, 'Slessor's Cook: The Imprudent Hero', *Australian Literary Studies*, Oct. 1971, 176–8.

37 *Tasman*: Abel Janszoon Tasman (*c.*1603–59), Dutch navigator who discovered Tasmania, New Zealand, Tonga and Fiji and explored the north-west coast of Australia.

39 *Bougainville*: see 'Captain Dobbin', line 131n.

II

This section also concerns Cook's first voyage in the *Endeavour*.

50 *Joseph Banks*: (1743–1820), British botanist who accompanied Cook in his voyage on the Endeavour.

51 *Latin*: the language used for scientific nomenclature.

53 *Gorgon*: in Greek mythology the Gorgons were three sisters whose glance turned observers to stone.

54 *horticulture*: the science of growing plants.

59 *Cook sailed at night*: In his 1965 lecture Slessor commented:

Usually, in strange waters, particularly in such an area of hidden reefs and unsounded depths, sailing was done in daylight only. But such was Cook's confidence in his navigation and seamanship that he kept his vessel sailing in darkness as well . . . (*BW*, 194; Haskell, 147)

73 *sextants*: astronomical instruments used for determining latitude and longitude. In his 1965 lecture Slessor said:

The episode in which the ship narrowly missed hitting a coral reef while officers stood on deck taking their sights for longitude has been described by Captain Cook himself . . .

This is what Cook wrote: 'The same sea that washed the side of the ship rose in a breaker prodigiously high the very next time it did arise, so that between us and destruction was only a dismal valley, the breadth of one wave, and even now no ground could be felt with 120 fathoms. Messrs Green, Clerke and Forwood were engaged in taking a sight for the longitude.'

Alan Villiers remarked: 'For three of the most important officers in the ship calmly to proceed with the accumulation of precise data to work out laboriously some reasonable approximation of the longitude of the ship, when that same ship was five minutes from one of the nastiest pieces of reef in the Coral Sea, and when the great swell was edging them to their deaths — this is on a level with the great moments of the sea.'

(*BW*, 194–5; Haskell, 147–8)

80 *phylacteries*: amulets, containers or scrolls of religious significance.

81 *ride broomsticks*: In European folklore witches and other magical figures could fly on broomsticks.
mesmerist: hypnotist.

III

This section deals with Cook's second voyage, on the *Resolution*. In his 1965 lecture Slessor said:

In *part 3*, the allusion is to an aspect of the second voyage which would have made it memorable in history even if nothing else had been achieved. This time Cook took with him two recently invented chronometers, installed by the Admiralty for a trial of the new method of discovering longitude . . .

In the episode described in *part* 2, the officers used the 'lunar' method, involving complicated calculations, which was only a little less unsatisfactory than the even older method of the log line. Sir Isaac Newton suggested a new way, by the comparison of two clocks, one marking Greenwich time and the other the local time by the sun at sea. The great problem was to construct a clock which would keep absolutely accurate time through the vast range of temperature and humidity of a sea-voyage. Two famous English watchmakers supplied the chronometers for this historic experiment. One was made by John Arnold, a friend of Sir Joseph Banks, the other by Larcum Kendal from a prototype invented by John Harrison. After both had been tested for many months of Cook's voyage, it was found that Kendal's chronometer lost time (7 minutes, 45 seconds in three years) while Arnold's gained time. For the purpose of the poem, it is

> imagined therefore that Kendal lived in the past and Arnold in the future. (*BW*, 195; Haskell, 148)

Slessor offered a few more details about the clocks in a note to the poem when published in *Voyager Poems*, ed. Douglas Stewart (Brisbane: Jacaranda, 1960), 115–16.

In a letter of 27 July 1953 Slessor described the poem as 'merely a fanciful exaggeration of the idea of one [clock] lagging and the other hurrying while, in the end, both become part of the distant past' (NLA MS 3020/1/152).

88 *Greenwich*: headquarters of the British Admiralty, now a suburb of London. Longitude and time were measured from Greenwich.

94 *Sandwich Isles*: Cook's name for the Hawaiian islands. It was here that Cook met his death, on 14 February 1779.

97 *haberdasher's*: seller of small clothing items, such as buttons and ribbons.

98 *yellow-haired boy*: i.e. Cook when young; he served an apprenticeship with a grocer and haberdasher.

IV

This section deals with Cook's third voyage, on the *Resolution*. In the 1965 lecture Slessor said:

> In *part 4*, the vision of Captain Cook on a workaday occasion during his third voyage is derived from some verses written by one of the midshipmen-aboard, later to become Captain Trevenen . . . The phrase 'cats to catch mice' was one of Cook's favorite admonitions to the lively boys who were his midshipmen. It is quoted by Trevenen with the explanation that the captain frequently told them that he didn't mind how much they kicked up their heels provided they did their duties first — his actual words were 'my cats have to catch mice before they get any milk'.
>
> So, after their routines had been finished, these young schoolboy-officers, to whom the whole voyage with all its perils and hardships was a glorious adventure, were often able to go with Cook in one of the ship's boats when he made small

excursions, noting details for his charts and getting fresh meat for the galley from birds and animals ashore. (*BW*, 195–6; Haskell, 148–9)

James Trevenen (1760–90) was an English-born mariner who sailed with Cook on Cook's last voyage. Thomson (25) quotes the relevant lines from Trevenen's poem:

> Oh Genius superior, in forming whom Nature
> Had an eye to the moulding of a great navigator;
> And tho' towards thy Mids thou wert not very nice,
> Declaring thoudst have no more cats than catch mice . . .
> Sometimes a shooting, and sometimes surveying,
> With pleasure still watching, with pleasure obeying,
> Through gulf, creek and inlet our jolly boat forcing,
> As if the old Devil himself had been coursing;
> Till pleased with our efforts thy features relax
> And thou givst us thy game to take home on our backs
> . . . he clothed in good nature his looks of authority,
> And shook from his eye brows their stern superiority.

Thomson also quotes Trevenen's prose account of these excursions on which 'we were sure of having plenty to eat and drink, which was not always the case on board the ship on our usual allowance'.

107 *plantains*: tropical fruits very similar to bananas.
110 *jolly-boats*: small work boats.
121 *fowling-piece*: a shotgun used for hunting wildfowl.

V

This section deals with Cook's third voyage, on the *Resolution*. In his 1965 lecture Slessor commented:

> The account of Cook in *part 5* comes in substance from the manuscript journal kept by Captain Alexander Home . . . Like Captain Trevenen, Alexander Home had been one of Cook's

company on his third voyage. Later, after many years at sea, he became almost totally blind and retired on a pension of 2s. 6d. a day to his home in Berwickshire in Scotland. Although Home did not witness the affray in which Cook lost his life, he wrote a narrative of it soon after the event, from statements made by those who had been ashore at the time. The references to Cook (such as his warning to deserters that he would get them back eventually 'dead or alive') are almost word for word from Home's journal . . . (*BW*, 196; Haskell, 149)

Alexander Home (1738–1823) sailed with Cook as an officer. In 1780, during the American War, he was partly blinded and in 1783 retired on half-pay to a small farm in Berwickshire, Scotland. In his 'The Account of Ottihiti and Our Transactions' (NLA MS 690, f. 17) Home describes Cook lecturing to his men against desertion: 'Amongst other things he told them they Might run off if they pleased. But they might Depend upon it he would Recover them again . . . His authority would bring them back and Dead or Alive he'd have them.'

126 *Yellow Sea*: part of the northern Pacific Ocean, between China and Korea.

161 *half-a-crown*: money amounting to two shillings and sixpence (equal to 25 cents).

166 *Greenwich Hospital to Cook*: In his 1965 lecture, misquoting his own line, Slessor commented:

The line 'Greenwich Hospital for Cook' alludes to the Admiralty's offer to give Cook an administrative post at the home for naval veterans, Greenwich Hospital. This was at a time when his proposals for further voyages were becoming a nuisance to the lethargic sea lords. For Cook, then aged 47, it was a dreadful vision of stagnation and he was reluctant to accept the offer. It would, indeed, have been like putting a seagull in a birdcage. (*BW*, 196; Haskell, 149)

In fact Cook applied to be one of the Captains of the Royal

Greenwich Hospital, but did feel ambivalent about the post. In the event he was sent on another voyage before he could take up the appointment.

177 *duchy's seal*: seal of a territory ruled by a duke or duchess.

187 *A prince in barter for a longboat*: Cook went ashore because the Hawaiian natives had stolen his ship's longboat (the largest workboat kept with a sailing ship). Cook considered taking one of the Hawaiian princes until the longboat was returned.
It was during this foray that Cook was killed.

188 *trumpery*: showy but rubbishy.

195 *a knife of English iron*: In his lecture Slessor said:

The details of the killing of captain Cook follow the accepted version given in many descriptions of the scene. It is a fact that Cook was stabbed with an English knife that had been traded to the Hawaiian natives only a few days before. (*BW*, 196; Haskell, 149)

Home's Log Book records the incident as follows:

Captain Cook Stood on the Edge of the Rock waiting for the Boat for the Captain Could Not Swim and when he Stood in that Possition one of the Chiefs Came Behind him and Stabed in the Back with an iron [dagger] From Siteer which had been Forged on board the Ships. The Indians being Desirous of such weapon and in Return they gave us Roots and Hogs. Captain cook being thus Mortily wounded Tumbled down the Rock into the Sea and his head fell into a gully Betwixt two Narrow Rocks. He attempted to get up could not and I Believe was Suffocated in the water . . . (NLA MS 690, f. 3).

211 *cardinal-birds*: types of finch, the male being a brilliant red colour.

A Bushranger

September 1931; (P)

In *CC* Slessor included a note which read:

Jackey Jackey, whose right name was William Westwood, became an almost fabulous hero amongst the old hands. The

> most incredible feats were attributed to him in the mythology which spread round his name, and the least of these were his power of travelling at an unearthly speed, his kissing of a Commissary's wife in the latter's carriage, and his reported conversation with the Governor in the most inexplicable and intellectual language.

On a tape recording made by Hazel de Berg on 6 March 1960 and now in the Berg collection of the NLA Slessor comments:

> All sorts of extraordinary feats were attributed to Jacky-Jacky. He was supposed to be able to ride at tremendous speeds, and he was a dead shot. He jumped all kinds of chasms in the mountains, and also he was reputed to be an extremely learned man, a man who could speak with the Governor in Latin and who could speak with boundary riders and station workers in their language, too, and he also at one time showed a touch of the highwayman in holding up a commissary's carriage and kissing the commissary's wife, so that altogether he was a remarkable person. I have used him as a figure of Australian mythology, to show how legend grows up in this country . . .

William Westwood (1821–47) was an Englishman transported to Sydney in 1837. In 1840 he began his bushranging career in New South Wales and Tasmania. He became somewhat legendary as a gentleman bushranger, with attributes which Slessor recounts in the poem. An account of him is given in Ch. VI of George Boxall's *History of the Australian Bushrangers*, first published in London in 1899 and then by Angus & Robertson in Sydney in 1916 and Cornstalk Publishing in Sydney in 1924; one of the latter two editions seems to have been Slessor's source book.

2 *carbines*: types of rifle.
hollo: shout.

3 *traps*: troopers.

8 *bulldog*: short-barrelled revolver.

10 *Mails*: coaches carrying the mail.

Long Tom Station: name of a fictional grazing property.

12 *cabbage-tree hat*: type of broad-brimmed hat worn in the Australian colonies, often taken to be a symbol of Australianness.

18 *prig*: (slang) steal.

bigwig: a person of social prominence. Boxall (84) notes:

More legends have collected round the name of Jackey Jackey than round that of any other of the bushrangers, and many of them are variants of the stories told of the historical highwaymen of England. For instance, Jackey Jackey is said to have bailed up the carriage of the Commissary; when he discovered that the Commissary's wife was inside he dismounted, opened the door and, sweeping the ground with his cabbage tree hat, as he bowed low before her, invited her to favour him with a step on the green.

20 *Patrick's Plains*: an ironic reference to an area in the Hunter Valley where the infamous James Mudie took a land grant which he called 'Castle Forbes'; he flogged his convicts so brutally that they rebelled in 1833. The convicts were recaptured and suffered terrible retribution.

The Country Ride

November 1930; (P)

Epigraph: from *The Diaries of Samuel Pepys*. Pepys (1633–1703) kept the most famous diary in English, from 1660 to 1669.

In his essay 'Modern English Poetry' Slessor said of the poem's technique:

By way of variation I have tried, not the matching consonants only or vowels only, but the repetition of a whole syllable, both vowels and consonants, so that it is not a rhyme but really the same word, or portion of the same word, reiterated. (Haskell, 158; Thomson, 145)

11 *pick-purse*: thief.

12 'Go and Be Hanged, That's Twice Good-bye': Pepys' diary records:

'There came Captn. Allen, and he and I withdrew and sang a song or two, and among others took pleasure in "Goe and bee hanged, that's good-bye"'.

14 *To kiss a little pretty dairymaid . . .*: Pepys' diary records: 'I met two little schoolboys going with pitchers of ale to their schoolmaster . . . and I did drink some of one of them and gave him twopence. By and by we came to two little girls keeping cows, and I saw one of them very pretty, . . . and telling her that I was her godfather . . . I gave her twopence'.

17 *greensleeve girl*: girl wearing green sleeves, with suggestions of unfaithfulness through association with the ballad 'Green-sleeves', first published 1580.

apprentice-equerry: apprentice groom of horses, or an attendant upon the sovereign.

19 *'Then Mr Sam says, "Riding's hot," he says . . .'*: Slessor's words, not Pepys's; Mr Sam seems to be Slessor's invention. Pepys's diary for 14 September 1660 mentions a Mr [Samuel] Samford, but in the entry for 11 April 1661 Pepys's companion is Captain Allen.

26 *cells . . . under tents of horn*: body cells under fingernails.

27 *bale*: evil, grief, misery; also, in Middle English 'bale' is a verb meaning 'to dance'.

28 *gallows-flesh*: Pepys's diary records, 'Mrs Anne and I rode under the man that hangs upon Shooter's Hill, and a filthy sight it was to see how his flesh is shrunk to his bones'. Shooter's Hill was a favourite spot for highwaymen, on the road between London and Dover; it was customary to erect gallows at the scene of a crime.

Elegy in a Botanic Gardens

April 1929; (P)

The details in the poem do not fit the Sydney Botanic Gardens; it seems that a fictional gardens is involved.

5 *Meleager*: in Greek mythology, a hero whose valour was foretold by the Fates; he led a successful hunt for a wild boar sent by Artemis to ravage the Aetolian area of Greece. He died once a brand

burning on the hearth when the Fates visited ceased to exist; or the reference could be to the Greek erotic poet and anthologist (active 1st century BC).

8 *Tristania*: The tree's name derives from Charles Tristan, but here suggests Tristan and Isolde (see 'Music, II', line 34n.) as well as a lovers' tryst. It is a Brisbane box tree.

15 Meryta Macrophylla: Dutton (150) points out that the tree's actual name is *Mertya macrophylla*. There are no common names for the *Mertya* genus of trees.

20 *Headlong Hall*: *Headlong Hall* (1816), a novel by Thomas Love Peacock, presents a Christmas party at the house of Squire Headlong. Slessor's list of objects derives from Ch. II; they belong to the odd guests, except for 'Cupid in a wig', which seems to be Slessor's addition.

Toilet of a Dandy

February 1931; (P)

3 *The Great Harry's*: Harry Trower, an uncle of Slessor's who lived in Weybridge, England; he was a wealthy reprobate. Slessor began a prose sketch based on him but never completed it (NLA MS 3020/19/Ms. diary dated 1 January 1927; Stewart prints part of the sketch at p. 131 and Dutton at pp. 155–6). The prose sketch mentions 'Transports of filed nerves', 'the excruciations and beatitudes of the decayed middle-aged voluptuary' and describes 'My uncle, the Great Harry . . . putting things on and off'. (See also 'To Myself', introductory n.)

7 *trees*: devices for shaping shoes.

8 *bootjacks*: devices for holding boots while taking them off or putting them on.

12 *Caruso's*: Enrico Caruso (1873–1921), Italian operatic tenor, known as 'The Great Caruso'. On Caruso's tomb is a statue of him in evening dress.

Serenade

September 1926; (P)

1 *Christus*: the Latin name of Christ.

4 *truckle*: submit obsequiously.

5 *cocker*: pampered.

6 *viand*: a choice food.

9 *lout*: bow, submit.

To Myself

April 1930; (P)

In *CC* the poem was titled 'Sentimental Soliloquy'.

Slessor commented on the poem at the end of his essay, 'The Quality of Magic':

> . . . moral or didactic purpose is no more essential to poetry than intellectual speculation and rational inquiry are to life itself, which is the same compound of starkness and enchantment as poetry, the ordinary transformed by passages of inexplicable magic. This is partly the view which I attempted to express a long time ago in a poem called 'To Myself' — though looking at it today I can see that it is probably just as obscure as some of the lines I have quoted [earlier in the essay] and without their transfiguring quality of magic . . . That is possibly the most 'private' poem I have ever written, and I am gloomily aware that, without the presence of magic, all such private codes of communication are doomed to failure. It is true that I did have an uncle, a dandy and an epicure, who appeared to live a perfect and happy life, paying courtesies to waiters and pretty women and without watching himself in the mirrors of introspection. Although, after forty years, the private allusions, personal associations and special memories still remain understandable to me, the writer, they must seem just as enigmatic as mad Alcaphra to anyone who does not share them. What the poem really tries to say is that the simple graces and pleasures of living

through the senses are in the end no more to be despised than the activities of the 'thin fluid mind'. (*S*, No. 4, 1971, 254–5)

7 *Hamlet's father*: At the beginning of *Hamlet* Hamlet's father has been murdered and calls on Hamlet to avenge his death and thereby release him from suffering.

11–12 *In the houses of dead kings* . . .: the imagery recalls 'Winter Dawn' (*E-V*) lines 17–18, 'Here lie those mummied Kings, / Men sleeping in houses, embalmed in stony coffins . . .'

Wild Grapes

March 1929; *Smith's Weekly*, 16 March 1929; (P)

This is the only one of Slessor's poems illustrated in *Smith's Weekly* which he included in a collection of his work, apart from *Darlinghurst Nights*. The *Smith's Weekly* version is slightly different, as noted below; it is included in *BBFB*. Thomson (35) claims that the poem is based on the murder of the Mulligan family, the fourteen-year-old daughter last, near Berrima, New South Wales, by John Lynch in the early 1840s. The murders are detailed in Ch. V of George E. Boxall's *History of the Australian Bushrangers*, which Slessor drew on for 'A Bushranger'; however, Slessor's poem does not conform with the details in Boxall and at most Boxall merely provides a starting point for Slessor's thought.

4 *or Hartigans, long drowned*: In the first, *Smith's Weekly* version, there was no comma.

7 *dogstars*: the brightest of the fixed stars, in the constellation of the Greater Dog.

9 *Isabella grapes*: a variety of large grape, in fact usually purple, sometimes green or red.

13 *Isabella, the dead girl*: to name the girl 'Isabella' is Slessor's conceit.

14 *Defiantly*: 'Mutinously' in *Smith's Weekly*.

18 *pins*: 'ear-rings' in *Smith's Weekly*.

20 *— or killed here —* :'and killed here — ' in *Smith's Weekly*.

Waters

January 1927; (P)

9–10 *And strangers . . . surf again*: In a letter to an inquiring student dated 4 April 1967 Slessor said about these lines:

> The lines mean roughly that these 'waters' (specifically Sydney Harbour) will outlast those who look at them and write about them — and after they have gone, when the city itself perhaps has returned to its original wilderness, future men ('strangers') may come camping among the trees of the headlands and see the Pacific on their seaward side. (NLA MS 3020/20/29)

13–14 *Like thieves . . . glassy-clear*: In the above-mentioned letter Slessor commented:

> It is dusk and the lights of the Harbour (i.e. navigation lights) are shining in the last of the daylight. They have appeared 'like thieves', 'too early' for darkness, and the image suggests that, as thieves, they have dropped a 'swag' of jewels (red, gold and green) into the depths of the water. (NLA MS 3020/20/29)

Burying Friends

May 1929; (P)

Epigraph: 'The Succubus' is a story published in *Vision*, Aug. 1923, 50–57, written by Norman Lindsay under the pseudonym 'Charles Partridge'. The words preceding those quoted are perhaps relevant:

> I found myself stirred to an emotion by Scadden's end that I hardly supposed him capable of arousing when alive. But he had been a figment of my life for years, and grief is wholly selfish. I came back from his funeral with that uneasy sense of dislocation which such an event leaves in the mind, for a little of our vital essence goes into the grave of a friend.

A succubus is a female evil spirit, or a whore. (Lindsay's story concerns a priggish Englishman who is driven to his grave by a selfish, low-life girl.)

Metempsychosis

June 1930; (P)

Metempsychosis: the transmigration of a soul, after death, into another body.

1 *John Benbow*: a fictional figure; in Robert Louis Stevenson's *Treasure Island* (1882) the inn kept by Jim Hawkins's mother is called the 'Admiral Benbow'.

3 *peajacket*: see 'Captain Dobbin', line 91n.

10 *'Turfbird's Tattle'*: a fictional newspaper title.

18 *peashooters*: tubes from which peas or pellets are fired by blowing through them.

Rubens' Hell

June 1929; (P)

Rubens: see 'Rubens' Innocents' (*TOTM*), introductory n.

This poem is based on Rubens' painting, 'The Toilet of Venus'.

1 *rosy-cloven*: reddish and split; both Pan and Satan are usually depicted as having cloven hooves.

7 *embayed*: bathed.

11 *croup*: hind-quarters, rump.
swagging: hanging loosely.

33 *butter-hatch*: small door behind which butter is kept; there is here also some suggestion of the verb 'hatch'.
flunkeys: see 'Glubbdubdrib', line 9n.

La Dame du Palais de la Reine

February 1927; (P)

Title: 'The Lady of the Queen's Palace' (French).

6 *minions*: servants.

17 *lime*: see 'City Nightfall', line 13n.

18 *Amor*: romantic dalliance.

Country Towns

February 1927; (P)

In his essay '"Five Bells" and Others' Slessor said of the poem:

> 'Country Towns' is a small and simple Australian bucolic which requires (I hope) no elucidation. It refers to no country town specifically but is a composite of many which have seemed the same. Its period is fading, or perhaps has already vanished, since farmers today prefer motors to mares and buggy-wheels are seldom heard. However, it is possible that the last of the Hogans still manage a few supermarkets and that the playbills of the Great Golightly Family may still be found under a layer of posters advertising pop singers.
>
> As a matter of accuracy, it might be mentioned that 'locusts' should properly be called cicadas and that the 'pepper-trees' are those feathery small trees, with bunches of red pellets, more scientifically known as Peruvian mastic. (*BW*, 199; Haskell, 152)

20 *schooner bees*: In a letter to a school student dated 27 Nov. 1962 Slessor said: '"schooner bees" means just what the words imply — big stately bees of the bumblebee kind, like schooners under full sail'. (NLA MS 3020/20/5)

Mephistopheles Perverted

May 1929; (P)

Mephistopheles: in German legend, the evil spirit to whom Faust (see 'The Nabob', line 2n.) sold his soul.

(Or Goethe for the Times): James McAuley in Kiernan (17) details the reference:

In the Auerbach's cellar scene in Goethe's *Faust*, Mephistopheles sings a subversive political song:

> '. . . There was once a king who had a great flea, which he loved as if it was his own son. He ordered his tailor to make the flea a handsome suit of clothes; and he placed ribbons and a cross on

the flea's coat so that he was a minister of state. Then all the flea's relatives came to court, and they plagued everyone, from the queen to the ladies-in-waiting, who didn't dare do anything to them — whereas we common folk know what to do, we crack a flea as soon as it bites us.'

22 *A King*: James I of England and VI of Scotland, who believed he had powers of healing.
scrofula: a disease chronically affecting the lymphatic glands, also known as 'King's Evil'.

Crustacean Rejoinder

December 1928; (P)

8 *Ethiop*: Ethiopian, or a black person generally.
12 *carapace*: shell.

Trade Circular

July 1929; (P)

1 *Bourbon-sugars*: whisky sweets.
3 *curricle*: see 'The Atlas', line 23n.

Fixed Ideas

July 1929; (P)

In *CC* the poem was titled 'Fixed Opinions'.

Slessor commented on the poem on three separate occasions. In 'Modern English Poetry' (1931) Slessor said:

> . . . the idea is fundamentally a contrast between the solidity and stiffness of rigid opinion, and the fluidity of the real stream of thought which besieges the human brain. The contrast is emphasized by the abrupt change from the first part, with its long, heavy lines, to the rapidly-running short lines of the second part. (Thomson, 140)

In 'Writing Poetry: The Why and the How' (1947) Slessor elaborated:

> My purpose was to study in a small way the flow of thought in a man's mind — the ceaseless ray-bombardment of mental reactions to the swarming stimuli of life, a waterfall of rapidly appearing, rapidly disappearing thoughts — and to compare this fluidity with the belief that a human being can, or should, have opinions firmly cemented into place by tradition, upbringing and experience. I tried to do this by a violent contrast in form . . . First, I attempt to show the solidity of the fixed opinions by square, heavy, rigid lines with images of solidity, squareness and rigidity . . . That was meant to produce a sensation of solidity by its shape, both physical and emotional . . . in the second part, the form is abruptly changed. The lines are short and running, the images are of fluidity instead of solidity, and the vowel-sounds are concentrated on the mercurial 'i' sound of the vowel, as in 'din' or 'in' itself. (Thomson, 153)

In his 1962 television interview with John Thompson, Slessor reiterated these thoughts on the poem, albeit in other words (see Kiernan, 5–6).

5 *precipitate*: a solid separated from the liquid in which it was dissolved.
6 *spar*: crystalline minerals.
7 *rhomboids*: diamond-shaped crystal solids.
9 *alabaster*: a mineral composed of lime and gypsum.
cartilage: gristle.
12 *Gorgon*: see 'Five Visions of Captain Cook', line 53n.
23 *Undo, loosen your bubbles!*: In his 1962 television interview Slessor commented that 'the last line, "Undo, loosen your bubbles" was always said to me by my old friend, Lennie Lower, whenever he saw me at the counter in the pub. He appealed to me to do this and buy him a glass of beer'. (Thomson, 6)

The Old Play

January 1929; (P)

Epigraph: 'Madam, do you know this old play? It is a very distinguished piece, only a little too melancholy.' These are the opening words of *Ideen Das Buch Le Grand* (1826), the second volume of *Reisebilder*. It was translated into French under the title *Histoire du tambour Legrand: Fragments* in 1832. Legrand is a *tambour*, or drum major, in Napoleon's army, and functions as a kind of artistic equivalent of Napoleon the emperor.

Heine: see 'Heine in Paris' (*E-V*), introductory n.

Douglas Stewart reported that Slessor wrote the poem, 'so he told me, because so many poets had written men's observations of the gods, and he thought it would be amusing to reverse the theme and relate the gods' observations of men' (Stewart, 82).

On 1 August 1966 Julian Croft wrote to Slessor, asking: 'Wallace-Crabbe describes "The Old Play" as an Eliotic experiment, did you intend it as such?' In notes he made towards a reply Slessor wrote: 'If so, must be entirely subconscious' and 'Based on conception of human life as a tragic comedy enacted in a theatre before all the deities whom humans had invented or postulated as a protection ag[ain]st "emptiness" — all the figures, Hequet, Mama Cocha, Marduk etc. are from the various mythologies'. (NLA MS 3020/1/581)

II

30 *colloquy*: conversation.

III

31 *Marduk*: the supreme deity of the Babylonians.
34 *pince-nez*: eyeglasses.
35 *Hequet*: Egyptian goddess of childbirth.
Mama Cocha: an Inca deity of rain and water.
37 *Hemlock*: poison made from hemlock plants or trees; it is famous as the poison given to the Greek philosopher Socrates.
42 *Thua*: not known, possibly a reference to one of the Tua de Danaan of Irish mythology.

IV

46 *mimes*: silent actors.
49 *minion*: see 'La Dame du Palais de la Reine', line 6n.

V

61 *Lucifers*: Satans.

67 *Azrael*: in Turkish and Mongolian mythology, the angel who introduced death into the world.

80 *Capuan*: from Capua, a city in Italy.

81 *Death with leather jaws . . .*: This image is repeated from 'Choker's Lane' (*DN*; written Sept. 1928) — 'The soft, unhurrying teeth of Death / with leather jaws come tasting men'.

VI

82 *Camazotz*: in Mayan mythology a bat-god, one of the demons of the underworld.

Anubis: an Egyptian god who introduced the souls of the dead to the other world.

83 coulisses: theatre wings.

90 *pomades*: scented ointments, especially applied to hair and scalp.

94 *tendrils*: thin shoots by which a plant attaches itself to another body.

103 *diadem*: rolled cloth worn on the head as a symbol of royalty by Persian monarchs; crown.

VII

108 *'Shang Ya! I want to be your friend'*: In *CC* Slessor included a note which read: 'The line "Shang Ya! I want to be your friend", is from an "Oath of Friendship" in *One Hundred & Seventy Chinese Poems*, translated by Arthur Waley. No. 1 of "Seventeen Old Poems" contains a fuller allusion to the Life-Parting, "the opposite to a parting by death".' The last phrase is quoted by Slessor from Waley's note. [Waley actually writes 'opposite of' rather than 'opposite to'.] 'Oaths of Friendship' no. 2 begins, 'Shang Ya!/ I want to be your friend / For ever and ever without break or decay', and ends, 'When Heaven and Earth mingle — / Not till then will I part from you' (*One Hundred & Seventy Chinese Poems*; for publication details see 'Old Chinese Poem' [*TOTM*], 37).

109 *termitary*: a termites' nest.

110 *cellules*: tiny cells; also pores.
115 *scullions*: the lowest class of servants.
119 *Napoleons*: French emperors.
120 *Though in Yuëh . . .*: 'Oaths of Friendship' (see line 108n.) has an introduction which reads: 'In the country of Yuëh when a man made friends with another they set up an altar of earth and sacrificed upon it a dog and a cock . . .' (Waley, 37).
123 *decalogue*: ten commandments.
127 *Han*: the Han dynasty ruled China 202 BC–220 AD. It was an expansionist, highly successful dynasty.
128 *Life-Parting*: see line 108n. No. 1 of 'Seventeen Old Poems' begins: 'On and on, always on and on / Away from you, parted by a life-parting'.
130 *On and on . . .*: see line 128n.
132 *ossification*: the process of bone formation.
134 *fissures*: cracks, openings.
136 *necessitude*: necessity; also a relation between people.
137 *that soft adhesive nag*: Douglas Stewart, who reads the poem biographically, sees this as a reference to 'the Pegasus he [Slessor] and Jack Lindsay rode in the *Vision* period' (80). Riding upon the winged horse of Greek mythology, Pegasus, is a traditional way of representing the inspired poet. Norman Lindsay provided such an illustration for Hugh McCrae's poem 'Creative Effort' in the first issue of *Vision*, May 1923.
139 *palfreys*: saddle horses for ordinary riding.
143 *On and on*: see line 130n.
144 *the Nine Lands*: see 'Amazement' (*TOTM*) line 14n.

VIII

151 *Excalibur*: the name of King Arthur's magical sword.
166 *quicklime*: burnt, unslaked lime.
171 *annuity*: an investment which yields receipt of an annual amount.
173 *Gutumdug*: not known.
Vukub-Cakix: a demon in Mayan myth who had to be overthrown before the human race could be created.

177 *Phew . . . heu . . .*: the sounds of breathing, or of snoring.

X

201 *Beli*: either a god of the Eddic myths of ancient Iceland and Scandinavia or a figure briefly mentioned in the Welsh *Mabinogion.*

203 *lachrymations*: weeping.

204 *champs:* chews.

comfiture: confection, or a preparation of drugs.

XI

210 *grape-shot*: see 'Crow Country', line 10n.

213 *expiation*: atonement.

220 *flagellation*: flogging.

242 *Gorgon's eyes*: see 'Five Visions of Captain Cook', line 53n.

Five Bells: XX Poems

(Sydney: Frank C. Johnson, 1939)

Dedication: J.A.R. McKellar (1904–32) published one book of poems, *Twenty-Six* (Sydney: Frank C. Johnson, 1931), the poems being selected by Slessor. He died suddenly from pneumonia.

Five Bells

completed January 1937; (P)

In his essay '"Five Bells" and Others' Slessor commented on the poem:

> Many hundreds of years ago, in an Arabian fairytale, a man dipped his head into a basin of magic water. In the few moments between submerging his face and withdrawing it, he dreamed that he had sailed on seven voyages, was cast up in a shipwreck, captured by pirates, discovered a diamond as big as a turkey's egg, married a princess, fought in many battles, and was brought to

execution . . . He had, in fact, lived an entire existence on another time-scale.

This is partly the idea of 'Five Bells', a poem which suggests that the whole span of a human life can be imagined, and even vicariously experienced, in a flash of thought as brief as the interval between the strokes of a bell. 'Five Bells' can be described as a kind of meditation at night, while looking at Sydney Harbour and hearing the cold fact of time, five bells or half-past ten, rung from a ship at its moorings below.

But in the three seconds or so which this mechanical process involves, between the double ding-ding and the single ding of the ship's bell, a sequence from a very different time-scale is interposed, compressing about thirty years of human life into the three seconds. For this reason the words '*five bells*' are repeated three times during the poem, to remind the reader that time, on the other scale, has occupied only a few moments, that the tongue of the bell is still moving and the sound is still suspended in the air.

The poem therefore is on two planes. First it attempts to epitomize the life of a specific human being, but fundamentally it is an expression of the relativeness of 'time'. Considered in this light, the personal allusions are unimportant. (*BW*, 196–7; Haskell, 149–50)

Five Bells: Notwithstanding the comments quoted above, there has been much discussion about the significance of the five bells, particularly since, as Dutton points out (170–1), this signal would never have been rung on a ship in harbour at night. Slessor's drafts of the poem refer to 'Four bells' and then 'Six bells' before he decided on 'Five bells' (see Dutton, 168–70).

Slessor's papers include a letter to Slessor from Sue Gowans, dated 31 July 1969, which says: 'After reading "Five Bells" my interest was aroused in the bell system on ships. I looked in the Encyclopaedia Britannica under Ship's Bells, and was interested to read that five bells are no longer rung on a ship as, since 1797, this has been the signal for mutiny . . . I should be very interested to know whether you had the mutiny signal in mind when you wrote "Five Bells".' Slessor's notes record: 'Replied 19/8/69 pointing out that 5 bells are omitted only during the second dog watch (6–8 p.m.) . . . your p[oin]t interesting one'. (NLA MS 3020/20/57)

2 *the flood that does not flow*: In notes for a reply to a letter received from two students on 2 September 1969 Slessor wrote:

Contrast is between conventional Time, measured by 'little fidget wheels' of clocks, and the Time, the *total* flow of human memory & emotion, The 'flood that does not flow' refers to both Time & memory — each of them mysterious — Obviously the first use of 'the flood that does not flow' refers to the second kind of Time, the flood of memory. (NLA MS 3020/20/58)

7 *Joe*: In his essay on the poem Slessor wrote:

The 'dead man' whose life is re-lived 'between the double and the single bell' was named Joe Lynch. He was a friend of my youth, a black-and-white artist of superb humour and talent whose work appeared in the '20s in many Australian periodicals and who was a member of the staffs of *Smith's Weekly* and Melbourne *Punch* when I, too, worked for them . . . One evening in the 1930s, Joe and half a dozen other artists and journalists left Circular Quay by ferry to go to a party on the north side of the Harbour. Joe sat on the lower deck-rail of the boat, clad in an ancient tattered raincoat, heavily laden with bottled beer in the pockets. There was a good deal of jollity until someone noticed that Joe had disappeared. The ferry hove to and there was a wide search, but no trace of Joe Lynch could be found. His body was never recovered and eventually he was presumed drowned. (*BW*, 197–8; Haskell, 150–1)

There has been a great deal of controversy about Lynch's drowning, which actually occurred on 14 May 1927. (See Stewart, 123–6; Haskell, 'Sheer Voice and Fidget Wheels: A Study of "Five Bells"', *Australian Literary Studies*, May 1988,

256–7; Dutton, 174–6; Peter Kirkpatrick, *Australian Literary Studies*, May 1988, 365–9.) Perhaps the most important comment of all comes in a letter Slessor wrote to a Sister M. Philippa on 10 June, 1963:

> Joe is not an actual figure from life but is founded on recollections of a dead acquaintance. He was drowned, after falling from a ferry, and did not deliberately commit suicide. (NLA MS 3020/20/8)

12 *the Cross*: Slessor wrote to Sister Philippa:

> The line means simply that the stars of the Southern Cross are reflected in the Harbour, and that the constellation is in such a position in the sky that its reflection is the reverse of how it is usually depicted. Of course, I do not mean that the Southern Cross or any other constellation can literally be seen in the lights reflected on the water. May I add that it is dangerous to attempt to find too much convoluted subtlety in most poetry? There is certainly no allusion intended here either to Christianity or to the burial of suicides — but, of course, the reader's personal word-associations may add overtones of implication to the straight-forward meaning of a line. (NLA MS 3020/20/8)

In his essay on the poem Slessor declared that 'the Cross' is '*not* . . . an allusion to the lights of Kings Cross' (*BW*, 198; Haskell, 151).

14 *flukes*: end parts of an anchor which hold the ship to the sea bed; instances of good luck.

24 *bumpkin*: awkward, clumsy.

25 *Life*: perhaps a reference to 'life' in the ordinary sense, perhaps a reference to 'Life' in the Lindsayan sense opposed to mere 'Existence' (see 'Realities' [*E-V*], line 30n.).

26 *pygmy strait*: i.e. the separation between Slessor and the 'dead man'.

36 *Darlinghurst*: a suburb of Sydney adjoining King's Cross.

39 *the talons of the rain*: There has been controversy over Slessor's use of this phrase, which also appears in R.D. FitzGerald's poem 'Ode

to Memory'. Criticised by Brian Elliott for copying FitzGerald, Slessor pointed out that 'Five Bells' was written before 'Ode to Memory' was published and therefore available for him to read. (See Thomson, 64–5; Slessor here dates the poem's writing Aug. 1935–Jan. 1937. Elsewhere he dated it Dec. 1934–Jan. 1937.) H.M. Green comments: 'FitzGerald tells me that he took this image over from an early poem that was printed in a Victorian literary periodical; Slessor also may have seen it there, and reproduced an unconscious memory' (*A History of Australian Literature*, rev. Dorothy Green [Sydney: Angus & Robertson, 1985], 948).

40 *Moorebank*: now a western suburb of Sydney. Slessor's friend Harley Matthews, also a poet, had a farm and vineyard there; it is referred to in 'The Knife'. Slessor wrote about Matthews in his essay 'Books of Verse and a Jug of Wine' (*BW*, 35–40).

46 *Milton*: John Milton (1608–74), great English poet and political radical, the author of *Paradise Lost.*
Rights of Man: a reference to the concept itself, or to *The Rights of Man*, a political tract by Thomas Paine published in 1791–2, which defended the French Revolution and argued for maximum individual freedom of thought and action.

56 *naphtha-flash*: an inflammable oil derived from coal, shale and petroleum, and used in lamps or as a fuel.

71 *Your journal*: In his essay on the poem Slessor commented:

In his bedroom at a North Melbourne boarding-house in the days when he worked for *Punch*, Joe found a battered, morocco-bound notebook, apparently the relic of some unknown lodger, and gave it to me for scribbling. It contained some pages of manuscript notes written by the lodger (or Joe) which, of course, I had really no right to see. One of these entries is reproduced literally in 'Five Bells'. Its misspellings ('photoes', 'differant', 'curioes') give it, I think, a peculiarly haunting and convincing flavour. I imagine that Labassa, at the beginning of the extract, is the name of another Melbourne lodging-house and that the writer is describing his bedroom 'at the top of the tower'. But for the purpose of the poem I have assumed that this is Joe's own entry. (*BW*, 198; Haskell, 151)

75 *Labassa*: a mansion with a tower in Manor Grove, North Caulfield, a suburb of Melbourne, and now owned by the National Trust of Australia. It was converted into a boarding house in 1923 (see Dutton, 96). See also line 71n.

85 *We argued about blowing up the world*: In his essay on the poem Slessor wrote:

> Joe was a devout nihilist and frequently contended (over a pint of Victoria bitter) that the only remedy for the world's disease was to blow it up and start afresh. He meant this literally and — long before the discovery of nuclear fission — conceived the notion of an explosive force that would destroy the entire globe at one go. (*BW*, 198–9; Haskell, 152)

101 *memory, the flood . . .*: see line 2n.

106 *sea-pinks*: the plant Thrift, a seashore plant with pink, white or purple flowers on leafless stems.

108 *Idea*: possibly a reference to Plato's concept of 'Ideas' — ideal and eternal patterns of archetypes; earthly things are imperfect copies of them and derive their existence from them.

121 *mackerel-backs*: a mackerel is a type of fish.

123 *Harbour-buoys*: Slessor commented in his essay on the poem:

> No pun on 'boys' is intended, as some critics have suggested, though there may have been a subconscious Empsonian instinct. It is an attempt to describe the Harbour navigation-lights, winking alternately on each side of the channel, so that it might appear that one was throwing a 'fireball' to be caught by the other. (*BW*, 199; Haskell, 152)

Sleep

December 1936; (P)

In his essay '"Five Bells" and Others' Slessor declared:

> 'Sleep' is explained by its title. It imagines the nightly human

mystery of going to sleep as a surrender to complete selflessness, in the form of a return to the unconsciousness of a child in its mother's body. Thus the nature of sleeping is pictured as the oblivion of pre-life and that of awakening as birth itself. Sleep, the state of unconsciousness, is personified as the mother addressing the child, the sleeper. The response 'Yes, utterly', comes from the sleeper — or child — consenting to the total immersion of 'body and no-body, flesh and no-flesh' (that is to say, body and mind) within the enveloping ocean of unconsciousness.

Technically this poem is an experiment in the narcotic effect of the repetition of certain consonant-structures and vowel-sounds. The significant vowel-sound is the long 'U' in such words and phrases as 'bear you', 'estuary', 'carry you', 'ferry you', 'take you', 'receive you', 'consume you', 'engulf you', 'huge cave' and 'huger waves'. There are also many internal rhymes and assonances such as 'ferry' and 'burial', 'cave', 'lave', 'waves', 'slumber', 'dumb', 'remorseless', 'forceps', and so on. (*BW*, 200; Haskell, 153)

10 *lave*: bathe.

19 *riving*: severing, tearing apart.

To the Poetry of Hugh McCrae

1936; *The Australian Writer's Annual* , Vol. 1, No. 1, 1936; (P)

Hugh McCrae (1876–1958) was an associate of Norman Lindsay and the Australian poet whom Slessor most admired. Slessor devoted an essay to McCrae's work. (*BW*, 110; abridged version in Haskell, 111–19)

7 *Meerschaum*: a magnesium silicate with a frothy appearance; or a tobacco pipe with a bowl partly made from meerschaum.

8 *blowzed*: made red and fat.

9 *baleful*: hurtful.

Kimberleys: the vast rugged region in the far north of Western Australia.

15 *Crusoes*: isolated individuals — from the main character of Daniel Defoe's *Robinson Crusoe* (1719), who was shipwrecked on an island.

Last Trams

Part I: January 1939, Part II: May 1939; (P)

20 *Röntgen diagrams*: X-rays, discovered by German scientist Wilhelm Conrad Röntgen (1845–1923) in 1895.

25 *fluorite*: also known as ‘fluorspar’, a mineral (Calcium fluoride) which is the source of the yellow gas fluorine.

37 *celluloid*: plastic material on which cinema films are imprinted.

Lesbia's Daughter

August 1935; (P)

The poem was originally conceived as part of ‘The Atlas’. See ‘The Atlas’ (*CC*), introductory n.

2 *amber*: tree resin that functions as a preservative; many ancient fossils have been preserved in amber.

10 *Lemuria*: a mythical lost continent.

Out of Time

December 1938; (P)

2 *foxed*: intoxicated.

3 *quince-bright*: a quince is a yellow, acid fruit.

slats: thin narrow strips.

7 *skulker*: malingerer.

20 *that pale and faceless host*: i.e. non-being, which must implore ‘Birth’ in order ‘to be flesh’, or ‘funeral’ in order ‘to be ghost’.

32 *meniscus*: crescent shape, especially at the top of a liquid.

North Country

May 1936; (P)

In his essay ‘“Five Bells” and Others’ Slessor said, ‘“North Country” and “South Country” are located in the coastal areas north and south of Sydney, and the contrast is between the densely timbered forests of the north and the bare, rolling cattle-grazing hills of the south’ (*BW*, 199; Haskell, 152).

2 *archers' volleys*: volleys of arrows fired by archers.

9 *bangled by greedy death*: In his essay Slessor explained that this phrase 'means "ringbarked"' (*BW*, 199; Haskell, 152).

16 *battue*: In his essay Slessor commented: '"battue" is intended to suggest that the dismembered trunks of felled trees resemble the bodies of animals slaughtered in a gameshooting hunt or "battue"' (*BW*, 199; Haskell, 152).

South Country

January 1939; (P)

See 'North Country', introductory n. In a letter to R.G. Howarth of 19 January 1949 Slessor said:

> Your assumption that the scene of the poem is on the upper south road is quite correct — but I don't think that a pinpointed location should be necessary, since the verse attempts to express the general feeling of all the area to Kiama and even farther south, and not of a particular 'view'. I mean the feeling of flatness, gentle undulation and space, contrasting with the crowded forests of the north. (NLA MS 1085).

1 *whey-faced*: 'whey' is the liquid that separates from the curds when milk coagulates.

11 *rotting sunlight*: Slessor commented in his letter to R.G. Howarth that the phrase was meant 'to indicate color — the sky colored by rotting sunlight as the sea might be colored by rotting seaweed. But the sunlight could certainly be visible in the air, either on clouds or as a reflection from below' (NLA MS 1085).

William Street

May 1939; (P)

William Street leads from Sydney city to Kings Cross.

In a 1936 newspaper article, 'The Sights of Sydney: Ten Things You Won't Find in the Guide Books', Slessor described one of the sights as:

> WILLIAM STREET ON A WET NIGHT, from the top of Park Street . . . a canal of liquid light, running and trickling with the spilt reds and greens of Neon . . . motor-headlights blazing and winking and blazing again . . . and, on the pavements, bright as mirrors, people walking on their own reflected heels . . . (*Smith's Weekly*, 17 Oct. 1936, 47)

In his text for *Portrait of Sydney* (Sydney: Ure Smith, 1952), reprinted in *BW* and Haskell, Slessor wrote:

> At night, after a slick of rain has fallen on it, turning the roadway to a long, black mirror, William Street comes out like a beautiful adventuress. It is dressed in Neon signs, the blazing arrows and the alphabets of light, in mandarin-yellow, tangerine-red, emerald and white, like the witch-fires of the Ancient Mariner, 'about, about, in reel and rout'. In the water silvering the pavement, people walk on their reflected heels. Their flesh is green or carmine or fluorescent blue as they move from one radiance to another, and in the juke-box bars the intense light exposes them as nakedly as if they were sliced and stained and gummed between slides for a microscope. (*BW*, 5; Haskell, 72–3)

In '"Five Bells" and Others' Slessor said of the poem:

> William Street is a sort of flashlight photograph of the swarming city channel that runs up the hill to Kings Cross, taken on a rainy night when the surface of the road is coated with a slick of reds and greens and whites reflected from the neon skysigns (the 'red globes' and 'pulsing arrows'). Here, too, there have been inexorable changes since the poem was written. The old fish-shops and '21 meals for £1' cafes have given way to pizza-counters and American hamburger-bars and second-hand clothes no longer hang in pawnshop windows. But the general reason for the poem remains, since it was intended as a defence of metropolitan fascinations against those who considered the city 'ugly' and found beauty only in the outback. (*BW*, 199–200; Haskell, 153)

In his essay 'Writing Poetry: The Why and the How', Slessor wrote:

> . . . in a poem called 'William Street', I have attempted to create a neon-lit, metallic and floozy atmosphere by the deliberate use of assonance — the kind of assonance used not so deliberately in the vulgar old comic songs which still delight me. You will see that I have rhymed in this way such words as 'green' and 'stream', and 'men' and 'condemn'. (Haskell, 162; Thomson, 155)

13 *dips*: pickpockets, or gangsters.
molls: gangsters' girlfriends, or prostitutes.
flip: flicking movement with the fingers; or an adjective, an abbreviation of 'flippant'.

Cock-Crow

November 1936; (P)

In 'Writing Poetry: The Why and the How' Slessor said that 'in "Cock-Crow", by using half-rhymes with an interlocking system of repeated vowel sounds and consonant sounds, I have tried to express the sense of remoteness and great distance which comes sometimes in a dream'. (Haskell, 161; Thomson, 155)

The Knife

August 1935; (P)

1 *Harley's field*: the vineyard of Slessor's poet-friend, Harley Matthews, at Moorebank (see 'Five Bells', line 40n.).

To a Friend

1932; (P)

In his television interview with Kenneth Slessor, John Thompson asked who the friend was. Slessor replied:

> Adam McKay [*sic*, a transcription error for 'McCay']. Adam McKay was one of the two men who most impressed me in my years of pupillage. One was Norman Lindsay and the other was

> Adam McKay. Adam McKay was a newspaper-man of a kind which, today, is almost extinct. A man of enormous erudition, great reading, classical knowledge; at the same time, an enormous humour, gusto, fondness for life, eating and drinking and so on. The poem we're talking about is quite true. It began at one time when Adam McKay said that my generation really knew nothing, that his generation was still much superior and that anything I could do, he could do better. So he began to show me, and he certainly showed me. I think we had a series of contests that lasted all day. We played billiards and he beat me. We played miniature golf — which was a pastime of those days — and he beat me at that. We played a pin game, where you put a penny in, and he beat me at that. Then he said he could drink four or five times as much beer as I could hold. We played some music and he recognized some works of Bach that I certainly hadn't been able to place — that was the references to the fugues, of course, — and so as you can see, he wiped the floor with me and he proved that he *could* do anything I did, better.

Slessor goes on to explain that McCay did not approve of the poem:

> Well, he didn't like my poetry very much. He was a complete Swinburnian, and he stopped, really, at Swinburne. And he didn't like the kind of poetry I was trying to write. Also I think he thought it was rather an intrusion on what had been a private day, a private amusement, to have it published. So I asked him if I could have it published, and he said no, he didn't like it. So I changed the name from Adam to Damon, which appears in the first version. (Kiernan, 7–8)

A portrait of Adam McCay is given by Penelope Nelson in *Australian Literary Studies*, Oct. 1984, 495–502.

1 *Adam*: 'Damon' in *FB.*

18 *catamountains*: leopards or panthers, or wild people.

27 *Abbey of Thélème*: an imagined community in the novel *Gargantua*

(1534) by François Rabelais (*c.*1483–1553). At the utopian abbey pupils so love learning that they are dedicated to it, studying all subjects and learning far more than at medieval universities. At one stage, in manuscript draft, the poem was titled 'Thélème'.

Vesper-Song of the Reverend Samuel Marsden

exact date not known, between 1932 and 1933; *The Australian Outline*, December 1933; (P)

Vesper-Song: evensong, or evening prayer.

Samuel Marsden: (1764–1838), Anglican priest who arrived in New South Wales in 1794. He was a fierce priest and brutal magistrate, known for the floggings he ordered as sentences. He was a pioneer sheep breeder and a very influential figure in the colony.

1 *cure*: district for which spiritual responsibility is held.

9 *knout*: whip.

12 *tinker's*: A 'tinker' was originally a tinsmith but the word came to be associated with unskilled workers, or low-life people of any kind.
litany: a form of prayer consisting of supplications and responses.

18 *vellum*: calfskin used as parchment.
veal: calf flesh.

24 *Cat*: whip, as in, for example, cat-o'-nine-tails.

25 *tails*: tresses on the whip.

26 *Overseer*: supervisor.

Full Orchestra

January 1935; *The Australian Author*; Authors Week [April 8–12], 1935; (P)

1 *footmen*: servants.

3 *dog-speech*: lesser speech, perhaps with the suggestion of barking or of following and trying to emulate.

4 *the Roman tongue*: i.e. the music of the trumpets, here associated with Ancient Rome, and perhaps with the Medieval period when Latin was the language of the church and of the learned.

6 *dingo*: Australian wild dog, which has a high-pitched howl but does not bark.

stops: devices on musical instruments used to produce particular notes.

7 *pear-tree*: The timber of pear trees is used in making musical instruments.

8 *quenched*: stifled.

your own: i.e. the orchestra's own music, which is entirely superior to that of the poet's 'words'.

10 *whet*: sharpen, make alert.

Advice to Psychologists

1934; (P)

The poem was completed, but not published, with the title 'Advice to Metaphysicians'.

2 *panes*: as in 'window panes', but with a pun on 'pains'.

Sensuality

June 1939; (P)

Cannibal Street

August 1935; (P)

The poem was included as epigraph in Frank Dalby Davison, *The White Thorn Tree* (Melbourne: National Press, 1968).

Perhaps of some relevance is Slessor's comment in a 1954 lecture on Kendall and Gordon: 'It is understandable, as H.M. Green has pointed out, . . . that "all poets are cannibals and feed to some extent on other poets"' (*BW*, 91; Haskell, 110–11).

7 *Helen's*: Helen of Troy, the archetype of female beauty.

9 *pedlar*: hawker, salesman.

13 *cleavers*: butchers' knives or hatchets.

from Poems

(Sydney: Angus & Robertson, 1957)

Polarities

exact date not known, between 1944 and 1948, possibly 1947–1948; *Southerly*, No. 2, 1948; (P)

The subject of the poem is Kathleen McShine, with whom Slessor lived in the late 1940s (see Dutton, 276–84). This was the last new poem which Slessor published.

Polarities: the possession of opposing tendencies.

2 *oriel window*: bay window.

9 *Sometimes, when she makes pea-soup or plays me Schumann*: In a letter to R.G. Howarth of 9 March 1948 Slessor wrote:

> The line about pea-soup and Schumann is, I am afraid, a private allusion, a practice which I won't attempt to excuse. It has a direct personal reference, but its first reference is to a line of a German poem with [for 'which'] has always haunted me — 'To a Dead Lady' by Detler von Liliencron. I know it only in its English translation by Jethro Bithell. Pea-soup and Schumann songs are among the rewards promised by the lady of the poem. But I realise perfectly well that 'pea soup' may jar, and I would like to suggest changing the whole line to: 'Sometimes, when she makes an omelette, or plays Schumann'. (NLA MS 1085)

Howarth did not like the suggestion, and the line remained.

An Inscription for Dog River

exact date not known, between 1942 and 1957, probably 1942–1945; (P)

Dog River is in Lebanon. The site of the inscription is on the Lebanese coast, just north of Beirut. Slessor visited the site as Australia's Official War Correspondent, both on 16 November 1941, before Blamey's inscription was cut, and on 18 May 1942, after it was cut. Slessor's war dispatch of 31 January 1942 describes the past inscriptions and the planned Australian addition without any hint of satire (see Haskell, 182; Clement Semmler, ed., *The War Despatches of Kenneth Slessor* [St Lucia: University of Queensland Press, 1987], 279–80).

1 *Our general*: General Sir Thomas Blamey (1884–1951) commanded the Australian military forces in the Middle East during World War II; from 1942 he was commander-in-chief of all Australian land forces.

3 *Ashur-Bani-Pal's*: a great Assyrian emperor, and creator of the first major library known to history.

4 *Nebuchadnezzar's*: famous King of Babylon.

Beach Burial

1942; *Southerly*, No. 3, 1944; (P)

In his essay '"Five Bells" and Others' Slessor comments on the poem:

> 'Beach Burial' comes from the period when Australian soldiers were fighting in the Western Desert of Egypt near El Alamein, where the German advance had been halted in 1942. Many of their camps were on the Mediterranean coast, and in the morning it was not uncommon to find the bodies of drowned men washed up on the beaches. They were buried in the sandhills under improvised crosses, identification usually being impossible. Most of them were sailors, some British, some German or Italian, some of them 'neutrals'. (*BW*, 200; Haskell, 153–4)

Slessor's war dispatch of 25 November 1941 describes stopping on the Lebanese coast to stand

> for a few moments at a little cluster of Australian graves. They were huddled together, as if taking cover on the slope of a hill . . . The crosses were the simple sides of packing cases nailed at right angles and the inscriptions, written with careful clumsiness in indelible pencil, had been smeared violet by the rain. (Haskell, 181; Semmler, *War Despatches*, 262)

In another of his war dispatches, Slessor wrote of:

> A beach in the Gulf of Arabs, two miles from El Alamein, dazzle-white in the morning sunlight and lined with slabs of driftwood over the sandy graves of 'unknown sailors' washed up in dozens with the tide. The guns were clubbing away in the west . . . (Semmler, *War Despatches*, 394)

1 *the Gulf of Arabs*: on the Egyptian coast, near El Alamein.

20 *the other front*: Slessor commented on this phrase in '"Five Bells" and Others':

> The superficial meaning, of course, is a military one. The verses were written at a time when there was pressure on the Allies to open a 'second front' against the Germans. However, there is a deeper implication which is really the theme of the poem. It is the idea that all men of all races, whether they fight with each other or not, are engaged together on the common 'front' of humanity's existence. The absolute fact of death unites them. Their hatreds, quarrels and wars should be dwarfed by the huger human struggle to survive against disease and cataclysms on this dangerous planet. (*BW*, 200–201; Haskell, 154)

The last phrase in this commentary is repeated from the last line of 'The Atlas' (*CC*).

The extended notion of 'another front' is apparent in Slessor's last newspaper article before leaving Australia to work as Official War Correspondent:

> . . . there is another front line, not such a dangerous one, certainly, but just as vital, and it is pitched, not on alien battlefields, but here among us in the streets and cities, the country towns, the farms and sliprail-fences and pub-verandahs of Australia. The war is being fought on this common, everyday front just as continuously as it is in France or Norway. Every Australian is a soldier in it. Every Australian has his part to play. (*Smith's Weekly*, 27 April 1940)

Funny Farmyard; Nursery Rhymes and Painting Book

(Sydney: Frank C. Johnson, undated [1933]), with drawings by Syd. Miller

Dated mss drafts of these poems do not exist but it is likely that the poems were written *c.* 1933. The book is on large page format and includes instructions for colouring the drawings. None of the poems was published elsewhere. Accordingly, the poems are listed below only if a note is necessary.

Timothy, the Terrier

4 *golosh*: a piece of waterproof footwear designed to fit over a shoe, and worn in wet weather.

Peter

1 *Peter*: mistakenly printed with a full stop after 'Peter' in *Funny Farmyard*.

2 *setter*: a hunting dog, in the spaniel family.

4 *Bitzer*: a mongrel dog.

Rufus Rooster

8 *Here's*: mistakenly printed as '"Here's' in *Funny Farmyard*.

Darlinghurst Nights

(Sydney: Frank C. Johnson, 1933; rpt Sydney: Angus & Robertson, 1981)

Darlinghurst: a suburb of Sydney, part of the King's Cross area. Slessor's essays 'A Portrait of Sydney', 'My King's Cross' (*BW*, 3–19; Haskell, 71–88) and *Life at the Cross* (Adelaide: Rigby, 1965; excerpts in Haskell, 170–2) have a general relevance to the poems. In 'My King's Cross' Slessor wrote: 'People who "go to the Cross" or "live at the Cross" may mean anywhere from Taylor Square to Wylde street. This doesn't matter. They are expressing a state of mind, just as the Cross itself is perpetually expressing a state of mind'. (*BW*, 15; Haskell, 84)

Dated mss drafts of these poems do not exist but it is highly likely that each poem was written close to its publication date. *DN* reproduced the poems exactly as published in *Smith's Weekly* except as noted. The poems were illustrated by Virgil Reilly who provided some revised illustrations for *Darlinghurst Nights*.

Delicatessen

Smith's Weekly, 6 October 1928

Delicatessen: In 1928 delicatessens were unusual shops in Australia. In his later book *Life at the Cross,* Slessor wrote:

> Delicatessen! If one word could evoke the essence of King's Cross to Australians abroad as hauntingly as burning gumleaves bring them an image of the bush, it might be those five German syllables. Like the stately homes of England, the delicatessen shops of King's Cross are both a heritage and a present joy . . . For the gourmet with money and imagination they are magic toyshops, piled with bottled, canned, and silver-wrapped loot from all the countries of the world. (11)

The word 'delicatessen' literally means dainty foods, or delicacies.

5 *someone*: mistakenly printed with a full stop after 'someone' in *Smith's Weekly*.

7 *Mammon*: wealth regarded as a false deity (see Matthew 6: 24 or Luke 16: 9, 11, 13).

9 *Smith and . . . Wesson*: a famous manufacturer of firearms.

14 *chauffeurs*: mistakenly printed as 'chaffeurs' in *Smith's Weekly*.

33 *on*: mistakenly printed with a full stop after 'on' in *Smith's Weekly*.

Country Eyes

Smith's Weekly, 13 April 1929

8 *Manhattans*: a type of cocktail.

10 *Tosti*: Francesco Paolo Tosti (1846–1916), Italian-born composer who became a British subject and wrote many popular drawing-room songs.

17 *sables*: furs taken from sables, mammals similar to weasels.

23 *Cuthbert de Vere*: a fictional character.

35 *Dresden princesses*: Dresden in eastern Germany is known for its fine porcelain, including porcelain figures.

The Green Rolls-Royce

Smith's Weekly, 11 August 1928

Rolls-Royce: *Smith's Weekly* printed this as 'Rolls Royce' throughout the poem.

1 *iceman*: man who delivered ice for ice-chests, used before refrigerators became common.

3 *Kelvinator*: a brand of refrigerator.

4 *Frigidaire*: a brand of refrigerator.

6 *sly*: bought from an illegal liquor trader.

13 *Black Marias*: police wagons with locked sections at the rear.

The Tiger in the Rose

Smith's Weekly, 2 June 1928

1 *the Stadium*: Sydney Stadium, the city's main venue for boxing matches.

4 *peck*: a large quantity.

5 *peschaniki*: fur made from the peschanik, a subspecies of the Suslik, from the Ural Mountains in Central Asia.

16 *triolets*: elaborate eight-line poetic stanzas with just two rhymes.

Choker's Lane

Smith's Weekly, 1 September 1928

Choker's Lane: a fictional street.

6 *Hades*: in Greek mythology, the underworld to which the dead were taken; colloquially, Hell.

15–16 *Death . . .*: See 'The Old Play', line 81n.

The Voice on the Wire

Smith's Weekly, 12 May 1928

1 *exchange*: telephone exchange.

6 *Nemesis*: in Greek mythology, the goddess of retribution.

7 *Kitto*: J.W. Kitto, Deputy Director of Posts and Telegraphs.

13 *monitor*: the switchboard operators' supervisor.

17 *ninety guineas*: ninety pounds and ninety shillings, a substantial amount of money.

21 *sylph*: an imaginary being supposed to inhabit the air, originally conceived by the Swiss alchemist Paracelsus (1493?–1541).

31 *eleven stone*: the equivalent of approx. 70 kg.

Kimono Cora

Smith's Weekly, 20 October 1928

1 *aurora*: spectacular streams of light in the sky.

7 *chiffon*: light, feminine fabric of silk, nylon or rayon.

14 *a brown*: a penny (equivalent to approx. one cent).

17 *attar*: perfume.

18 *potage*: soup, as described on an à la carte menu.

19 *plethora*: superabundance.

32 *track*: mistakenly printed without a full stop in *Smith's Weekly*.

35 *serges*: types of woven fabric.

Carmen of the Chorus

Smith's Weekly, 31 August 1929

4 *Zeiss*: a brand of binoculars or opera glasses.

8 *Euclid*: Greek geometrician (active 300 BC).

10 *porous*: allowing through water, air etc.

13 *In*: printed as 'in' in *Smith's Weekly* but this would seem a typographical error.

17 *pirouettes*: whirling on the points of the toes, as in ballet dancing.

19 *pantalettes*: long drawers with frills at the end of each leg.

The Girl in the Window

Smith's Weekly, 13 October 1928

16 *Heidsieck*: a brand of champagne.

It, If and Also

Smith's Weekly, 11 January 1930

2 *Burgundy*: wine of many varieties similar to that originally produced in Burgundy, France.

17 *chinchilla*: a fur, made from rabbit or other animals.

21 *Glynnish*: Elinor Glyn (1864–1943) wrote romantic novels and short stories; her novel *It* (1927), once filmed in Hollywood, made the word 'it' a synonym for sex appeal.

Gardens in the Sky

Smith's Weekly, 25 October 1930

1 *hocus-pocus*: mystification, trickery.

3 *crocus*: a type of deep yellow flower.

4 *William Street*: See 'William Street', introductory n.

5 *Roman candles*: types of firecrackers with showers of sparks.

8 *the Alps of Darlinghurst*: In Melbourne *Punch* on 5 March 1925 Slessor published an article titled 'Points of Discovery, No. 7 — The Alps of Darlinghurst. A Study in Flats'; it is a comic piece which describes 'this garden of gutter-tiles and metal flowers'.

13 *Mr Villon*: François Villon (pseudonym of François de Montcorbier or François des Loges; 1431–after 1463), French lyric poet who lived a criminal life and spent much time in prison. In many poems he wrote about the underworld life of Paris.

16 *lightwells*: spaces designed to let light into buildings.

Ticket in Tatts

Smith's Weekly, 26 May 1928

Tatts: Tattersall's sweep, a form of subscription betting.

3 *Flemington*: a racecourse in Melbourne.

4 *Remington*: a brand of typewriter.

5 *Pitman*: a method of shorthand.

6 *comptometers*: old types of calculators.

7 *chronometers*: clocks.

11 *gastronomy*: the art of good eating.

20 *Moët*: an expensive brand of champagne.

21 *truffles*: type of edible fungi regarded as a delicacy; or a chocolate resembling truffles.
venison: deer meat.

22 *Sir Samuel*: Sir Samuel Hordern (1876–1956), at one time Governing Director of Anthony Hordern & Sons, and a director of other companies.
Denison: Hugh Robert Denison (1865–1940), prominent businessman, racing identity and philanthropist.

23 *George Cohen*: (1842–1937), prominent businessman, a director of the Commercial Banking Co.

24 *spats*: short gaiters worn over shoes, a form of flash dressing.

Good-bye Iceman

Smith's Weekly, 27 October 1928

Iceman: See 'The Green Rolls-Royce', line 1n.

10 *Casanova*: Giovanni Giacomo Casanova (1725–98), adventurer and libertine, now a byword for male lovers.

25 *dumb-waiter*: a stand near a dining table, or a set of shelves which can be moved up and down a shaft.

Mannequins

Smith's Weekly, 24 August 1929

1 *taffeta*: a type of fabric, mainly of silk or rayon.

4 *Ninety Guinea*: See 'The Voice on the Wire', line 17n.

6 *Lanvin*: Jeanne Lanvin (1867–1946), French designer of elegant women's clothing.

Poiret: Paul Poiret (1879–1944), French designer of radical and glamorous women's clothing.

10 *Dowagers*: widows of a king, duke etc.; colloquially, any dignified elderly ladies.

11 *adiposity*: fat.

13 *Champs Élysées*: one of the main streets of Paris, and a principal area in world fashion.

15 *Redfern*: an inner Sydney suburb, very much working class at the time.

Paquin: Mme Paquin (?–1936), French designer of glamorous, romantic women's clothing.

16 *Kissproof*: a slogan used by various cosmetics manufacturers.

17 *steerage*: section of ship allotted to passengers travelling for the cheapest fare.

19 *jitneys*: cheap taxis (originally charging a five cent fare).

20 *Crown Street*: an inner city street which runs between Redfern and Darlinghurst.

23 *FIVE BOB*: five shillings, the equivalent of fifty cents.

27 *Woolworth's*: a chain of department stores which sell inexpensive goods.

the Sack: termination of employment.

Caretakers' Daughters

Smith's Weekly, 7 September 1929

3 *mezzanine*: a floor in between two other storeys.

10 *parapet-edges*: walls at the edges of balconies; also the edges of defensive walls, as in forts or castles.

17 *declares*: mistakenly printed with a full stop after 'declares' in *Smith's Weekly*.

Eleven O'Clock

Smith's Weekly, 16 February 1929

3 *Pitman*: See 'Ticket in Tatts', line 5n.

4 *Whitman*: Walt Whitman (1819–92), American experimental

poet, who wrote in free verse and coined many new words.

5 *Underwood*: a brand of typewriter.

13 *loco*: locomotive, a steam train.

26–7 *rhine-stone*: an artificial gem made of paste.

30 *in loco*: in residence.

The Lady in the Lift

Smith's Weekly, 18 January 1930

8 *Otis*: a manufacturer of lifts; in 1930 lifts were never automatic but had drivers.

23 *Standard Waygood*: a manufacturer of lifts (later to merge with the Otis company).

Pay-Day

Smith's Weekly, 15 February 1928

3 *Mammon*: See 'Delicatessen', line 7n.

5 *Astors and Fords*: two wealthy American families.
Infantas: See 'The Embarkation for Cythera', line 19n.

7 *houris*: alluring women, especially oriental women.
dowries: money or gifts given to a spouse, especially to a groom, on marriage.

10 *bisons*: a type of American buffalo.

12 *Jimmy Tyson's*: James Tyson (1819–98), wealthy pastoralist but down to earth character. He is celebrated in a poem, 'T.Y.S.O.N.' by Banjo Paterson.

14 *talkies by Warner*: films with sound made by Warner Brothers.

15–16 *Mr Heather-/shaw's*: James Heathershaw (1871–1943), Secretary to the Commonwealth Treasury 1926–1932.

17 *Woolworth's*: See 'Mannequins', line 27n.

21 *Romano's*: a fashionable (and expensive) Sydney restaurant and nightclub.

22 *rajahs*: princes, kings or rulers in India, Burma and Java.

24 *kippers*: dried, smoked or salted fish, especially herring.

Residential

Smith's Weekly, 18 August 1928

11 *paint*: make-up.

13 *Molong*: a town in western New South Wales, near Orange, where Slessor was born.

16 *Yes*: mistakenly printed as '"Yes' in *Smith's Weekly*.

Cucumber Kitty

Smith's Weekly, 28 December 1929

3 *Roger and Gallet's*: a brand of scents, hair-lotions and soaps.

17 *punkahs*: ceiling fans.

18 *gin-rickey*: a drink made with gin and lime or lemon juice.

The Beauty Parlor

Smith's Weekly, 15 September 1928

8 *henna*: reddish-orange dye, originally made from the leaves of the henna plant.

11 *Mr Cohen's*: See 'Ticket in Tatts', line 23n.

12 *Middle Harbor*: a harbour joining Sydney Harbour at Middle Head.

17 *Lady Angelina Guelph*: a fictional character.

Underground Roses

Smith's Weekly, 28 September 1929

Underground: The Sydney rail network runs underground in the central city area.

10 *chokers*: tight necklaces.
the Rockdale Through: train running from the city to Rockdale, in Sydney's south-west.

11 *Black Narcissus*: a type of rose.

12 *canaries*: canaries were used in underground coal mines to detect the presence of explosive gas.

13 *Museum*: a station on the underground network.

16 *St James*: a station on the underground network, one stop from Museum.

17 *The Queen*: Above St James station is Queen's Square, where a statue of Queen Victoria stands.

19 *the Saint*: Saint James; the station is named for St James's Church, built in 1820, which stands above the station.

21 *buffer*: an extended part of a railway carriage designed to absorb jolts and vibrations.

23 *Hades*: See 'Choker's Lane', line 6n.

The Gunman's Girl

Smith's Weekly, 8 June 1929

In *Smith's Weekly* the poem had a domestic illustration, showing a woman at a stove looking to a man wearing a suit standing near her, and a table set for dinner behind them. In *DN* the poem was given a more dramatic illustration.

2 *opossum*: possum, an Australian marsupial; mistakenly printed as 'oppossum' in *Smith's Weekly*.

4 *Snowdrops*: cocaine takers; see 'Snowdrops' (*DN*).

12 *Dangerous Dan's*: a fictional character.

14 *hang-dog*: pitiful, self-denying.

15 *Smith & Wesson*: See 'Delicatessen', line 9n.

22 *rookery*: swindling, crime.

The Girl at the Wheel

Smith's Weekly, 3 May 1930

19 *Alfred Montgomery Pye*: a fictional character.

22 *chauffeurs*: mistakenly printed as 'chaffeurs' in *Smith's Weekly*.

32 *wireless*: radio.

Going Home

Smith's Weekly, 14 April 1928

1 *a Yellow*: a taxi.

3 *Marmon*: a brand of luxury motor vehicle.

8 *Orpen*: William Orpen (1878–1931), Irish-born portrait painter.

12 *Michael Arlen*: original name Dikran Kouyoumdjian (1895–1956),

Bulgarian-born British novelist and story writer who depicted fashionable British society after the Great War.

21 *buffer*: See 'Underground Roses', line 21n.

26 *St Mary's*: St Mary's Cathedral, between Sydney's Domain and Hyde Park.

Tête-à-Tête

Smith's Weekly, 21 June 1930

Tête-à-Tête: an intimate, important conversation between two people.

1 *Underwood*: See 'Eleven O'Clock', line 5n.

9 *Contessa*: an Italian countess.

10 *garçon*: waiter (French).

20 *Lido*: a beach resort near Venice.

24 *truffle*: See 'Ticket in Tatts', line 21n.
Marchesa: an Italian marchioness.

26 *Romanoff*: the dynasty that ruled Russia from 1613 until the 1917 Russian Revolution.

31 *Romano*: See 'Pay-Day', line 21n.

32 *deener*: one shilling.

35 *Hispano-Suiza*: a brand of luxury car, built in both Spain and France.

38 *Mr Menjou*: Adolphe Menjou (1890–1963), American film actor, known for his fine dress.

39 *Maraschino*: liqueur made from marasca cherries.

41 *one and three*: one shilling and threepence (equivalent to approx. twelve cents).

44 *the Quay*: Circular Quay, the northern end of central Sydney, on Sydney Harbour.

Serenade

Smith's Weekly, 11 October 1930

3 *tango*: a Spanish dance
mantillas: silk or lace headscarfs or capes worn by Spanish women.

4 *Alcazar*: The flats are named after the Alcazar palace in Segovia, Spain.

8 *bizonk*: a word of Slessor's coinage, presumably meaning 'silly' or 'nonsensical'.

12 *Carmens*: women like the passionate central character of the opera *Carmen*, by French composer Georges Bizet (1838–75).

17 *San Antonio*: the name of another block of flats.

18 *Roneo*: a brand of copying machinery used in offices.

32 *cronk*: fraudulent.

34 *La Paloma*: There are a number of Spanish and South American folk tunes or songs titled 'La Paloma' (The Dove); the most likely reference is to that written by the Spanish composer, Sebastian Yradier, or Iradier (1809–1865).

39 *permanent wavery*: A permanent wave is an artificial curling of the hair meant to last for some time.

44 *he will insist on coming*: Although printed as 'he will insist coming' in *Smith's Weekly*, the line presumably should read 'he will insist on coming'.

The Night Express

Smith's Weekly, 12 January 1929

In *Smith's Weekly* the poem had an illustration which showed a woman sitting alone on a train in the top left hand corner and a steam train tearing through the night underneath the poem, culminating in the engine in the bottom right hand corner. The illustration in *Darlinghurst Nights* shows two women in sleeping bunks, and was originally used in a cartoon in *Smith's Weekly* on 21 March 1931 with the caption:

'Do you think you should stop a married man kissing you?'
'Yes, it makes them more persistent.'

3 *Bogan's Hill*: a fictional place.

19 *port-mant-eau*: a case or bag.

The Vestibule

Smith's Weekly, 5 January 1929

6 *cool*: mistakenly printed with no comma following in *Smith's Weekly*.

12 *Shepheard's*: the most famous hotel in Cairo.
Scott's: one of Melbourne's best hotels.

Miss Pillion

Smith's Weekly, 17 August 1929

4 *country pillion*: cushion attached behind a saddle, especially as a seat for a woman.

12 *bob-tailed nag*: horse with its tail cut short.

13 *Indian Scout*: a brand of motorbike.

14 *tam-o'-shanter*: a type of Scottish cap.

21 *Canterbury Road*: a suburban main road in Sydney, running through Canterbury, a south-western suburb.

23 *B.S.A.*: a brand of motorbike.

25 *Armstrong-Siddeley*: a brand of motor vehicle.

Snowdrops

Smith's Weekly, 29 June 1929

Snowdrops: cocaine users.

8 *Coke-Tree*: cocaine is obtained from coca leaves.

16 *sniff*: cocaine is sniffed through the nostrils.

27 *basic wage*: minimum wage, at this time set by the Court of Conciliation and Arbitration.

The Road to Mandolin

Smith's Weekly, 24 March 1928

3 *calico*: a type of cotton cloth.

15 *Disraeli*: Benjamin Disraeli (1804–81), English prime minister and novelist.

30 *plaid*: material with pattern of different colours crossing each other, as in a tartan.

31 *The Gay Bandolero*: 'The Bandolero', a popular song of the period, written by English songwriter Leslie Stuart (pseudonym of Thomas Barrett, 1866–1928).

33 *flappers*: young women free of traditional social restraints.

35 *Romano*: See 'Pay-Day', line 21n.

In A/C with Ghosts

Smith's Weekly, 1 March 1930

A/C: abbreviation for 'account'.

8 *at Three*: In 1930 banks closed their doors to customers at 3 p.m.

13 *nabobs*: See 'The Nabob' (*CC*), introductory n.
bobs: one-shilling coins.

14 *Midas*: In Greek mythology Midas was a Phrygian king whom Dionysus gave the power to turn everything he touched into gold.

15 *double entries*: accounting entries.

17 *pass-books*: bank books used for savings accounts.

18 *the forests of the Four Per Cent*: records of borrowers, or of lenders, with loans accruing 4% p.a. interest.

19 *ledgers*: principal accounting records.

21 *bogies*: ghosts.

23 *crinoline*: type of coarse cotton material, or a hooped skirt.

27 *opulent*: affluent.

Mademoiselle — All of Them

Smith's Weekly, 28 April 1928

9 *Mademoiselle from Armentières*: the title of a song popular during the Great War. Armentières is in the north of France, near the Belgian border.

12 *A.I.F.*: Australian Imperial Forces.

25 *grenadiers*: elite unit of soldiers; or grenade-equipped unit of soldiers.

26 *fusiliers*: name of certain army units (originally soldiers who carried fusils, or muskets).

27 *bombardiers*: artillery regiments.

Lonely

Smith's Weekly, 22 December 1928

7 *willow-pattern*: a blue and white design, especially used on crockery, based on a Chinese legend.

9 *a guinea*: one pound and one shilling.

13 *the 'Herald'*: the *Sydney Morning Herald* newspaper.

14 *schooner*: sailing ship with at least two masts.

Gruner: Elioth Gruner (1882–1939), Australian (although born in New Zealand) landscape painter.

15 *Pymble*: a northern suburb of Sydney.

17 *Black Narcissus*: See 'Underground Roses', line 11n.

18 *Edward Gibbon*: (1737–94), English historian, best known for *The History of the Decline and Fall of the Roman Empire.*

20 *Parramatta*: a western suburb of Sydney.

21 *lubra*: an Aboriginal woman.

Maroubra: a southern suburb of Sydney.

Wangaratta: a town in northern Victoria.

27 *a poker-work machine*: a machine for ornamenting wood by burning designs into it.

33 *Coty's crystals*: a brand of bath salts.

mercery: material, fabrics.

Evolution

Smith's Weekly, 4 April 1931

2 *'Little White Lies'*: a popular song written by American songwriter Walter Donaldson (1893–1947).

5 *slinky*: slender and flowing.

6 *timed-to-the-tick*: timed to the tick of the clock — i.e. up to date, modern.

7 *minky*: made of mink.

8 *coupe*: a two door car with only one set of seats.

dinky: dainty and smart.

11 *Romano's*: See 'Pay-Day', line 21n.

14 *chic*: fashionable and stylish.
Talgai: a reference to the Talgai skull, discovered in Queensland in 1884 and estimated to be 10,000–25,000 years old.

20 *shale*: a type of stone.

35 *Marie Corelli*: pseudonym of Mary Mackay (1855–1924), English author of popular romantic and melodramatic novels.
Lang: Jack (John Thomas) Lang (1876–1975), controversial Premier of New South Wales 1925–1927 and 1930–1932. See 'Jack-in-the-box' (*UP*).
Ned Kelly: Edward Kelly (1855–80), the most famous of all Australian bushrangers and a folk hero.

The Snow Maiden

Smith's Weekly, 16 June 1928

1 *gaiters*: cloth or leather covering worn over ankle and part of the shoe.

3 *Kelvinators*: See 'The Green Rolls-Royce', line 3n.

6 *five degrees*: i.e. five degrees Fahrenheit, on which scale 32 degrees is freezing point.

20 *Firing a funeral mute*: dismissing an employee who has worked as a professional mourner at funerals.

26 *Frigidaire*: See 'The Green Rolls-Royce', line 4n.

27 *Hillier*: Ern Hillier, proprietor of refreshment rooms in Pitt Street and in George Street, Sydney.

The Ballad of the Knee

Smith's Weekly, 28 July 1928

5 *bombazine*: a type of fine fabric, once used often for formal dress.

6 *taffeta*: lustrous silk or rayon fabric.

9 *bustles*: pads or frames worn above the buttocks to expand dresses, popular in Victorian times.

14 *patellas*: kneecaps.

16 *antimacassars*: coverings for the backs and arms of chairs, common in the nineteenth century.

21 *peignoirs*: dressing gowns or negligees.

23 *Dundrearies*: long side-whiskers, common in the nineteenth century.
26 *gavotte*: a type of dance, in quick time.
27 *contracted the Jeebies*: became nervous, or were revolted; usually written as 'heebie-jeebies'.
35 *flappers*: See 'The Road to Mandolin', line 33n.
Manhattan: See 'Country Eyes', line 8n.

The All-Night Taxi Stand

Smith's Weekly, 22 September 1928

1 *Yellow*: See 'Going Home', line 1n.
6 *Usher's*: an up-market Sydney hotel and restaurant.
7 *Glengarriff*: a town in the south-west of Ireland, near Bantry Bay; mistakenly printed as 'Glengariff' in *Smith's Weekly* and *DN*.
17 *Black Jacks*: suspicious-looking men, criminals.
22 *the Count of Hot Dogs*: a footpath hotdog seller.

Good-bye Chorus Lady

Smith's Weekly, 23 August 1930

5 *a Yellow*: See 'Going Home', line 1n.
7 *Vitaphones*: a process of recording and playing sound tracks of films.
8 *Magnavox*: a brand of speakers used in cinemas.
18 *Paramount*: a company making motion pictures.
19 *Daisy de Vere*: stage name of a fictional chorus lady.
30 *Columbine*: a traditional female comic character.
39 *Chrysanthemum Alley*: a fictional street.
40 *Western Electric*: an American company involved in making talking films.
corps-de-ballet: company of ballet dancers.

Up in Mabel's Room

Smith's Weekly, 7 November 1931

13 *Choker's Lane*: See 'Choker's Lane', introductory n.

17 *fifty shilling pride*: pride, or self-importance, from renting rooms for fifty shillings (equal to $5) per week.

25 *nebulae*: galaxies of stars.

Backless Betty from Bondi

ed. Julian Croft (Sydney: Angus and Robertson, 1983)

These poems were collected by Julian Croft twelve years after Slessor's death, following the success of the reprint of *Darlinghurst Nights* in 1981. As with *Darlinghurst Nights*, dated mss drafts of these poems do not exist but it is highly likely that each poem was written close to its publication date. These poems were also illustrated by Virgil Reilly. The general introductory note to *Darlinghurst Nights* is equally applicable to *Backless Betty from Bondi*.

The Man Who Came Back

Smith's Weekly, 6 August 1932

The Man Who Came Back: i.e. came back from dejection and unemployment, and thus came back to buying *Smith's Weekly*. The poem provides a reminder that the context for all the poems in *DN* and *BBFB* is the Great Depression.

Epigraph: 'Oigle' was a character in the comic strip 'Li'l Abner', published in *Smith's Weekly*.

20 *Indian ink*: a black ink, used by pen and ink artists and cartoonists.

Night of Romance

Smith's Weekly, 30 August 1930

1 *Bailiffs*: rent collectors.

11 *Otto*: Sir Otto Niemeyer (1883–1971) was Chairman of the Bank of England, to which the New South Wales Government owed money. See also 'Virgil and Slessor Throw a Party on the Strength

of the Lang Party's Return to Office' (UP).

L.S.D.: pounds, shillings and pence.

12 *Otto*: partly a pun on 'attar', perfume of roses.

Mademoiselle from Everywhere

Smith's Weekly, 11 May 1929

Mademoiselle from Everywhere: a play on the song title, 'Mademoiselle from Armentières'; see 'Mademoiselle — All of Them' (*DN*).

1 *Putney*: a south-western suburb of London.

4 *Beckenham*: a southern suburb of London.

6 *punt*: a ferry, usually running on cables, which carried people, vehicles etc. across a river.

8 *Tipperary*: a city and a county in Ireland. 'It's a Long Way to Tipperary' was a popular song during the Great War.

9 *the Front*: the battle front.

13 *seventeen stone*: the equivalent of approximately 108 kg.

18 *A.W.L.*: Absent Without Leave (from military duties).

19 *Calais*: a city on the north coast of France, where boats and ferries dock after crossing the English Channel.

20 *Beersheba*: a city in what is now central Israel.

21 *Palais*: palace (French). Many dance halls used the word 'Palais' in their titles.

24 *vanishing cream*: make-up supposed to remove wrinkles.

28 *bungs.*: bungalows; this is the word used by the English for what Australians call 'houses', and the abbreviation is used in real estate advertisements.

De Sotos: a brand of motor vehicle, manufactured by Chrysler.

Nocturne

Smith's Weekly, 25 August 1928

Nocturne: a term generally used in painting or music to indicate a night scene or music (often pensive) appropriate to the night.
Epigraph: *The Daily Telegraph Pictorial* and the *Sun* were Sydney evening newspapers at the time.

8 *minx*: a pert and flirtatious woman.
20 *trull*: a prostitute.
32 *drab*: a prostitute.
35 *midden*: dunghill.

The Girl at the Gate

Smith's Weekly, 21 December 1929

4 *Lochinvar*: the hero of a ballad in the poem *Marmion* by Sir Walter Scott (1771–1832).
10 *the Nine Mile Gate*: Australian country roads sometimes have gates in order to prevent cattle or sheep escaping.
21 *Packard*: a brand of motor vehicle.

Firefly

Smith's Weekly, 29 December 1928

Firefly: literally, a beetle whose abdominal organs produce light; colloquially applied to cinema or theatre ushers and usherettes.

2 *flambeau*: a torch, originally a flaming torch and used on grand occasions.
5 *Clovelly*: an eastern suburb of Sydney.
7 '*Vendetta*': a novel by Marie Corelli.
Marie Corelli: See 'Evolution' (*DN*), line 35n.
9 *Halley*: Edmund Halley (1656–1742), English astronomer; he was the first to realise that comets revisit the earth, including the one named after him, every 74–79 years.
13 *Mae*: Mae West (1892–1980), American film actress.
Dolores: Dolores Costello (1905–79), American film actress.
14 *Greta Garbo*: (1905–90), Swedish film actress (real name, Greta Lovisa Gustafsson).
18 *Wurlitzer*: a brand of organ. Organs were often played at cinemas before films were shown.
21 *St Peter*: colloquially, keeper of the gates to Heaven.

As We Pine in a Line

Smith's Weekly, 11 February 1928

1 *half-an-inch*: equivalent to a little over 1 cm.; Slessor's line alludes to the opening of Alfred Lord Tennyson's 'The Charge of the Light Brigade': 'Half a league, half a league'.

2 *punt*: See 'Mademoiselle from Everywhere', line 6n. Punts were reasonably common in Australia at the time.

3–7 *Austins, Packards, Buicks, Hupmobiles*: brands of motor vehicle.

20 *Oh, well for the rollicking medico's boy*: Slessor's line alludes to the second stanza of Tennyson's 'Break, Break, Break': 'O, well for the fisherman's boy'.

24 *cadges*: begs and borrows.
B.M.A. badges: badges signifying membership of the British Medical Association. Doctors had rights of precedence.

Come Aboard

Smith's Weekly, 2 February 1929

4 *bo'suns*: boatswains — warrant officers on warships or petty officers on merchant ships, responsible for anchors, cables etc.

6 *stokers*: See 'Captain Dobbin' (*CC*), line 160n.

12 *sea-legs*: ability to walk on a boat or ship rocked by the sea.

13 *Blue Peter*: flag hoisted on ships to indicate that they are about to leave port.

16 *Duco*: a type (originally a brand) of paint used on motor vehicles.

29 *glister*: glistening.

Butterflies

Smith's Weekly, 10 August 1929

6 *Burgundy*: See 'It, If and Also' (*DN*), line 2n.

8 *Moth*: a Gypsy Moth biplane.

11 *Wapiti*: Westland Wapiti, a brand of aeroplane.

14 *Marmon*: See 'Going Home' (*DN*), line 3n.
Hup: Hupmobile, a brand of motor vehicle.

15 *Packards*: a brand of motor vehicle.

21 *Widgeon*: a type of duck, also a British biplane, the Westland Widgeon.

Underwood Ann

Smith's Weekly, 25 June 1932

Underwood: See 'Eleven O'Clock' (*DN*), line 5n.

3 *the bell*: the bell on old typewriters which signalled the end of a line.

35 *Napoleon*: Napoleon Bonaparte (1769–1821), French military leader who became Emperor; here, the archetypal commander.

Skis and Shes

Smith's Weekly, 9 July 1932

9 *Kosciusko*: Mt Kosciusko, the highest mountain in Australia, and a place where skiing is popular in winter.

19 *hoi-polloi*: the common people (Greek for 'the many').

She Keeps on Walking

Smith's Weekly, 23 July 1932

7 *tam-o'-shanter*: See 'Miss Pillion' (*DN*), line 14n.

18 *centipedes*: a class of insects with numerous legs.

19 *billy*: a container for boiling water and making tea, much used in Australian folklore.

25 *dryad*: in Greek mythology, wood nymphs.

27 *jeremiad*: lamentation.

She Shoots to Conquer

Smith's Weekly, 4 November 1933

She Shoots to Conquer: 'Shoots' in the sense of catches the waves. The title puns on the title of the play *She Stoops to Conquer*, by Oliver Goldsmith (1728?–1774).

10 *the belt*: the belt sometimes worn by surf lifesavers when making rescues.

11 *beach-patrols*: surf lifesavers patrolling the beach for swimmers in trouble.

Nightingale — 1930

Smith's Weekly, 23 November 1929

4 *nightingales*: both the bird and nurses, so called after Florence Nightingale (1820–1910), famed for her nursing of British soldiers in the Crimean War and for founding trained nursing as a profession.

6 *A Lady went forth with a Lamp*: Florence Nightingale was known as the 'Lady of the Lamp'.

11 *Röntgen and radium*: X-rays; see 'Last Trams' (*FB*), line 20n.

16 *iodoform*: a type of antiseptic.

18 *Fahrenheit*: a method of measuring. temperature, named after German physicist Gabriel Fahrenheit (1686–1736).

20 *Gloaming*: a champion racehorse of the period.

29 *St George*: the patron saint of England since the reign of Edward III; in mythology slaying a dragon is one of his achievements.

36 *Probationer Jones*: Jones is in a trial period as a nurse.

The Girl on the Corner

Smith's Weekly, 14 May 1932

15 *CLARK GABLE*: William Clark Gable (1901–60), American film actor.

16 *SCOTT*: Randolph Scott (1903-), American film actor.

38 *the Quay*: See 'Tête-à-Tête', line 44n.

Little Theatre Girl

Smith's Weekly, 24 June 1933

11 *Mrs Patrick Campbell*: (1865–1940), English theatre actress.

17 *Pirandello*: Luigi Pirandello (1867–1936), Italian playwright, novelist and short story writer.

19 Othello: *Othello, the Moor of Venice*, by Shakespeare (1564–1616).

20 *O'Neill*: Eugene O'Neill (1888–1953), American playwright.

21 *D.H. Lawrence*: (1885–1930), controversial English novelist, poet and playwright.

25 *Strindberg*: August Strindberg (1849–1912), Swedish playwright.

27 *Lindbergh*: Charles Lindbergh (1902–1974), American pioneer aviator.

Streamer's End

Smith's Weekly, 15 March 1930

1 *steamer*: steamship.

25 Orsova: a famous passenger ship of the period.

27 *Casanova*: See 'Good-bye Iceman', line 10n.

Spring

Smith's Weekly, 14 September 1929

1 *pipits*: a type of bird, similar to larks.

Great-grandmother Speaks

Smith's Weekly, 1 April 1933

17 *RUDY*: Rudy Vallee (1901–1986), American popular singer, the first to be called a 'crooner'.

18 *Mr. CRUMMIT*: Frank Crummit (1889–1943), American popular singer.

28 *Ginger Blue quadrille*: a type of square-dance of French origin, usually performed by four couples.

46 *saxophone*: The saxophone was invented by Adolphe Sax (1814–94) in 1846.

Moving Day

Smith's Weekly, 18 June 1932

2 *boarders*: people paying for accommodation and meals.

7 *Gladstone bag*: a light travelling bag named after the English statesman, William Ewart Gladstone (1809–98).

22 *Bourke Street Main*: for 'Main' see 'The Embarkation for Cythera' (*TOTM*), line 12n. Bourke Street runs through inner Sydney suburbs, including Darlinghurst.

28–31 *pan-tech-ni-con*: furniture removalist's van.

35 *Arabian Nights*: The phrase plays on the *1001 Arabian Nights*, which Slessor enjoyed, plus notions of the original Arabs as nomads and the moving by night of the characters in the poem.

The Girl in the Gods

Smith's Weekly, 28 May 1932

the Gods: colloquially, a reference to (cheaper) seats high up in a theatre.

1 *Donizetti*: Gaetano Donizetti (1797–1848), Italian composer of *Lucia di Lammermoor* and other operas.

4 *Upper Circle*: seats high up in a theatre.

6 *Mr ROSSI*: Mario Rossi (1902–), Italian conductor.

9 *the damsel of Rossetti*: a reference to the poem 'The Blessed Damozel' by English poet and painter, Dante Gabriel Rossetti (1828–82); its first two lines read, 'The blessed damozel leaned out / From the gold bar of Heaven'.

12 *Carmen*: the passionate main character in the opera *Carmen*; see 'Serenade' (*DN*), line 12n.

13 *APOLLO*: See 'Realities' (*E-V*), line 21n.

14 *prima donna*: the principal female singer in any opera.

17 *allegrettos*: musical directions for a fairly fast tempo.

19 *stilettos*: narrow-bladed daggers.

20 *Roseville*: a northern suburb of Sydney.

21 *altos*: female singers with relatively deep voices.
contraltos: female singers with relatively deep voices, between soprano and tenor.

23 *Rialtos*: markets resembling the Rialto, a market island and district in Venice.

27 *Prince of Parma*: a character in any one of three seventeenth-century English masques: *The Bashful Lover* by Philip Massinger (1583–1640), *The Duke's Mistress* by James Shirley (1596–1666) and *Love and Honour* by William Davenant (1606–68).

28 *Mon Repos*: the name of a house, French for 'My Place of Rest'.

29 *Artarmon*: a northern suburb of Sydney.

My Lady's Maid

Smith's Weekly, 11 June 1932

3 *prinking*: fussing, altering for show.

29 *Midas*: See 'In A/C with Ghosts' (*DN*), line 14n.

30 *modiste's bill*: bill from a maker or dealer in fashionable clothing.

Passers-by

Smith's Weekly, 19 January 1929

11 *Furies*: in Greek mythology avenging deities who dwelt in the Underworld.

22 *Doreen*: Slessor's poem was inspired by a letter sent to *Smith's* by Doreen Crook, who lived at Wycliffe Well, in the outback, north of Alice Springs. *Smith's* published the letter, with illustrations, on p. 15 of this issue under the title, 'Doreen From The Burning Centre Tells Her Story'.

Wild Grapes

Smith's Weekly, 16 March 1929; P

A revised version of this poem was included in *CC* without an illustration. For notes and variants see *CC*.

Silence

Smith's Weekly, 16 March 1929

2 *ocarinas*: types of flute, usually made of terracotta, sometimes played by children, and often used in folk music; mistakenly printed as 'occarinas' in *Smith's Weekly* and *BBFB*.

3 *riff-raff*: common people.

10 *Jupiter*: the planet Jupiter.

15 *harmoniums*: types of reed organ.

17 *euphoniums*: tenor tubas.

30 *Blue Heaven*: 'My Blue Heaven', a popular song written by American Walter Donaldson (1893–1947).

The Girl in the Window

Smith's Weekly, 7 December 1929

11 *Mousseline-de-soir*: an evening dress made of stiff silk or rayon.

32 *Nine Pounds Four*: nine pounds, four shillings, equivalent to $18.40, a substantial sum for a dress at the time.

Eve — of Ottawa

Smith's Weekly, 30 July 1932

Epigraph: In Ottawa, the capital of Canada, heads of the countries of the British Empire met for a month, beginning on 22 July, in order to discuss trade agreements and other matters. The *Sydney Morning Herald* is Sydney's most famous morning paper.

11 *girl from Armentières*: See 'Mademoiselle — All of Them', line 9n.

19 *LILY of Laguna*: a song by Leslie Stuart; for Stuart, see 'The Road to Mandolin' (*DN*).

23 *The MAID of Athens*: a song by Irish songwriter Henry Robinson Allen (1809–76) from a poem by Lord Byron.

MARY of Argyle: a song by English composer Sydney Nelson (1800–62) and English lyricist Charles Jefferys (1807–65).

24 *ELAINE of Astolat*: the heroine of 'Lancelot and Elaine' in *Idylls of the King*, by Alfred Lord Tennyson (1809–92), English poet; part of the poem was set to music by English composer Frederick Nicholls (1871–1952) as 'Elaine's Song'.

25 *ROSE of Tralee*: a song by English songwriter Charles Glover (1806–63). Tralee is a town in the south-west of Ireland.

26 *TILLY of Bloomsbury*: not known.

old Drury's NELL: Nell Gwynn (1650–87), actress in London, where Drury Lane marked the theatre district, and mistress of Charles II.

27 *SALLY of Our Alley*: 'Sally', a song written by English composer Will E. Haines (1876–1961) in 1929 and made famous by Gracie Fields (1898–1979) when she sang it in her first film, *Sally in Our Alley* (1931).

33 *Hansards*: the official record of parliamentary proceedings.

Eating by Yourself

Smith's Weekly, 4 June 1932

2 *the Guelph*: a restaurant in Florence.

3 *Trocaderos*: The Trocadero was Sydney's best-known venue for dancing.

7 *fricassee of mutton*: mutton stewed and served in a white sauce made from the resulting stock. Slessor was a renowned gourmet.

8 *terrapin ragouts*: turtle meat in a highly seasoned stew.

9 *claret of Lugano*: claret from Lugano, on Italy's northern border with Switzerland.

11 *Ferdinand Romano*: the proprietor of Romano's restaurant. See 'Pay-Day' (*DN*), line 21n.

32 *Foggitt, Jones*: a brand of canned foods.

The Moth and the Candle

Smith's Weekly, 19 October 1929

1 *Gypsy*: Gypsy Moth aeroplane.

3 *tipsy*: slightly drunk.

5 *Vandal*: one of the Germanic people who in 455 AD sacked Rome.

6 *a Goth*: one of the Teutonic race who invaded the Roman Empire.

13 *sideslip*: to lose height, voluntarily or involuntarily, by slipping with one wing down.

14 *Mercury*: See 'Realities' (*E-V*), line 10n. Mercury was sometimes depicted wearing winged sandals.

15 *Pegasus*: in Greek mythology a winged horse that could fly.

28 *Waghorn*: Flying Officer H.R.D. Waghorn of the RAF won the Schneider Trophy in 1929, setting a new world speed record of 532 kilometres per hour.
Schneider: Jacques Schneider, a wealthy Frenchman, in 1912 inaugurated the Schneider Trophy seaplane race, with a valuable trophy and prizemoney.

29 *Hinkler*: Herbert (Bert) Hinkler (1892–1933) pioneer Australian aviator. See 'Hinkler Picks the Lorry' (*UP*).

32 *the Jaguars*: a brand of aeroplane engine.

Lucky Dogs

Smith's Weekly, 7 May 1932

This is the poem as held in Slessor's papers at the NLA (MS 3020/4/305); it is a copy of the *Smith's Weekly* publication on which Slessor has crossed out the 'Overture' plus stanzas 2 and 4, all the stanza numbers, and 'BY KENNETH SLESSOR'. The word 'While' in line 15 has been changed by Slessor to 'Whilst'. This would seem to be Slessor's final version. The *Smith's Weekly* inclusions are:

Overture

Oh, where are they tugging them, why are they hugging them,
What are they lugging them FROM?
A pug and a collie run circles round Polly,
While Pauline goes past with a Pom.

Stanza 2:

Such quantities of dog-and-girl are going to-and-from,
For Mollie has a collie she can follow with aplomb.
And Poppy has a Pekinese to tangle round her Milanese,
And in and out the pepper-trees, it's Pom, Pom Pom!

Stanza 4:

The merrier the terriers, the more they meet and squeak,
Flirtations with Alsatians make the pavement give a shriek,
But ladies waving handkerchiefs ignore the little darlings' tiffs —
Surrounded by a sea of sniffs, they speak Peke Peke!

2 *With bottled things to eat*: See 'Delicatessen' (*DN*).

11 *Sealyham*: a Welsh terrier with a shaggy white coat.
a black-and-tan: a terrier of black and tan colouring.

12 *a pug*: a breed of dog with wrinkled face and curled tail.

13 *tooth-and-nail*: a conventional phrase usually used to describe fighting.

16 *Cochin China*: a region of Vietnam which provides the name of 'cochins', a breed of large domestic fowls.

17 *puppy-love*: a pun on the phrase colloquially used to indicate juvenile infatuation.

Rejected Stanzas:

a Pom: a Pomeranian, a breed of dogs with long silky hair.
Milanese: stockings.

pepper-trees: See 'Country Towns' (*CC*), introductory n.
Peke: Pekingese, a breed of small, long-haired Chinese dog.

Pantette

30 April 1932

Pantette: a type of women's lingerie, designed to be partly visible, as with pantalettes.

3 *Garbo*: See 'Firefly', line 14n.
9 *Caledonia*: Scotland.
14 *rosette*: rose-shaped gathering of material.
20 *plaid*: See 'The Road to Mandolin', line 30n.
26 *georgette*: sheer silk or rayon crepe.
35 *jugular*: any one of the large veins in the neck.

Backless Betty from Bondi

Smith's Weekly, 19 November 1932

Bondi: a Sydney suburb and Australia's most famous beach.

11 *Euclid*: geometry; see 'Carmen of the Chorus', line 8n.
29 *INSPECTORS*: Councils employed beach inspectors; one of their jobs was to send from the beach anyone wearing a costume that was too daring, or at least to make them cover up.

Extra Hand

Smith's Weekly, 17 December 1932

1 *Ninepenny*: the equivalent of approx. 8 cents.
10 *Fourpenny*: the equivalent of approx. 3 cents.
12 *a rocket*: In large department stores dockets were sent to cashiers and accounting staff by means of pneumatic tubes.

Poor Little Rich Girl

Smith's Weekly, 19 August 1933

1 *damask*: table linen woven with patterns.
4 *Dresden ware*: fine crockery; see 'Country Eyes' (*DN*), line 35n.
9 *Lanvin*: See 'Mannequins', line 6n.

12 *Pommery*: a brand of champagne.

15 *a third-floor-back*: a flat in the back of the third floor of a building, generally an unattractive position.

16 *Woolloomooloo*: an inner suburb of Sydney, adjoining Darlinghurst. Slessor describes it in his essay, 'A Portrait of Sydney' (*BW*, 7; Haskell, 75–6).

Uncollected Poems

These poems are arranged in chronological order according to the date of composition where that is known. Poems for which this date is completely unknown are presented at the end of the section.

Jerusalem Set Free

written 1917; first published in *The Torchbearer* (magazine of the Church of England Grammar School) and various newspapers, 23 May 1918

The poem won first prize for a poem on the subject of 'Jerusalem Set Free' organised by the Victoria League in London for British subjects living outside Britain. A sketch by Norman Lindsay showing Australian soldiers of the Great War with Crusaders and other historical figures was published in the *Bulletin* on 1 February 1917.

The Crusaders Retreating A.D. 1192: The Third Crusade (1189–92) was led by King Richard I of England and intended to win back the city of Jerusalem from the Muslim leader, Saladin, but failed to do so.

2 *the Lion-Heart*: Richard I was known as 'Richard the Lion Heart'.

5 *Saracen*: any Muslim or Mohammedan.

The Crusaders Advancing A.D. 1917: Jerusalem was captured from the Turks by British and Australian forces in December 1917.

14 *the Wall*: probably a reference to the walls of Jerusalem.

Goin'

written 1917; first published *Bulletin*, 19 July 1917.

This was Slessor's first poem accepted for publication by a magazine. In his notes for a 1962 television interview Slessor said of the poem, 'I blush inwardly to think of it' (Haskell, 249). In notes written toward a reply to a request for permission to reprint the poems in an anthology of First World War literature, dated November 1969, Slessor wrote, 'I think these verses ["Goin'" and "France–1918"] shockingly bad'. (NLA MS 3020/1/856) 'I had hoped that these frightful lapses of my youth had gone into oblivion for ever and their exhumation somewhat embarrasses me'. (NLA MS 3020/1/860)

5 *Anzac*: the battle at Gallipoli, where Australian, New Zealand and other troops landed before dawn on 25 April 1915 and where many were killed before the Gallipoli campaign ended in January 1916. See also 'April 25' (*TOTM*), general n.

10 *Manly! Mosman! Middle 'Arbor!*: Manly, Mosman and Middle Harbour are areas of Sydney served by Sydney Harbour ferries.

12 *the music on the boat!*: musicians played on ferries at this time.

15 *Fort Denison*: a martello tower built in 1857 on a once rocky outcrop in Sydney Harbour. It was named after William Thomas Denison, Governor of the colony in 1857.

Southern Song

1917, before 30 July

2 *curvetting*: leaping in a way that has all four legs off the ground.

5 *brumbie's*: 'brumby' is an Australian term for a wild horse.

9 *beat the stragglers round*: drive straggling sheep or cattle into the main group.

21 *a restless gum*: a gum tree in the wind.

France — 1918

exact date not known, probably 1918; *Bulletin*, 9 May 1918

16 *A station on the Darling*: a property near the Darling River, the longest river in Australia, which runs through Queensland and New South Wales.

Ophelia

1918

Ophelia: the young lover of Hamlet in Shakespeare's play *Hamlet*, who drowns in a brook. Slessor may have had in mind the painting 'Ophelia' by the Pre-Raphaelite, John Millais (1829–96).

4 *cups*: the lily flowers.

9 *even*: evening.

Untitled ('I sing the Epic . . .')

not known, probably 1919; *Smith's Weekly*, 5 July 1919

Epigraph: The *Emden* was a German cruiser destroyed by HMAS *Sydney* near the Cocos Islands on 9 November 1914. Hyde Park is the main park in the central city area of Sydney.

8 *Oxford-street*: a main road which runs from the south-east corner of Hyde Park to Bondi Junction.

26 *Michael Meagher*: presumably a misprint for 'Richard Meagher', correctly named in the epigraph.

M.L.C.: Member of the Legislative Council, the upper house of the New South Wales Parliament; Meagher had been Lord Mayor of Sydney and a Member of the Legislative Assembly, the lower house of the New South Wales Parliament.

30 *Thomas Nesbitt*: Town Clerk of Sydney for more than twenty years from 1901.

To a Forgotten Portrait

not known; *Bulletin*, 10 July 1919

4 *Georgie the Third*: King George III of Britain (1738–1820); he reigned 1760–1820, during which time the Australian colonies were founded, but was acknowledged insane in 1811.

a tourist to Botany Bay: Many convicts were transported to Botany Bay during the reign of George III.

5 *primrosy path*: Shakespeare's play *Macbeth* (II. iii) describes 'The primrose way to the everlasting bonfire' and *Hamlet* (I. iii)

mentions 'the primrose path of dalliance' pursued by the 'puff'd and reckless libertine'.

6 *the Pump Room at Bath*: Bath was a fashionable spa town west of London. The Pump Room, built in the eighteenth century, provides access to natural hot springs and baths once used by the Romans.

The Uncharted

not known; *Bulletin*, 7 August 1919

Epigraph: from 'Elegy Written in a Country Churchyard' by Thomas Gray (1716–71)

2 *furze*: an evergreen shrub with yellow flowers, better known in Europe than in Australia.

3 *spin-drift*: continuous driving spray.

4 *cobble*: a rounded stone, or a piece of clumsy mending or joining.

5 *couche*: couch, bed.

The Buccaneers

not known; *Bulletin*, 18 September 1919

2 *Watson's Bay*: a suburb of Sydney on South Head, the entrance to Sydney Harbour.

10 *spars*: See 'The Embarkation for Cythera' (*TOTM*), line 13n.

12 *the Cross*: the Southern Cross star formation.
Caribbee: the Caribbean; printed as 'Caribee' in the *Bulletin*.

13 *One thousand leagues*: equivalent to approx. 5000 km.
Circular Quay: See 'Tête-à-Tête' (*DN*), line 44n.

14 *east-nor'-south*: a nonsense direction.
wot: reckon.

18 *Cremorne*: a northern suburb of Sydney, on Middle Harbour.

20 *a dolphin steed*: in some ancient mythologies dolphins escorted the dead to the Islands of the Blessed.

26 *Spanish Main*: See 'The Embarkation for Cythera' (*TOTM*), line 12n.

31 *ken*: know.

Poetic Licence

not known; *Bulletin*, 24 July 1919

Poetic Licence: Printed as 'License' in the *Bulletin*; 'poetic licence' is a freedom with language or with factual truth customarily allowed to poets.

4 *Indenture*: legal agreement. Slessor's poem takes the form of a contract between himself and the Muse.

8 *Parnassian*: related to Mt Parnassus, in Greek mythology the home of the Muses.

15 *twang the Lyre*: In classical art the Muses were often depicted playing the lyre.

18 *THALIA*: in Greek mythology, the Muse who presided over comedy and idyllic poetry, and also one of the three Graces, the patroness of festive meetings.

19 *1st of April*: April Fools' Day.

20 *Kirribilli*: a northern suburb of Sydney.

29 *permute*: interchange, transmute.

31 *factorial n*: to a mathematical factor of n.

37 *sward*: a poeticism for grass-covered soil.

38 *zephyr*: a poeticism for breeze.

39 *meads*: a poeticism for meadows.

ford: a place of shallow water where crossings may be made.

41 *dells*: a small vale with trees or plants.

49 *paean*: a song of praise or thanksgiving.

54 *callow*: naive.

Ella Wheeler Wilcox: American poet (1850–1919), known for romantic, sentimental verse.

Civilisation

not known; *The Triad*, 10 March 1920

In *The Triad* the spelling 'Civilization' was used, and the poem was number III of three 'Songs from the Chinese'. The poem is given here in the form of Slessor's manuscript.

Yuan Chieh: (719–772), Chinese poet who was concerned with the moral dimension of literature; Slessor's poem is an adaptation of a translation by Arthur Waley in *One Hundred and Seventy Chinese Poems* (see 'The Old Chinese Poem' [*TOTM*], introductory n.), which reads:

Civilization

To the south-east — three thousand leagues —
The Yüan and Hsiang form into a mighty lake.
Above the lake are deep mountain valleys,
And men dwelling whose hearts are without guile.
Gay like children, they swarm to the tops of the trees;
And run to the water to catch bream and trout.
Their pleasures are the same as those of beasts and birds;
They put no restraint either on body or mind.
Far I have wandered throughout the Nine Lands;
Wherever I went such manners had disappeared.
I find myself standing and wondering, perplexed,
Whether Saints and Sages have really done us good.

1 *a thousand leagues*: See 'The Buccaneers', line 13n.

2 *Yuan*: Yuan River, approx. 800 km long, a major river in Hunan and Kweichow provinces, which empties into the Tung-t'ing Lake at Ch'angte and thence into the Yangtze River.
Hsiang: Hsiang River, also approx. 800 km long, which discharges into Tung-t'ing Lake.

13 *The Nine Lands*: See 'Amazement' (*TOTM*), line 14n.

Songs from the Chinese

not known; *The Triad*, dates as shown below

i

The Scarlet Cockatoo

The Triad, 10 October 1919

A poem by Po Chü-I (see 'An Old Harp' [*TOTM*], introductory n.). In *The Triad* this poem and 'The Birth of His Son' (see below) are contained in a letter written by Slessor. They are introduced with the comment: '. . . what is so fascinating in this ancient poetry is its truth as applied to the twentieth century. I give below two little poems which might have been penned this morning, so true and pregnant are they still'. The poem is given here in the form of Slessor's manuscript. The poem is translated in Waley (see 'Civilisation' above), pp. 149–50, as follows:

The Red Cockatoo

Sent as a present from Annam —
A red cockatoo.
Coloured like the peach-tree blossom,
Speaking with the speech of men.
And they did to it what is always done
To the learned and eloquent.
They took a cage with stout bars
And shut it up inside.

1 *Annam:* central Vietnam.

ii

The Birth of His Son

The Triad, 10 October 1919

A poem by Su Tung-p'o (1037–1101), also known as 'Su Shih', a Szechwan poet known for his mastery of an enormous range of Chinese literary forms and for the setbacks in his political career, which enriched his poetry. The poem is translated in Waley (who gives his birth date as 1036), p. 98, as 'On the Birth of His Son':

On the Birth of His Son

Families, when a child is born
Want it to be intelligent.
I, through intelligence,

Having wrecked my whole life,
Only hope the baby will prove
Ignorant and stupid.
Then he will crown a tranquil life
By becoming a Cabinet Minister.

15 *cit:* citizen.

iii

Cockcrow Song

The Triad, 10 March 1920

An anonymous poem from first century BC China. In *The Triad* the poem was published as 'Songs of the Chinese', number I (see 'Civilisation' above). The poem is translated in Waley, pp. 30–1:

Cock-Crow Song

In the eastern quarter dawn breaks, the stars flicker pale.
The morning cock at Ju-nan mounts the wall and crows.
The songs are over, the clock run down, but still the feast is set.
The moon grows dim and the stars are few; morning has
  come to the world.
At a thousand gates and ten thousand doors the fish-shaped
  keys turn;
Round the Palace and up by the Castle, the crows and
  magpies are flying.

21 *Ju-nan*: a city in Shandong Province, central eastern China, not far from the Yellow Sea.

22 *The clocks have run dry*: the Chinese used water clocks.

iv

In Protest

The Triad, 10 March 1920

A poem by Ts'ao Sung (flourished *c.*870–920). In *The Triad* the poem was published as 'Songs of the Chinese', number II and titled 'Ts'Ao Sung's Protest' (see 'Civilisation' above). The poem is translated in Waley as 'A Protest in the Sixth Year of Ch'ien Fu (AD 879)', pp. 97–8:

A Protest in the Sixth Year of Ch'ien Fu

The hills and rivers of the lowland country
  You have made your battle-ground.
How do you suppose the people who live there
  Will procure 'firewood and hay'?
Do not let me hear you talking together
  About titles and promotions;
For a single general's reputation
  Is made out of ten thousand corpses.

Youth

not known

The only known copy of this poem appears in the Frank C. Johnson papers in the Mitchell Library (ML MSS 1214/33/111), where it is attributed to Jack Lindsay, as are other poems definitely by Slessor. The poem is in Slessor's handwriting.

1 *Ooling*: O-ling, a lake in the Kunan Mountains in south central China.

2 *caparisoned*: with ornate trappings over their horses.

8 *Tartar*: See 'Marco Polo' (*TOTM*), line 25n.

The Drunken Poet

1919

The poem exists in corrected typescript in Slessor's papers (NLA MS 3020/21/194)

1 *Castlereagh-Street*: a street in central Sydney.

5 *Thessalian*: from Thessalia (in ancient Greece, 'Thessaly'), a district of northern Greece, south of Macedonia.

7 *heather-ale*: an imagined drink.

12 *moulder*: waste away.

In an Old Book Shop

1919; *The Triad*, 10 January 1920

In *The Triad* and in a pamphlet form in which the poem was later published by James Tyrrell, it was titled 'In Tyrrell's Book Shop'. Slessor has made corrections in his copy of the poem in the NLA (MS 3020/4/295). James Tyrrell was the best known of Sydney's secondhand booksellers; the poem most likely refers to his Castlereagh Street shop (see Stewart, 93–5).

2 *pinions*: literally, birds' wings; here the arms of the clocks' mechanisms.

6 *motey sun-shaft*: ray of light with dust specks visible.

11 *cleft from onyx*: carved from onyx, a type of quartz.

13 *Damascene*: decorated with etching or with inlaid precious metals.

14 *Boule*: cabinets with inlaid designs, after the manner of Andre-Charles Boulle (1642–1732), French cabinetmaker.

16 *Dresden*: See 'Country Eyes' (*DN*), line 35n.

21 *querulous*: complaining.

23 *those*: 'the' in *The Triad* and the pamphlet.

24 *darkling*: in the dark.

29 *Cicero*: Marcus Tullius Cicero (106–43 BC), Roman orator and politician.

31 *brindled duodecimo*: pages formed from sheets of paper folded to form twelve double-sided pages, now grey or tawny with spots or streaks.

32 *leaves*: pages.

A Chaplet

not known; *Bulletin*, 22 January 1920

Chaplet: a string of beads, in Roman Catholicism a string of beads used for counting prayers.

11 *Treasure Island*: See 'Metempsychosis' (*CC*), line 1n.

14 *Caribbee*: See 'The Buccaneers', line 12n.

15 *'Haroun Alraschid'*: (766–809), Arabian caliph.

20 *minarets*: towers or turrets of a mosque.

22 *Pompadour*: Jeanne-Antoinette Poisson, Mme de Pompadour (1721–64), friend of Voltaire and influential mistress of Louis XV and a patron of literature and the arts generally.
23 *Versailles*: grand palace of the French kings.
24 *Tritons*: See 'Realities' (*E-V*), line 20n.
26 *carp*: a type of fish.
29 *'Forty-four*: perhaps a reference to 1544; in 1544 Henry VIII sent English armies to Scotland, burning villages, slaughtering the people, devastating Edinburgh, including Holyroodhouse, and many border abbeys.
30 *Holyrood*: an abbey in Edinburgh, founded 1128; or possibly a reference to Holyroodhouse, which adjoins the abbey and is the monarch's official residence in Scotland.
31 *Araby*: a poeticism for Arabia.
Bath: See 'To a Forgotten Portrait', line 6n.
33 *cabala*: occult or esoteric lore.

Magnanimous Manly

not known; *Bulletin*, 12 February 1920

Manly: a north-eastern beachside suburb of Sydney.
Epigraph: The Prince of Wales is the heir to the British throne, in this case later to become Edward VIII and then to abdicate.
Sydney Pickles: (1894-), pioneer Australian aviator; a pilot with the Royal Navy Air Service in the Great War, Pickles had recently (in 1919) flown a Sydney to Broken Hill survey flight.

1 *the Corso*: a main street of Manly.
3 *the festal main*: the ocean prepared for a festival.
4 *bunting*: flags and streamers.
the Steyne: the street running parallel to Manly Beach, and to North Steyne and Queenscliff beaches.
8 *Pierrots*: masqueraders or buffoons, named after a male character, Pierrot, in French pantomine.
9 *Doges*: chief magistrates in the old city-states of Venice and Genoa.
16 *H.M.S. Renown*: the battleship used by the Prince of Wales on his

visit to Australia. Slessor wrote newspaper articles about the ship and the Prince's visit, printed in the *Sun* on 22 June and 19 August, 1920.

Wayside Pipers

not known; *Bulletin*, 1 April 1920

Epigraph: The *Sun* was a Sydney newspaper for which Slessor worked at the time. Ascham is a private girls' school at Edgecliff, near Kings Cross.

5 *the Domain*: an area close to the city, used as a Speakers' Corner, especially on Sundays.

7 *Bolshevik*: a supporter of Lenin's Social Democratic Party which took power in Russia after the 1917 revolution.

8 *quacks*: frauds, pretenders to knowledge, especially medical knowledge.

9 *Ryan*: Thomas Joseph Ryan (1876–1921), MHR for West Sydney and Deputy Leader of the Labor Party.
Hughes: William Morris ('Billy') Hughes (1864–1952), Australian Prime Minister at the time; in November 1917 Hughes prevented publication of an anti-conscription speech by Ryan, at that time Premier of Queensland, under wartime censorship regulations. Ryan repeated his comments in Parliament and Hughes tried, unsuccesssfully, to seize the copies of *Hansard* in which Ryan's comments were reported.

10 *Rabelaisian*: See 'To a Friend' (*FB*), line 27n. Rabelais is known as a brilliant satirist.

11 *Brobdingnagian*: gigantic, after the country of giants, Brobdingnag, in Swift's *Gulliver's Travels* (see 'Gulliver' [*CC*], introductory n).

13 *Pymble*: a northern suburb of Sydney.

14 *Hyde Park*: See 'Untitled ("I sing the Epic . . .")', introductory n.

16 *patricians*: aristocrats.
steerage: See 'Mannequins' (*DN*), line 17n.

17 *willy-nilly*: willingly or unwillingly.
the Rocks: the area to the west of Circular Quay (where the settlement of Sydney began).

Kirribilli: a suburb of Sydney on the opposite Harbour shore from Circular Quay.

18 *oligarchs*: the few people holding power in a society.

19 *gambol*: caper, spring.

Stanzas Written by a Bard Who is Morbidly Anxious to Know Exactly What *Professor Einstein Discovered about Newton*

not known; *Bulletin*, 22 November 1920

Professor Einstein: Albert Einstein (1879–1955), German-born physicist whose General Theory of Relativity, published in 1916, declared that gravity was not a force, as Newton had envisaged it, but a curved field in the continuum of space and time caused by the presence of mass. Einstein's theory was declared proven in November 1919 when the Royal Society of London made observations and subsequent calculations of a solar eclipse. Isaac Newton (1643–1727), English physicist, is regarded as Einstein's greatest predecessor.

2 *'Varsity*: university.
Mr Wellisch: properly spelt 'Wellish'; Edward Wellish (1882–1948) was lecturer (and later Associate Professor) in Applied Mathematics at Sydney University.

3 *parabola*: in geometry, a plane curve.
philander: flirt, make love irresponsibly.
quadratics: the branch of algebra that treats equations involving squares of numbers.

4 *cycloid*: a circle, or in geometry a curve generated by a point on the circumference of a circle rolling on a straight line in its plane.

5 *pundits*: people who suppose themselves to be experts.
collegiate: pertaining to a college, or university.

6 Did *what went Up come Down?*: a reference to the colloquial explanation of gravity, 'What goes up must come down'.

7 *that 'Varsity election*: the election of members of the Senate, the governing body, of Sydney University.

9 *Hades*: See 'Choker's Lane', line 6n.
deflection: Einstein's General Theory of Relativity was proven, as he had suggested, by measuring the deflection of starlight as it travelled close to the sun, the starlight being visible only during a total eclipse.
16 *Michael*: presumably the archangel Michael, who was supposed to know the secret of the 'word' by which God created Heaven and Earth, and who spoke to Moses on Mt Sinai (Acts 7: 38).
17 *Cambridge*: Cambridge University, where Newton was once a professor.
18 did . . . *the Apple drop?*: Newton said that his conception of gravity was prompted by the falling of an apple.

Blind

not known; *The Sun*, 28 November 1920

2 *Cockatoo*: Cockatoo Island in Sydney Harbour, close to Balmain.
3 *Balmain*: an inner western suburb of Sydney.
6 *men-of-war*: warships; Cockatoo Island was a naval dockyard.
7 *Greenwich*: a suburb of Sydney on the Harbour, almost opposite Balmain.
8 *louis d'or*: a gold coin first issued in the reign of Louis XIII of France.
11 *Pyrmont*: an inner western suburb, between Balmain and the city.
12 *Temeraire*: a reference to the painting 'The Fighting Temeraire' by J.M.W. Turner (1775–1851). It depicts the *Temeraire*, which had sailed directly behind Nelson's *Victory* at the Battle of Trafalgar, being towed by a steamer in early morning light.

Ave!

not known, probably close to publication date; *Sun*, 7 September 1921

In the *Sun* the poem had above it a headline, 'Lord Northcliffe in Sydney Today' and a photograph of Viscount Northcliffe. Alfred Harmsworth (1865–1922) was an extraordinarily successful newspaper publisher and the founder of modern popular journalism. He was made a Viscount in 1917 for heading the British war mission in the USA and was director of propaganda in enemy countries in 1917–18.

23 *when our guns were one to nine*: In 1917 Northcliffe exposed the British Army's shortage of shells in the pages of his paper, the *Daily Mail*.

The Ego of Aaron

close to publication date; *Sun*, 25 October 1922

In the *Sun* newspaper Slessor published a small number of book reviews in verse, none of great consequence. This poem-review of D.H. Lawrence's novel *Aaron's Rod* is included as an example of such work.

Henley on Crayfish Swamp

not known; *Punch* (Melbourne), 23 October 1924

Crayfish Swamp: an imaginary place.

4 *Yarra*: the river that flows through the city of Melbourne.

6 *Henley*: Henley-on-Thames in Oxfordshire, England, is the site of an annual rowing regatta.

7 *punts*: shallow, square-ended boats.

9 *poles*: poles used for moving a punt by pushing on the waterbed. *tad*: i.e. tadpoles.

Passenger by Greycliffe

between 3 and 11 November 1927; *Smith's Weekly*, 12 November 1927

On 3 November 1927 the liner *Tahiti* ran into the ferry *Greycliffe* in Sydney Harbour and forty people, including many schoolchildren, drowned. Slessor's poem accompanied an article about the tragedy.

10 *sepulchre*: grave.

The Office Lunch

not known, probably close to publication date; *Smith's Weekly*, 25 February 1928

1 *Haydn*: Franz Joseph Haydn (1732–1809), Austrian composer.
3 *a tether*: a lead.
14 *a draper*: a dealer in textiles.

Hinkler Picks the Lorry

not known, probably close to publication date; *Smith's Weekly*, 3 March 1928

Hinkler: See 'The Moth and the Candle'. Hinkler was born in Bundaberg, North Queensland. He was a shy and modest person.

1 *proletariat*: the working class.
14 *Hudson*: a brand of motor vehicle.
Rolls-Royce: mistakenly printed as 'Rolls Royce' in *Smith's Weekly*.
15 *Packards*: See 'Butterflies' (*BBFB*), line 15n. Packards were fairly luxurious.

With Regrets

not known, probably close to publication date; *Smith's Weekly*, 17 March 1928

6 *down*: mistakenly followed by a full stop in *Smith's Weekly*.
9 *Moët*: See 'Ticket in Tatts' (*DN*), line 20n.
10 *chickens*: chicken was an expensive meat in Australia at the time.
11 *wattle*: yellow-flowering acacia trees, common in Australia.

from Heine

not known; *The London Aphrodite*, No. 2, October 1928

Heine: See 'Heine in Paris' (*E-V*), introductory n. Slessor's translation is of section 3 of 'Yolante und Marie', a poem in four sections.

3 *Chablis*: a type of dry white wine.
4 *camisoles*: patterned underbodices, worn under blouses.

The Vanishing Army

not known, probably close to publication date; *Smith's Weekly*, 9 March 1929

cobbers: mates. Charles Abbott (1886–1954) served in the AIF 1914–1919.

7 *centurions*: in the Roman Army, commanders of 100 men.

Economics

exact date not known; between 1921 and 1929

The poem is included in Janet Lindsay's papers in the Mitchell Library (ML DOC 2261c).

1 *Unemployment?*: The poem reflects the conditions in the period leading up to the Great Depression, 1929–1933.

Sally in Our Alley

not known, probably close to publication date; *Smith's Weekly*, 22 February 1930

Sally in Our Alley: See 'Eve — of Ottawa' (*BBFB*), line 27n.

'Mo': a clown portrayed by Roy Rene, stage name of Henry Van der Sluys (1892–1954).

'Cressy' O'Reilly: Walter Creswell O'Reilly (1877–1954), Commonwealth Film Censor.

LICENCE: mistakenly printed as 'LICENSE' in *Smith's Weekly*.

twill: fabric woven like serge.

'Take a Pair of Sparkling Eyes'

a song by W.S. Gilbert (1836–1911) and Arthur Sullivan (1842–1900), from *The Gondoliers*

1 *horn-rimmed specs*: spectacles made with horn or tortoiseshell.

10 *cot*: the 'cot' in the original is a poeticism for 'cottage'.

'Hallelujah, I'm a Bum'

a popular song by the American, Harry Kirby McClintock (1882–1957) based on the traditional hymn 'Revive Us Again'

'At Seventeen'

a song from the operetta *The Student Prince*, music by Sigmund Romberg (1887–1951), text by Dorothy Donnelly (1880–1928), filmed in 1927

'Come Into the Garden, Maud'

the first stanza of *Maud, a Monodrama*, XXII, by Alfred Lord Tennyson (1809–92)

31 *chiropterous*: bat-like.

33 *chaperone*: an older person who accompanies young unmarried women and men for propriety's sake.

'Gin a Body Meet a Body'

a poem by Robbie Burns (1759–96)

38 *Gyx*: a nonsense word. 'Gin' in the original Scots means 'if'.

39 *O.T.*: foreign area (abbreviation for 'over there').

40 *Spa*: see, espy.

42 *Ilka*: every (Scots).

45 *Postum*: a brand name of a coffee substitute, made from cereal.

Footnote: *Change here*: a pun on the instructions given to train travellers. Milparinka is in the New South Wales outback; Onkaparinga is a river in South Australia and became the name of a woollen mill; 'Ilka' and 'Bilka' are fictional names.

'Drink to Me Only'

a part of the poem 'To Celia' by Ben Jonson (1572?–1637). The music was first published in 1780, composer uncertain.

47 *pledge*: the Temperance pledge to refrain from alcohol.

48 *Flytox*: a brand of fly spray.

52 *Schweppe's Sarte*: a brand of soft drink.

53 *Gorgonzola*: blue-veined type of Italian cheese.

Footnote: a joke based on a notice given on trains, buses and trams which did not collect passengers at stops.

'I Wonder Who's Kissing Her Now'

a song by American songwriter, Joseph Howard (1878–1961)

56 *pince-nez*: See 'The Old Play' (*CC*), line 34n.

60 *tract*: a statement of doctrine.

'Mademoiselle from Armentières'

See 'Mademoiselle — All of Them' (*DN*), line 9n.

67 *conversation-lolly*: a sweet with a message imprinted on it.
Vino Gattino: a brand of wine, perhaps fictional ('gattino' is Italian for 'kitten').

Virgil and Slessor Throw a Party on the Strength of the Lang Party's Return to Office

not known, close to publication date; *Smith's Weekly*, 1 November 1930

Virgil: Virgil Reilly, black and white artist who illustrated many of Slessor's poems.
Lang Party's: With the Great Depression prevailing, the New South Wales Labor Party, led by John Thomas (Jack) Lang (1876–1975), won an overwhelming victory in the 1930 election and was sworn into office on 4 November.
Indian ink: See 'The Man Who Came Back' (*BBFB*), line 20n.

5 *pecker*: courage.
7 *the Ritz*: a luxurious hotel in London.
Checker: a type of American car, frequently used as taxis.
8 *foxtrots*: a type of dance.
16 *Otto*: Otto Niemeyer; see 'Night of Romance' (*BBFB*), line 11n.
37 *linnet*: a small bird, like a finch, known for its singing.

Earth Speaks

exact date not known, between 2 and 13 February 1931; *Smith's Weekly*, 14 February 1931

On 2 February 1931 the Hawkes Bay area in the north island of New Zealand suffered a series of earthquakes, followed by serious fires.

6 *pinions*: See 'In an Old Book Shop' (UP), line 2n.
14 *ecstasy*: mistakenly printed as 'ecstacy' in *Smith's Weekly*.

Once a Year

not known, probably close to publication date; *Smith's Weekly*, 29 August 1931

2 *the dole*: unemployment relief.
3 *dimity*: See 'The Man of Sentiment', Part One (*TOTM*), line 115n.
16 *organdi*: fine cotton fabric.

Vicar of Wakefield, M.H.R.

not known; *Smith's Weekly*, 3 December 1931

Vicar of Wakefield: *The Vicar of Wakefield*, a novel written in

1761–2 by Anglo-Irish author Oliver Goldsmith (1728–74).

M.H.R.: Member of the House of Representatives, the lower house of Federal Parliament.

Richard Foster: Richard Witty Foster (1856–1932), federal member for Wakefield. He was known as a blunt, outspoken and independent politician.

1 *Stanley Melbourne*: Stanley Melbourne Bruce (1883–1967), Prime Minister of Australia.

2 *the House*: the House of Representatives.

6 *the Speaker*: the chairperson of the House of Representatives.

11 *beadle*: a parish officer.

She'll Say:–

not known, probably close to publication date; *Smith's Weekly*, 5 December 1931.

16 *Kingsford Smith*: Charles Kingsford Smith (1897–1935), Australian pioneer aviator.

24 *lasso*: mistakenly printed as'lassoo' in *Smith's Weekly*.

Birds of a Feather

not known, probably close to publication date; *Smith's Weekly*, 21 May 1932

7 *Glengarry*: a type of hat worn by Scottish Highlanders, originally as part of military dress (named after a valley in Inverness-shire, Scotland).

8 *Robin Hood*: a hat similar to that worn by Robin Hood, the legendary Medieval English outlaw.

11 *Dolly Vardons*: The surname should be spelt 'Vardens'; flower-trimmed bonnets, named after the heroine of Charles Dickens's 1841 novel *Barnaby Rudge.*

13 *cash-and-carry*: a general shop which did not deliver goods.

25 *Burwood*: a western suburb of Sydney.

27 *forest of Sherwood*: Sherwood Forest, in Nottinghamshire, was the home of Robin Hood.

28 *Wynyard Square*: an area in the centre of Sydney city.

Jack-in-the-Box

between 21 and 24 June, 1932; *Smith's Weekly*, 25 June 1932

Jack-in-the-Box: a toy, with a figure in a box which springs out suddenly when the lid is opened; and a reference to Jack Lang (see 'Virgil and Slessor Throw a Party . . .' [UP]) in the witness box at the Goode Inquiry, a Royal Commission into the conduct of Charles Goode, Chief Transport Commissioner, while employed by the Railway Commissioners. Goode had been dismissed by the Railway Commissioners. Lang, who had had Goode draft transport legislation, gave evidence on 20 June 1932. In late July the Royal Commission found Goode guilty of misconduct.

5 *the book*: the Bible.
the vow: the promise to tell the whole truth.
9 *Cabinets*: groups of ministers responsible for government of the nation.
15 *bloke*: man.

Sugar Daddy

not known, probably close to publication date; *Smith's Weekly*, 16 July 1932

Sugar Daddy: a middle-aged or older man whom women accompany or have sex with because of his wealth and the presents he gives them.

3 *coney coats*: coats made of rabbit fur.
9 *flappers*: See 'The Road to Mandolin' (*DN*), line 33n.
10 *teeny*: tiny.
17 *pecks*: kisses.
20 *a million quid*: a million pounds (equivalent to $2,000,000).
35 *Sir Robert*: Sir Robert Gibson (1864–1934) was Chairman of Directors of the Commonwealth Bank. At the Premiers' Conference held in early July 1932, the state premiers argued for loans in order to finance jobs for the unemployed and their own budget deficits. At the conference the Prime Minister, Joe Lyons, had the premiers confer at length with Sir Robert Gibson.

Camille

not known, probably close to publication date; *Smith's Weekly*, 16 September 1932

6 *Onoto*: a brand of fountain pen.

24 *rosella*: a type of brightly coloured parrot.

And That's That

not known, probably close to publication date; *Smith's Weekly*, 31 December 1932

1 *bailiff*: See 'Night of Romance' (*BBFB*), line 1n.

2 *suet*: hard fatty tissue covering the loins and kidneys of cattle and sheep.

5 *doles*: welfare payments or other handouts.

14 *limpets*: types of sea molluscs with cone-shaped shells that attach themselves to rocks.

19 *Hope springs eternal in the*: 'Hope springs eternal in the human breast', Alexander Pope (1688–1744), *An Essay on Man,* i, line 95.

20 *the wame*: the belly.

22 *a pint*: a pint of beer.

28 *mizzle*: to give up.

Epitaph for a Dead Dog

not known, probably close to publication date; *Smith's Weekly*, 11 February 1933

An Australian Spring Song that is Different

not known, probably close to publication date; *Smith's Weekly*, 16 September 1933

3 *rosellas*: See 'Camille' (UP), line 24n.

9 *In*: printed with a small 'i' in *Smith's Weekly*.

11 *No gods on mouldy leopards*: The gods of classical mythology were sometimes depicted as riding leopards (or 'pards').

15 *Pan*: See 'Pan at Lane Cove' (*TOTM*).

17 *Peter*: Peter Pan was a champion racehorse; it won a number of races carrying heavy weights, and in fact did so in the Melbourne Cup in the following year, 1934.

18 *9 stone 5*: nine stone, five pounds (equivalent to approx. 59.5 kilograms).

21 *Strephons*: Strephon is the shepherd-lover in Sir Philip Sidney's pastoral romance, *Arcadia* (1590).

22 *Helens*: parallels to Helen of Troy.

23 *Hades*: See 'Choker's Lane' (*DN*), line 6n.

26 *naiads*: in Greek mythology, water nymphs.

27 *Merino*: a Spanish breed of sheep from which an Australian breed was developed.

29 *andantino*: a musical direction to play slowly and distinctly.

Melinda in a Hurry

not known, probably close to publication date; *Smith's Weekly*, 14 October 1933

2 *flapjack*: type of thick pancake.

10 *pantette*: See 'Pantette' (*BBFB*).

georgette: type of silk or rayon crepe, dull in texture.

18 *Ritz*: See 'Virgil and Slessor Throw a Party . . .' (UP), line 7n.

Not Understood

not known, probably close to publication date; *Smith's Weekly*, 4 November 1933

Thomas Bracken: Irish-born poet and journalist (1843–98) who wrote a set of verses titled 'Not Understood'.

1 *retrenches*: dismisses people from employment. The Depression was still serious at this time.

13 *candour*: printed as 'candor' in *Smith's Weekly*.

Armistice Day — Military Hospital

not known, probably close to publication date; *Smith's Weekly*, 11 November 1933

Armistice Day: 11 November of each year, commemorating the signing of the peace treaty which ended the Great War, and all those who have died in war.

Triumphal Ode

not known, probably close to publication date; *Smith's Weekly*, 27 January 1934

Ode: a lyric poem in a lofty vein, sometimes composed for grand occasions.

Dedication: Thomas Walter White (1888–1957), MHR for Balaclava (Victoria), Minister for Trade and Customs.

8 *bumpkin*: a clumsy, ignorant person.

16 *Mr MOSES GABB*: Joel Moses Gabb (1882–1951), MHR for Angas (South Australia). 'Gabb' is Australian slang for undirected talk.

18 *PERKINS*: John Arthur Perkins (1878–1954), MHR for Eden-Monaro (New South Wales).

19 *GANDER*: Joseph Herbert Gander (1888–1954), MHR for Reid (New South Wales). 'Gander' is Australian slang for a look at something or someone.

23 *HOLMAN*: William Arthur Holman (1871–1934), MHR for Martin (New South Wales).

HUGHES: Billy Hughes; see 'Wayside Pipers' (UP), line 9n. At this time Hughes was Minister for Health and Minister for Repatriation.

Daniels: Daniel in the Old Testament book named after him was a wise man and prophet.

24 *PARKHILL*: Robert Archdale Parkhill (1879–1947), MHR for Warringah (New South Wales), Minister for Defence.

CHARLIE MARR: Charles William Marr (1880–1960), MHR for Parkes (New South Wales), Minister without a portfolio.

WHITE: Thomas White; see dedication.

GREEN: Roland Frederick Green (1885–1947), MHR for Richmond (New South Wales).

27 *The arch-Malthusian of the Apple Isle*: Joseph Lyons (1879–1939), Prime Minister. Lyons believed in the balanced budgets of orthodox economics and was a strong opponent of Jack Lang. Thomas Malthus (1766–1834) was an English economist and demographer who claimed that population growth will always outrun food supply. Lyons fathered eleven children. An Australian census was taken on 29–30 June 1933. The 'Apple Isle' is Tasmania, Lyons's home state.

30 *Curl-papers*: paper used for curling the hair, mentioned in various eighteenth-century satires on which Slessor's poem is modelled.
Hansard: See 'Eve — of Ottawa' (UP), line 33n.

31 *incarnardined*: made blood-red. The famous usage is in Shakespeare's *Macbeth*, II. ii. 62, where the murderer Macbeth says of his own hand that the seas could not wash it clean. Rather, his hand would 'The multitudinous seas incarnadine'.
Morocco-red: type of leather made from goatskin, originally made in Morocco.

36 *gord*: God.

God Save the Duke of Gloucester

not known, probably close to publication date; *Smith's Weekly*, 24 November 1934

The Duke of Gloucester made an official visit to Australia in 1934.

1 *the cannon's fearful bang*: the military salute for a visiting dignitary.

2 The Herald: *The Sydney Morning Herald*; see 'Eve — of Ottawa' (*BBFB*).
The Star: a Melbourne evening tabloid newspaper.

3 *Mr Lang*: See 'Virgil and Slessor Throw a Party . . .' (UP).

4 *Mr Marr*: See 'Triumphal Ode' (UP), line 24n.

8 *odes*: See 'Triumphal Ode' (UP).

11 *Associated News*: presumably a reference to Associated Press, a co-operative news agency founded in New York in 1848, famous for its photography.

17 *Leagues*: various social and cultural organisations.

19 *colic*: abdominal pain caused by wind.

20 *shivers*: In *Smith's Weekly* this word was 'jeebies'.

22 *Parramatta*: a western suburb of Sydney.

24 *swallowtails*: coats with forked tails like those of swallows.
spats: See 'Ticket in Tatts', (*DN*), line 24n.

Body-Line!

not known, probably close to publication date; *Smith's Weekly*, 26 January 1935

Body-Line: In cricket, a type of fast bowling aimed at the batsman rather than the wicket, controversially introduced by English captain Douglas Jardine in the 1933 Ashes tour of Australia. It was subsequently banned from the game.

1 *crinoline*: See 'In A/C with Ghosts' (*DN*), line 23n.

2 *postman's-knock*: a kissing game.

4 *battledore*: a shuttlecock racquet.

8 *First Wicket Down*: after the first batsman is out; generally the position for the best batsman in the team.

9 *Tennyson's*: See 'Eve — of Ottawa' (*BBFB*), line 24n.

11 *The 'Nineties*: the English 1890s.

19 *square-leg*: a fielding position, in a straight line behind the batsman's legs.

22 *Ours is the theory*: Bodyline was officially known as 'leg-theory'.

Dad's Toast

not known, probably close to publication date; *Smith's Weekly*, 9 February 1935

This poem employed the same illustration as used for 'And That's That', (UP).

3 *THE KING*: George V, who reigned 1910–1936.

6 *a rum kind er place*: a rough, difficult place.

7 *a six o'clock gaol*: By law pubs had to close at 6 p.m.

8 *schooners*: large glasses of beer.
threepence: the equivalent of approx. two cents.

10 *Franz Josef lager*: a brand of beer named after the Emperor of Austria.

11 *the Troc.*: the Trocadero; see 'Eating by Yourself' (*BBFB*), line 3n.

12 *West's Pitchers*: Western Suburbs Cinemas' theatre in Pitt Street.

13 *'Ughes*: Billy Hughes; see 'Wayside Pipers' (UP), line 9n.

14 *Central exchange*: the Sydney central telephone exchange.

15 *H.M.S.* Powerful: An armed cruiser, the largest warship in the Royal Navy when launched in the late 1890s.

16 *Signor Gasparri sung Tosti's 'Good-Bye'*: No record can be found of a singer named 'Gasparri'. 'Goodbye' was a popular song written by (Francesco) Paolo Tosti; for 'Tosti' see 'Country Eyes' (*DN*), line 10n.

17 *Mr Mark Foy*: (1865–1950), Sydney businessman who had with his brother Francis founded the department store, Mark Foy's.

18 *a penny*: the equivalent of approx. one cent.

The Star: See 'God Save the Duke of Gloucester', line 2n.

The Taxpayers' Marsellaise

not known, probably close to publication date; *Smith's Weekly*, 17 August 1935

The Marseillaise: The French national anthem, written by Rouget de Lisle as a revolutionary song in 1792 and officially adopted in 1795.

2 *Form 92*: the taxation return form, which provided the basis of individual income tax assessment.

6 *backblocks*: the outback.

7 *the nobs*: the well-to-do.

8 *half-crowns*: coins, equivalent to approx. twenty-five cents.

16 *Blue Gum Creek*: There are three places in or near Sydney with this name, in Annangrove, Kurrajong Hills and West Lindfield. Slessor's reference is probably to West Lindfield.

29 *primage*: loading and shipping charges.

30 *probate*: a tax on the processing of a will.

42 *Mr Sikes*: presumably Bill Sikes, the burglar in Dickens's *Oliver Twist* for whom Fagin acts as a fence. (There is no record of a politician, councillor or prominent public servant named 'Sikes' at the time.)

43 *impale a few heads on our pikes*: an act traditionally performed upon defeated enemies or executed wrongdoers.

This battle hymn of the republic: American civil war song, tune traditional, words by Julia Ward Howe.

licence: printed as 'license' in *Smith's Weekly*.

Pat Malone: not known; 'Pat Malone' is rhyming slang for 'on your own'. Slessor seems to suggest the action of Tim Finnegan in the Irish folk song, 'Finnegan's Wake'.

a bit bent: The lines of the poem were printed in irregular curves in *Smith's Weekly*.

Lady Spider

not known, probably close to publication date; *Smith's Weekly*, 7 September 1935

1 *Arachne*: In Greek mythology Arachne was a young woman who challenged Athena to a weaving contest and was turned into a spider.

3 *hackney*: See 'The Atlas' (*CC*), line 69n.

9 *Humber*: a brand of motor vehicle.

Slow Coach

not known, probably close to publication date; *Smith's Weekly*, 12 October 1935

2 *Twenty-one*: printed as 'Twenty one' in *Smith's Weekly*.

13 *the fearful Post*: the distance post on the road, here marking the age of twenty-one.

16 *trolley-bus*: a bus which draws power from overhead electric wires; mistakenly printed as 'trolly-bus' in *Smith's Weekly*.

Outboard

not known, probably close to publication date; *Smith's Weekly*, 7 December 1935

outboard: a motor which sits on the back of a boat.

5 *concertina*: a small accordion.

6 *uke*: ukelele.

7 *signorina*: a young unmarried woman (Italian).

9 *Doge's*: See 'Magnanimous Manly' (UP), line 9n.

10 *the street*: the canal, in Venice.
fins: of boats, as in gondolas.

13 *basso*: a singer with a bass voice.

15 *Tasso*: Torquato Tasso (1544–95), Italian poet.

17 *gondolieri*: gondoliers.

27 *Balmoral*: a northern waterside suburb of Sydney.

31 *La Scala*: the opera house in Milan.

Hands

not known, probably close to publication date; *Smith's Weekly*, 14 December 1935

3 *permanent waving*: See 'Serenade' (*DN*), line 39n.

20 *Burgundy red*: the colour of burgundy wine.

King's Cross Gardens

not known, probably close to publication date; *Smith's Weekly*, 4 January 1936

1 *Where the flats are crowded flatter*: 'The Green Rolls-Royce' (*DN*) includes the line, 'And the flats are rather flatter'.

16 *beds that fold in walls*: beds that fold up flat against walls when not in use.

To a Town Hall Pigeon

not known, probably close to publication date; *Smith's Weekly*, 1 August 1936

Town Hall: Sydney Town Hall

8 *Dr Purdy*: John Smith Purdy (1872–1936), Sydney city Health Officer.

28 *Archibald*: J.F. Archibald (1856–1919), whose will provided a bequest for erection of the Archibald Fountain in Hyde Park.

36 *St Andrew's*: St Andrew's Cathedral, next door to the Sydney Town Hall.

When I Was King

not known, probably close to publication date; *Smith's Weekly*, 14 August 1937

Epigraph: Mr. Hughes is Billy Hughes, Prime Minister of Australia from 1915 during the Great War. (See 'Wayside Pipers' [UP], line 9n.)

W.E. Henley: William Ernest Henley (1849–1903), English poet and editor; Slessor's poem is modelled on Henley's poem, 'Or Ever the Knightly Years Were Gone', which is also written in stanzas of 4–6–4–6–4 lines, and which begins: 'Or ever the knightly years were gone / With the old world to the grave, / I was a King in Babylon / And you were a Christian Slave'.

1 *the War Precautions Act*: An act of Federal Parliament passed on 29 October 1914 which, with an amendment passed on 30 April 1915, gave the government very wide powers in order to secure 'the public defence of the Commonwealth'.
High Court: the highest court in Australia, the crucial court in interpretations of the Australian constitution. During the war Hughes sought to transfer powers over commerce and industrial relations from the state governments to the Commonwealth Government; the transfer was secured by the 1916 High Court case of Farey *v.* Burett.

8 *flummery*: humbug.

9 *scuppered*: sank.

18 *Babylon*: in the Bible (Genesis, 11), an ancient city where language was confounded; also mentioned in Henley's poem.

20 *Swan*: quill.

Come to Sydney

not known, probably close to publication date; *Smith's Weekly*, 4 September 1937

Epigraph: J.M. Dunningham was John Montgomery Dunningham (1884–1938), minister in charge of Australia's sesquicentenary celebrations.

19 *by Jove*: a conventional colloquialism; 'Jove' is another name for Jupiter, the Roman god of light.
Lane Cove: See 'Pan at Lane Cove' (*TOTM*).

Truthful Bob

not known, probably close to publication date; *Smith's Weekly*, 6 January 1940

Bob: Robert Gordon Menzies (1894–1978), Prime Minister at the time.
Bret Harte: Francis Bret Harte (1839–1902), American fiction writer and poet; Harte first gained fame through 'The Heathen Chinee', a poem about a card shark and confidence trickster named Ah Sin.

1 *Kew*: a well-to-do inner Melbourne suburb.
12 *with a thimble and a pea*: i.e. by taking bets on which of three (or more) thimbles covers a pea.

Second-Class Ballad of the North Shore First

not known, probably close to publication date; *Smith's Weekly*, 13 January 1940

'*The Gondoliers*': See 'Take a Pair of Sparkling Eyes', part of 'Sally in Our Alley' (UP).

1 *czar*: pre-revolution Russian monarch, with virtually dictatorial powers.
3 *N.S.W.G.R.*: New South Wales Government Railways.
7 *Hawkins, Jorkins, Mr Crick*: Francis Harold Hawkins, MLA for Newcastle at the time; 'Jorkins' is a fictional name; Stanley Sadler Crick (1888–1955), Lord Mayor of Sydney at the time.
8 *Sir Marcus and Sir Walter*: not known, possibly representative names.
12 '*Second Smoking*': second-class, smoking carriage.
14 *Potts and Watts*: representative names rather than the names of particular individuals.
15 *straps*: for passengers to hold in order to keep their balance while standing.
17 *what change*: Travel on Sydney metropolitan trains became one class from 1 January 1940. The North Shore included some of Sydney's wealthier suburbs, and some councils protested about the change.
26 *Sir Alf*: not known, possibly a representative name.
30 *Sir Arthur's*: not known, possibly a representative name.

An Inscription for the Graves at Bergoulive

after May 1942, probably before 1945

Bergoulive: a town in Lebanon, north of Tyre.

This poem, which is closely related to 'An Inscription for Dog River' (*P*), is included in Slessor's papers in the NLA (MS 3020/21/192).

1 *Maximus Martius*: a fictional name, based on the names of Roman emperors; Slessor's target is Thomas Blamey.
3 *Ashur Bani Pal's*: (7th century BC), last major king of Assyria (reigned 668–627 BC); he assembled the first organised library.
4 *Nebuchadnezzar*: See 'An Inscription for Dog River' (*P*), line 4n.

Not That There Here

not known, probably close to publication date; *The Sun*, 3 August 1945

This poem was printed anonymously in the paper but Slessor worked for *The Sun* at the time and kept a copy of the poem in his papers (NLA MS 3020/5).

Epigraph: Forbes Street, Woolloomooloo, is part of the King's Cross area; apart from its role in bohemian life it has sometimes been associated with prostitution.

2 *Narrabeen and Avalon*: northern beachside suburbs of Sydney.
4 *Hurlstone Park*: a south-western suburb of Sydney.
5 *Pymble, Hornsby and St Ives*: northern suburbs of Sydney.
6 *stone the crows*: a common colloquialism, indicating surprise and frustration.
7 *Palm Beach and Collaroy*: northern beachside suburbs of Sydney.
8 *Gin-rummy*: a type of card game.
10 *Chowder Bay*: a bay of Sydney Harbour, in Mosman.
La Perouse: a southern suburb of Sydney.

Lovett Bay

probably 1951, before 24 March

This poem was written by Slessor in the visitors' book of his friend, actor Chips Rafferty (real name, John Goffage), on 24 March 1951 (ML MSS 5190/1). Rafferty and his wife lived at Lovett Bay, which is in the Pittwater area, in Sydney's northern suburbs.

F.W. Sidney: Frederick W. Sidney (dates uncertain, active in surveying from 1833), sailor and surveyor; Sidney surveyed the Pittwater area between 1868 and 1872 and gave the name 'Night Bay' to what is now known as 'Lovett Bay'. Slessor assumes that the new name came from a shire councillor; in fact, John Lovett was an early settler there, in 1836, before Sidney mapped the area. (See Charles Swancott, *Dee Why to Barrenjoey and Pittwater* [Sydney: D.S. Ford, 1967], p. 66.)

4 *the other*: Morning Bay, which is just north of Lovett Bay.

20 *Emoh Ruo*: a name once sometimes used for houses, an instance of bad taste; it is 'Our Home' spelt backwards.

A Short History of K. Slessor

exact date not known, between September 1954 and 1957

The poem is included in Slessor's papers in NLA (MS 3020/8/7).

1 *Orange*: Slessor's birthplace, a town west of Sydney (see Dutton, 6, 11).

2 *Shore*: Sydney Church of England Grammar School in Sydney, where Slessor attended high school (see Dutton, 22–7, 30).
The Sun: the Sydney newspaper which provided Slessor with his first job, in 1920 (see Dutton, 39–41).

3 *the* Melbourne Herald *and* Punch: a Melbourne newspaper and magazine respectively. Slessor worked for them from 1924 to 1925 (see Dutton, 88–99).

4 Smith's: *Smith's Weekly*, Sydney weekly newspaper for which Slessor wrote from 1927 to 1940 (see Dutton, 114–40).
Stan Cross, Joe Jonsson, George Finey: Stan Cross (1888–1977), Joe Jonsson (1890–1963), George Finey (1895–1987), cartoonists and sketch artists with whom Slessor worked on *Smith's Weekly.*

6 *Official War Correspondent*: Slessor was Australia's Official War Correspondent in World War II.

8 *New Guinea, Great Britain . . .*: For details of Slessor's travels as war correspondent, see Clement Semmler, ed., *The War Diaries of Kenneth Slessor* (St Lucia: University of Queensland Press, 1985) and *The War Despatches of Kenneth Slessor* (St Lucia: University of Queensland Press, 1987), and Dutton (178–254).

9 *back with* The Sun: Slessor resumed work for *The Sun* after resigning from his position as War Correspondent in 1944.

no more use for the Muse: Slessor all but stopped writing poetry relatively early in his life and apparently at the height of his powers; he wrote very little from 1937, when 'Five Bells' was completed. (See Dutton, 315, 337; Haskell, 260–1; and Dennis Haskell, '"My rather tedious hero": A Portrait of Kenneth Slessor', *Westerly*, September 1991, 30–34.)

10 *Tito*: Josip Broz Tito (1892–1980), then President of Yugoslavia. *SEATO*: South East Asian Treaty Organisation, a regional defence organisation which operated 1955–1977; in another version (MS 3020/8/8), rather than 'Tito and SEATO', this line reads 'international money reform'.

12 *Elizabeth Bay*: a Sydney suburb in the Kings Cross area. *a wife*: Pauline, whom Slessor married in 1950 (see Dutton, 284–96). *Paul*: Paul Slessor, born August 1951; in the other version this line reads 'but at least he's happily married, with one little boy called Paul'.

Lines Written on the Occasion of the Transposition of the Ladies' and Gents' Lavatories on the 9th Floor

1947; privately printed, 1947

A copy of the poem is held in Slessor's papers at the NLA (MS 3020/21/184), and the poem is reproduced in Alexander MacDonald, *The Ukulele Player under the Red Lamp* (Sydney: Angus & Robertson, 1972). MacDonald comments that the poem was 'privately printed (on copy-paper) to commemorate an important event which took place in the Sydney *Sun* building in Elizabeth Street in 1947' (262).

4 *our daily motions*: both planetary and bodily motions.

8 *privvies*: toilets.

24 *alabaster*: a type of gypsum, often used for ornamental purposes.

26 *Hades*: See 'Choker's Lane' (*DN*), line 6n.

32 *button*: men's trousers at this time had buttoned, not zippered, flies.

I Wish I Were . . .

April 1962

Class 5A of Orange Primary School, where Slessor's mother had been a teacher, sent Slessor congratulations on his birthday in 1962; Slessor sent the poem in reply. (See Stewart, 24–5.)

1 *Orange*: See 'A Short History of K. Slessor', line 1n.

5 *cicadas*: insects, which in summer in eastern Australia make loud, shrill noises.

The Peep-Hole

not known

The poem is included in Slessor's papers in the NLA (MS 3020/21/201); it may be a draft rather than a final version. The style, and the spelling 'kisst', indicate that this is an early poem.

7 *rondeau*: a poem of ten or thirteen lines, using just two rhymes.

Young Death

not known

The poem is included in Slessor's papers in the NLA (MS 3020/21/202); it may be a draft rather than a final version. The style indicates that this is an early poem.

13 *ruth*: sorrow or grief.

Ode on the Enlightened & Liberal Patronage Bestowed on the Arts by Their Majesties, The King and Queen of Great Britain

not known, possibly 1920s

The poem is included in Slesssor's papers in NLA (MS 3020/19/107).

The King and Queen: King Edward VII and Queen Alexandra.
Refpect: Slessor is playing on the use until the eighteenth century of a long 'f' to signify 's'.

Maecenas: Gaius Cilnius Maecenas (*c.*70–8 BC), Roman diplomat and patron of the arts, including of the poets Virgil and Horace.
the Mufical Halls: a form of popular entertainment.
the Late King Edward VII: Edward VII reigned 1901–1910. He was an affable and popular monarch, interested in sport and social activities, flamboyant and ostentatious.

4 *The Laureate Pen*: the pen of the poet laureate, at this time Robert Bridges, who was Laureate 1910–1930.
Phidian Clay: Phidias (*c.*490–430 BC), Greek sculptor, creator of enduring images of the Greek gods; Slessor is playing on notions of human clay.

6 *Q---n M--y's*: Queen Mary, wife of George V.

8 *Raphael*: Raphael Sanzio (1483–1520), Italian Renaissance painter and architect.
TUCK: possibly a reference to Henry Scott Tuke (1858–1929), landscape artist and portraitist.

10 *great G----e's*: George V, who reigned 1910–1936. One of his hobbies was stamp collecting.

13 *Albion*: poetic name for Britain.

Untitled ('Oh what a pleasure . . .')

not known; *The National Times,* 27 September–2 October 1976

This poem is attributed to Slessor by Clement Semmler and included by him in an article on Slessor, 'What Kenneth Slessor was writing during his 30 silent years'. The location of Slessor's manuscript is now unknown.

2 *Doctor Johnson*: Samuel Johnson (1709–84), English essayist, poet and critic.

3 *Mount Kosciusko*: Australia's highest mountain.

8 *With*: mistakenly printed as 'with' in *The National Times*.

10 *Mrs Thrale*: Johnson lived with Henry and Hester Thrale, and Hester Thrale helped Johnson with his work.

15 *buried cells*: both hidden regions and brain cells.

18 *seraglios*: harems.

Popular Song

not known; *The National Times,* 27 September–2 October 1976

This poem is attributed to Slessor by Clement Semmler and included by him in an article on Slessor, 'What Kenneth Slessor was writing during his 30 silent years'. The location of Slessor's manuscript is now unknown.

2 *billy*: See 'She Keeps on Walking' (*BBFB*), line 19n.; the poem mentions a number of Australian icons.

3 *jackeroo cherub*: an angel acting like a sheep or cattle station worker.

4 *damper*: a type of bread made with a simple flour and water mixture, and often cooked in bush campfires.

10 *leavings*: leftovers.

Appendix: Selections of poems as published by Slessor

Poetry in Australia, 1923
A Surrender
Mangroves
Incongruity
Thief of the Moon
Pan at Lane Cove
The Embarkation for Cythera
The Mask
Good-night!
Rubens' Innocents
Thieves' Kitchen
Nuremberg
The Ghost
Adventure Bay
The Man of Sentiment [Part One only]

Poems (1957)
Earth-Visitors
Nuremberg
Pan at Lane Cove
Taoist
Rubens' Innocents
Marco Polo
Chessmen
Mangroves
Thief of the Moon
Heine in Paris
Winter Dawn
A Surrender
The Man of Sentiment, Part One
The Man of Sentiment, Part Two

Thieves' Kitchen
Stars
The Ghost
Undine
Next Turn
City Nightfall
Adventure Bay
The Night-Ride
A Sunset
Realities
Music
Captain Dobbin
The Atlas
To Myself
Elegy in a Botanic Gardens
Trade Circular
Five Visions of Captain Cook
Wild Grapes
La Dame du Palais de la Reine
Waters
Glubbdubdrib
Rubens' Hell
Burying Friends
Crow Country
Serenade
Talbingo
Country Towns
A Bushranger
Gulliver
Fixed Ideas
The Country Ride
The Nabob
Toilet of a Dandy

Metempsychosis
Mephistopheles Perverted
The Old Play
Crustacean Rejoinder
Out of Time
Sleep
Sensuality
Lesbia's Daughter
The Knife
Cock-Crow
North Country
South Country
Last Trams
Advice to Psychologists
Vesper-Song of the Reverend Samuel Marsden
To a Friend
William Street
Cannibal Street
To the Poetry of Hugh McCrae
Full Orchestra
Five Bells
Polarities
An Inscription for Dog River
Beach Burial

The Penguin Book of Modern Australian Verse (1961)
The Nabob
Captain Dobbin
Sleep
South Country
Beach Burial
Five Bells

Index of titles

Index of first lines